SPECIAL EDUCATIONAL & ADDITIONAL LEARNING NEEDS

Sara Miller McCune founded SAGE Publishing in 1965 to support the dissemination of usable knowledge and educate a global community. SAGE publishes more than 1000 journals and over 800 new books each year, spanning a wide range of subject areas. Our growing selection of library products includes archives, data, case studies and video. SAGE remains majority owned by our founder and after her lifetime will become owned by a charitable trust that secures the company's continued independence.

Los Angeles | London | New Delhi | Singapore | Washington DC | Melbourne

SPECIAL EDUCATIONAL & ADDITIONAL LEARNING NEEDS

AN ESSENTIAL GUIDE

JANICE WEARMOUTH

Los Angeles | London | New Delhi
Singapore | Washington DC | Melbourne

Los Angeles | London | New Delhi
Singapore | Washington DC | Melbourne

SAGE Publications Ltd
1 Oliver's Yard
55 City Road
London EC1Y 1SP

SAGE Publications Inc.
2455 Teller Road
Thousand Oaks, California 91320

SAGE Publications India Pvt Ltd
B 1/I 1 Mohan Cooperative Industrial Area
Mathura Road
New Delhi 110 044

SAGE Publications Asia-Pacific Pte Ltd
3 Church Street
#10-04 Samsung Hub
Singapore 049483

Editor: Delayna Spencer
Production editor: Imogen Roome
Copyeditor: Sarah Bury
Proofreader: Leigh Smithson
Indexer: Adam Pozner
Marketing manager: Lorna Patkai
Cover design: Wendy Scott
Typeset by: C&M Digitals (P) Ltd, Chennai, India
Printed in the UK

Library of Congress Control Number: 2021952308

British Library Cataloguing in Publication data

A catalogue record for this book is available from
the British Library

ISBN 978-1-5297-1205-6
ISBN 978-1-5297-1204-9 (pbk)

At SAGE we take sustainability seriously. Most of our products are printed in the UK using responsibly sourced
papers and boards. When we print overseas we ensure sustainable papers are used as measured by the PREPS
grading system. We undertake an annual audit to monitor our sustainability.

CONTENTS

Much effort has been made to ensure that descriptions of, and references to, legislation across the UK and Northern Ireland that is associated with special educational, additional learning, and/or support, needs and disability are accurate at the time of writing this text. However, it may well be that some changes in the law are made in the lifetime of this book.

PREFACE

This book, and the bespoke companion website with its links to assets on the SAGE Education web pages, is an important resource that enables pre-service and more experienced teachers, students studying at various levels on courses related to special and/or additional learning and support needs and disabilities across the UK, to develop their understanding of children and young people with special educational, and additional support, needs within Early Years settings, schools and colleges, and will give them the confidence to address these needs effectively. It has also been designed to support governing boards of educational institutions, parents and carers to be more aware of young people's entitlements to special and/or additional support and provision and the kind of partnerships between home and school/college that predispose to positive working relationships, to the benefit of all concerned. This volume has been developed in consultation with focus groups of students at undergraduate and postgraduate level who have a specific interest and concern for supporting young people with special or additional learning and support needs and disabilities in educational contexts. These students have expressed very clear views about what they would find useful and supportive to them in classrooms as well as on their academic assignments. Key elements in the chapters reflect their views.

This book offers, firstly, a critical edge of understanding of how and why the statutory rights and entitlements of young people with special and/or additional learning and support needs and disabilities and their families, and the accountabilities of teachers, educational institutions and local authorities in meeting needs, have been extended over the years. Secondly, it is intended to support educators to carry out their duties, and young people and their families to know what they might reasonably expect from others, from a thoughtful, confident position that is very well-informed in practice, theory and critical understanding of the issues in the field.

Important assets have been included on the website:

- resources, including links to YouTube and other video clips, for reflective activities that support discussion among teachers during training, or among new and experienced teachers during continuing professional development sessions. These invite readers to reflect on policy and practice in provision for special and/or additional learning and support needs and disability and on their own position, values and beliefs regarding the rights and legal entitlements to education of all young people;
- examples of different kinds of assessment tools and interventions that will support new teachers and others to try out and evaluate tried-and-tested interventions for themselves;
- checklists of effective inclusion practices for self-audit of teaching practices;
- examples of setting/school/college policy documents, e.g. school/college SEND policy, school/college dyslexia policy;
- examples of classroom and individual student observation tools;
- templates for understanding and assessing difficult behaviour and planning for improvement.

Summary of chapters

Chapter 1. Introduction. Special and/or additional learning and support needs and disabilities

Chapter 1 includes definitions and consideration of 'need' in a variety of contexts. Reflective activities are introduced to clarify the link between 'need' and the context in which it occurs.

The principle of equity in law is introduced with reference to visual images to explain the principle. Reflective activities invite readers to consider possible positive and negative consequences of the equity principle: the requirement to assess for negative difference to demonstrate the case for special or additional funding to provide required resources and, hence, support positive progress. The potential negatives of labelling and stereotyping are discussed and also the possible positives where provision is sensitive and responsive to individual learners' interests and strengths as well as difficulties.

Chapter 2. Understandings of human learning. Influence of discourses

Major questions addressed in this chapter are: how are teacher expectations and learners' motivation associated with progress and achievement? What theories of human learning lie at the root of approaches commonly employed to address difficulties in learning and behaviour? What may be the strengths and limitations of each in devising ways to address difficulties in learning and behaviour most positively?

Across time, a range of social or psychological understandings have underpinned interventions. It is really important to recognise these in order to evaluate their likely appropriateness for use in supporting individuals' learning and progress in context. For this reason, a number of models of learning and behaviour are introduced, discussed and critiqued. These include behaviourism, constructivism and social-constructivism, attachment theory, therapeutic approaches, and so on. Readers are invited to reflect on the significance, effectiveness and ethical implications of the use of these models through examples of practice in the book, and/or through links uploaded on the website.

Chapter 3. A historical background of the special sector in education

In order to understand approaches to current policy and provision in education across the UK it is important to have a grasp of its history. In Chapter 3 there is an outline of developments from the beginning of the nineteenth century through the twentieth, and up to the development of the concept of 'special educational needs' introduced by Warnock in 1978. This outline is intended to illustrate the association between the national political contexts and contemporary policy and practices in education in general terms, and in relation to those learners who experience difficulties in particular. Readers are invited to read and reflect on the discussion in the text.

Chapter 4. Legal accountabilities in educational institutions

Knowledge and understanding of legislation can provide firm ground on which practitioners can stand when they are involved in decisions about, or make cases to request, special and/or additional learning and support provision. Such understanding also enables families and young people to be aware of their legal entitlements.

In Chapter 4 there are clear, straightforward outlines of the main principles of disability law across the UK, as well as law related to special and/or additional learning and support policy and provision. The various Codes of Practice for each country are referenced and discussed in principle, including their origin and status. Reasons why students might experience special or additional learning and/or support needs are conceptualised somewhat differently in the different countries of the UK. In England and Northern Ireland, the term 'special educational needs' continues to be used, in Scotland the term is 'additional support for learning', and under the most recent legislation in Wales the term is 'additional learning needs'.

Reflective activities focused, for example, on comparisons between aspects of the various laws, and on the differences between the frames of reference used to denote 'need' across the different countries of the UK, and what they may imply, have been designed to encourage understanding of legal definitions and their implications.

Readers are invited to consider implications of the law for individual educational institutions.

Chapter 5. Difficulties in communication and interaction

At any level in the education system learners need to be able to use language competently in order to access the curriculum. Language development is critical to thinking and learning, and, in most circumstances, to making friends and becoming a contributing member of the learning community in settings, schools and colleges. Major questions addressed in Chapter 5 are: what particular needs are experienced by learners with difficulty in the acquisition of speech, language and communication? What kind of approaches can be effective in addressing these needs? How can we understand autistic spectrum disorders and how can we address the needs of learners who experience autistic spectrum disorder (ASD) and ensure that they are included in settings, schools and colleges?

Chapter 6. Difficulties in cognition and learning

The term 'cognition' relates to the processing of information and includes a range of functions that are crucial to human learning, for example memory, problem-solving, reasoning, comprehension and production of language, and perception. Difficulties in cognition are associated with a wide range of needs in education, including moderate learning difficulties (MLD), severe learning difficulties (SLD), profound and multiple learning difficulties (PMLD), and specific learning difficulties (SpLD) such as dyslexia, dyscalculia and dyspraxia. In Chapter 6 we address the question of what we can do to ensure that young people who experience difficulties in cognition and learning can access the curriculum most effectively and be included in the education system.

Chapter 7. Social, emotional and mental health difficulties and associated behavioural issues

Chapter 7 adopts a view that all young people, including those with challenging behaviour, have a fundamental need to belong. There is discussion of the needs of the learners with, and ways to address:

- social and emotional upset, exceptionally shy/withdrawn behaviour in classrooms, and behaviour associated with attachment difficulties and bereavement – with additional practical examples of both the behaviour and the strategies, made available on the website;
- more extreme behaviour, including attention deficit/hyperactivity disorder (AD/HD), and bullying behaviour – including practical examples of both the behaviour and appropriate interventions;
- anger, and potential approaches to encouraging anger management.

Chapter 8. Sensory and/or physical difficulties

Addressing needs relating to sensory and/or physical difficulties is a legislative requirement included in both disability law across the UK and also law that pertains to special or additional learning and/or support needs in the various countries. Both within-person factors, that is the sensory or physical disability, and contextual factors relating to the environment in educational institutions and family circumstances interact to influence learning and achievement.

In Chapter 8 we consider the kinds of sensory and physical difficulties that are commonly experienced in settings, schools and colleges across the UK, how these difficulties can create barriers to learning and progress, and how these barriers might be addressed in educational institutions.

Chapter 9. Assessment and planning

A thoughtful and well-informed assessment of need that is sensitive to the learner's individuality is a very important aspect of determining whether there is a barrier to learning in the first place, and then working out what kind of provision will be effective in addressing the need. A major issue framing Chapter 9 is the place of assessment in addressing learning and behavioural needs that is appropriate to the age of the learners, the kind of difficulties that are either experienced or are a matter of concern for the learners, family, or teachers, and the curriculum area. We discuss the principles of different kinds of assessment, roles and functions: the significance of understanding the barriers to learning from the young people's and families' perspective, and frameworks for planning provision within the curriculum.

Chapter 10. Difficulties in literacy acquisition

Major questions in Chapter 10 are how teachers and others can understand difficulties in literacy acquisition in ways that enable them to problem solve what they can do to support young people in educational institutions at different ages and stages, and at home. Examples of what we discuss are ways of understanding the reading/writing process as a frame of reference within which literacy difficulties can be understood, common difficulties in literacy acquisition, and a range of practical reading/writing/spelling initiatives designed to address these difficulties at different ages and stages, including at home.

Chapter 11. Numeracy difficulties

Gaining competence in the range of skills that we might see as comprising 'numeracy' can be very important to a learner's future life chances. A major question for Chapter 11 is how teachers and others can understand difficulties in numeracy in ways that enable them to support numeracy acquisition for these young people in settings/schools and colleges, and at home. Chapter 11 discusses and illustrates what different kinds of numeracy difficulties 'look like' to teachers, and 'feel like' to young people. It goes on to offer an overview of practical initiatives to address these difficulties at different ages and stages, and at individual, group or family level.

Chapter 12. Inclusive practices in schools and classrooms

The focus of Chapter 12 is the kind of learning environments, and the kind of pedagogies, that can be responsive to the learning and positive behaviour of all young people.

Some of the questions addressed are: what could an inclusive classroom look like at different ages and stages of education? Are there any principles that could guide decisions about inclusive classroom practice and pedagogy? Is teaching that encourages progress in learning and behaviour for young people with special educational or additional learning needs necessarily qualitatively different from that of all other learners? If so, in what way(s)?

Chapter 13. Working in partnership with families and outside agencies

Topics addressed in Chapter 13 include professional relationships and partnership work between schools/colleges, parents and families, and between schools/colleges and outside agencies. It outlines also statutory rights and potential roles of parents and families in the education system. It considers the role of specialist external agencies in supporting provision for SEND in schools and colleges: when and how to seek advice. In doing so it acknowledges challenges in relation to partnership work – with examples of what can happen in practice, effective and ineffective.

Postscript

The Postscript summarises the importance of policy and practice in this area of education, and some of the inherent challenges. It raises issues of belonging with an understanding that, for many young people, identification with, or failure in, and alienation from, school may have long-lasting and deep effects throughout their lives. Support for addressing difficulties that are experienced as a result of special educational, additional or support needs and/or disabilities is therefore crucial. The conclusion adopts the view that, while finding ways to address the difficulties that learners may experience can be challenging and demanding, it can also be exciting and very rewarding for the individual learner. Well conceptualised, thoughtful provision designed to engage learners' interests and engagement has the potential to make a difference to an individual's learning and future life chances. This is beyond price.

ABOUT THE ONLINE RESOURCES

This textbook comes with additional online resources to support your learning, provide further reading and encourage critical reflection.

Extra resources to support *Special Educational and Additional Learning Needs*, in the form of **Activities** that can be used alongside each chapter to further understanding and encourage critical reflection on content, can be found at **https://study.sagepub.com/wearmouth**

ABOUT THE AUTHOR

Janice Wearmouth had many years of experience of teaching in mainstream schools, first on voluntary service in Cameroon, and later, in Bermuda, London, Northamptonshire and Bedfordshire, until she changed career to teach and research in universities. She began her career by teaching English Language and Literature, Latin and Classical Studies before moving into the area of Special Educational Needs and Disability and working as a special educational needs co-ordinator (SENCO) and Head of Education Support.

Prior to joining the University of Bedfordshire, she was Director of the Centre for Curriculum and Teaching Studies at the Open University, and then Professor of Education at Victoria University of Wellington in New Zealand. Currently, Janice is Professor of Education at the University of Bedfordshire, teaching on both undergraduate and postgraduate programmes in Education, and supervising research students to doctoral level. She is course leader of the National Award for Special Educational Needs Co-ordination (NASENCO) in the Master's Programme and has recently co-developed a new BA (Hons) Special Educational Needs and Disability degree.

1

INTRODUCTION: SPECIAL AND/OR ADDITIONAL LEARNING AND SUPPORT NEEDS AND DISABILITIES

Major questions addressed in this chapter are:

- What might constitute 'need' in relation to young people in educational contexts?
    - Is it what learners 'need' to do to meet what is expected of them?
    - Is it what learners require in order to be able to do what is expected?
    - Is it what schools and colleges 'need' young people to do to meet institutional targets and goals?
- Who might decide whether a learner has a need, and what that need might be?

Key terms

Needs in education, human rights, equality, equity, eugenics, labelling

Introduction

Children and young people identified as needing special or additional learning, support or provision in educational institutions are human beings with the same degree of humanity, individuality and entitlement to respect, dignity, excitement and engagement in learning as their peers. (See discussion of Human Rights legislation later in this chapter.) Sometimes, however, in our quest to categorise and label according to identified 'conditions', we seem to lose sight of this.

Over time, a number of terms have been developed and become important in the world of special educational, additional learning or support needs and disability (SEND), or additional support needs.[1] The terms we use when we speak or write about other people are really important. This applies in educational institutions, too. They are linked to what we might call our 'frame of reference'. This is, broadly, the way we, as individuals, look at and interpret the world and our surroundings. It can come, for example, from our families, teachers, the experiences we have had, our culture, education, the media (television, newspapers, the radio), social media, and so on. In a similar vein, Michel Foucault (1980, p. 131), the French sociologist, talked about 'discourses' which are used within any particular society as 'regimes of truth', that is, particular ways of speaking or writing that dominate our thinking and make it difficult to see things from a different perspective. It is important to recognise types of discourse and common frames of reference as they are used in educational contexts and have a grasp of how they are used in order to understand policy, practice and provision. It is also important to acknowledge the extent to which the labels associated with these frames of reference, rather than the individuality of the learner, can come to dominate our thinking about those young people.

Marginalising discourse

We might illustrate the point about the importance of personal awareness of the influence of common discourses with reference to the whole issue of what the labels associated with the field of special educational, and/or additional learning or support needs and/or disability do, or do not, tell us about learners. Of course, some young people experience sensory and/or physical difficulties, multiple and profound difficulties in learning, language issues, and so on. However, giving a learner a label may be highly problematic. We might exemplify this point by the disrespectful remark of a doctor when a colleague took her daughter to hospital for a check-up: 'Here comes the Down's'.

Discourses or frames of reference associated with needs labels and the way in which they may carry positive or negative connotations in relation to individual children bear a strong relationship to the social and political context in which they develop and are used. We discuss this issue later in Chapter 2, but for now it is instructive to look back at the way in which Down's syndrome was viewed in the nineteenth century.

---

[1]'Special educational needs and disability' is the term used in England and still, at the time of writing, in Northern Ireland also. In Wales and Scotland, the related term is somewhat different: 'additional learning' and 'additional support' needs, respectively.

LEARNING POINT
DANGERS OF MARGINALISING DISCOURSES
AND ASSOCIATED PRACTICES

In the nineteenth century, the German physiologist and anthropologist, Johann Friedrich Blumenbach, noted that a small group of children shared facial similarities such as folds in the upper eyelids (epicanthal folds) with those of the Mongolian race. In 1866, a British physician, John Langdon Down, wrote a paper entitled 'Observations on an Ethnic Classification of Idiots', which, broadly, is about what is now known as Down's syndrome, named after him. He, however, classified this group as 'congenital idiots', for which he used the term 'mongoloid'. He wrote in this paper:

A very large number of congenital idiots are typical Mongols. So marked is this, that when placed side by side, it is difficult to believe that the specimens compared are not children of the same parents. The number of idiots who arrange themselves around the Mongolian type is so great, and they present such a close resemblance to one another in mental power, that I shall describe an idiot member of this racial division, selected from the large number that have fallen under my observation. (Down, 1866, p. 259)

What are the dangers, do you think, of calling other human beings 'congenital idiots'?

What do you know of some of the immoral and, sometimes, downright evil acts that were performed in some countries less than 100 years ago against people with Down's syndrome?

With the rise of the eugenics movement in the latter part of the nineteenth and first half of the twentieth century, a number of countries, including certain states in the United States, began programmes of forced sterilisation of individuals with Down's syndrome. 'Action T4' was a programme of the systematic murder of individuals with Down's syndrome and other comparable disabilities in Nazi Germany, for example (Lifton, 2000). Since the Second World War, however, laws relating to such sterilisation programmes have been repealed.

In 1961, a number of geneticists wrote to the editor of The Lancet, suggesting that the term 'Mongolian idiocy' had 'misleading connotations', had become 'an embarrassing term', and should therefore be changed (Gordon, 1961). The Lancet advocated using the term Down's syndrome. The World Health Organization (WHO) officially dropped references to mongolism in 1965 after a request by the Mongolian delegate (Howard-Jones, 1979).

Power in decision-making over other individuals' lives when those individuals have been identified as different in some way can, as the reference to 'Action T4' suggests, have catastrophic consequences.

Web activity WA1.1
Reflecting on the immorality of eugenics and
past treatment of disabled people

We have uploaded an article reflecting on the use of eugenics in past time, together with an activity, on the website. You might choose to access this material now.

Down's syndrome cannot be cured, but the learning and other difficulties associated with it can be addressed if people with the syndrome are offered appropriate help and if other people accept and include them. Above all, it is important to stress that children with Down's syndrome are individuals with their own abilities and achievements.

> ## LEARNING POINT
> ## SUPPORTING LEARNERS TO MAKE PROGRESS
>
> When you think about the discussion so far in this chapter, you might like to consider how far the following protocol might help you, in the first instance, to begin to support learners who experience difficulties of various kinds to make progress in learning and/or behaviour:
>
> - find out as much as possible about the learner. In particular, find ways to talk with him/her and observe behaviour in various contexts;
> - learn about his/her experiences of what helps/hinders him/her to learn, socialise with others, be included in school;
> - find out about his/her strengths and interests as well as the difficulties s/he experiences;
> - find out what can really engage him/her in his/her learning;
> - think about the barriers to learning in the learning environment;
> - consider what will best address those barriers to help the learner to achieve in the classroom/setting/ school/college, how to draw on interests and build on strengths.

'Need' in educational contexts

There is nothing 'set in stone' about the term 'need' in the context of education. As we discuss below, this term is a construction that some might think of as an administrative convenience that is useful for identifying differences in relation to expected pupil/student progression in schools and colleges. Only when these differences have been identified can we make a case for additional resources to enable young people to make expected progress.

LEARNING POINT
REFLECTIONS ON THE CREATION OF 'NEED'
IN EDUCATIONAL CONTEXTS

Think about one or more of the young people in your experience who have, or have had, difficulties in the context of school or college. Note down your responses to the following questions:

- What creates/has created those difficulties?
- What would help to address those difficulties?
- Is it something to do with amending the task(s) or expectations that are made, or the resources that are available?
- Is it something to do with the individuals concerned?
- Is it a mixture of both?
- What do you think?

Now think about a difficulty that you experienced yourself in school, college or university. What created that difficulty?

Can you see any parallels between the difficulties and what creates/created them as you identified them for the young people and for yourself?

What does this mean about 'need', in your view?

Teachers and others in settings, schools and colleges, as Fulcher (1989) points out, may react to learners' difficulties in a number of ways. Some might interpret a need as a child's problem: what is 'wrong' with the child and how this 'problem' can be dealt with. If we focus on what is wrong with a learner, it emphasises ways in which s/he is different or deficient. The assumption then is that these 'deficiencies' can be 'treated' like an illness – the so-called 'medical model'. It can often be experienced, especially by the learners themselves, as a very negative way of meeting needs.

Some people might be concerned about young people's well-being and their own moral responsibility to help them. They feel sympathetic to the child's struggles. Or sometimes children's difficulties may be seen as a tragedy, and the child treated as a 'charity case'.

Another way of understanding difficulties is to view the learning context, including the physical environment, resources, teaching approaches, the difficulty and/or interest level of the classroom activity as a potential barrier to engagement and progress. In a broader context, social factors, for example economic deprivation and poverty, can contribute to creating barriers to learning. We might then think about the extent to which 'learning difficulties' arise from the social context in which those young people live. It might be economic factors, government policy, institutional practices, broader social attitudes or inappropriate physical surroundings that stop people from doing things.

Case study: Interpretations of 'need'

Sometimes personal experiences with students can open our eyes to some of the issues related to the labels we give to students. Please read the following text.

The current author first met 'Jimmy' as a 13-year-old. His father and one brother were in prison, and the author knew that his mother had difficulty feeding and clothing Jimmy and his siblings. In the middle of the winter Jimmy came to school with no jacket or coat, and he was frequently hungry. He had a long record of stealing from peers and the local shops. He took peers' possessions, pens, pencils, anything lying on the desk, when they were not looking. At the end of one lesson the author realised that he had stolen her Parker pen, a gift from her deceased uncle, so very precious to her. One of the other pupils had seen him putting it into his bag. His peers imposed their own punishment on him by avoiding him and refusing to talk to him. Some time later he was transferred to a pupil referral unit where the head teacher was sure he could cure him of his thieving – until Jimmy crept into his office and stole money from his desk.

Viewing this situation through Fulcher's framework, we might interpret his 'needs' in different ways, as did his teachers and the educational psychologist. Which, if any, of Fulcher's interpretations of need do you consider fits the situation most accurately?

The use of the word 'need' is extremely sensitive in the context of education. On the surface, the notion of fulfilling a 'need' conveys a sense of kindliness. In practice, however, the kind of special or additional provision that is made may imply a value placed on learners (Salmon, 1995). There may be an assumption of agreement between all the interested parties about what is 'needed', which often (but not always, of course) ignores 'crucial issues' of the lack of power that may be allowed to learners and their families in the decision-making process. There is also a question about appropriate expectations of children identified as 'having' needs. As we discuss in Chapter 2, there is a strong relationship between teachers' expectations and student achievement, self-esteem and development that has been well documented since the seminal work of Rosenthal and Jacobson (1968). Salmon (1995) comments on her perception that the term SEN (now SEND) used in England and Northern Ireland is too often associated with a sense of failure to come up to the mark. Instead of signifying belonging and entitlement, she sees the terms *special* and *need* as 'weasel words' with connotations of helplessness and inadequacy.

Not all educators take the same view, however. Of course some young people experience sensory and/or physical difficulties, multiple and profound difficulties in learning, language issues, and so on. Some educators, for example Cole (1990), argue that identifying children's 'special educational needs' has a very humanitarian aim. This is to provide additional resources, develop specialist methods to address particular difficulties in learning, or overcome the effects of a disability in order that children can benefit from their education. Without identification of individual needs, it is impossible to justify individual resourcing.

Case study: Consideration of the need for an informed label

Read the text below.

The current author still remembers 'Will', whom she first met as a 14-year-old. He had been placed in a class of 'slow learners' who experienced a range of difficulties in conceptual development: language, problem-solving, communication and abstract thinking. Will could barely read or write, was identified as 'having learning problems', and appeared quiet, compliant and very depressed. In conversation with him one day, the author introduced him to an audio recording of Roald Dahl's novel *Boy* that she gave him with a copy of the text. Will loved it, and asked for more Roald Dahl books. Before too long he progressed to other 'talking books', most notably recordings of Tolkien. In a few weeks Will was walking into the classroom with his head held high, face held up to the sun, instead of looking at his shoes, as he did before. There was a clear disjunction between the label 'slow-learning' and the author's new observation of him as articulate and engaged when he talked about the books he was reading, assisted by the recordings. He was clearly dyslexic. In his case, the label 'dyslexic' brought with it a completely different – and positive view – of this young man, opened the door to informed support to address his needs and, albeit late in his education, had the potential to facilitate enhanced life chances.

Have you ever met a learner like 'Will'?

What would you do to help him address the barriers to his learning and achievement?

Implications of Human Rights legislation in education

These days, the fundamental rights and freedoms that everyone in the UK is entitled to, including in the area of education, are set out in the Human Rights Act 1998, which came into force across the UK in October 2000. The Act incorporates into domestic British law the rights set out in the European Convention on Human Rights (ECHR). Protocol 1, Article 2 protects learners' right to an effective education. It states: 'No person shall be denied a right to an education' (www.equalityhumanrights.com/en/human-rights-act/article-2-first-protocol-right-education, accessed 26.10.2021). The courts have ruled that the right to education relates to the education system that already exists. This is very important when we consider learners who experience difficulties, because a question then arises about how to make what exists accessible to all in a way that is fair and reasonable.

Two of the strategies that we can use to try to ensure fairness in accessing education relate to equity and equality. Equity in education means that schools and education systems provide equal learning opportunities to all students (Organisation for Economic Co-operation and Development (OECD), 2018, www.oecd.org/pisa/Equity-in-Education-country-note-UK.pdf, accessed 26.10.2021) and give learners what they need to be successful. Equality aims to promote fairness by treating everyone the same, but it can only work if everyone starts from the same place and needs the same help.

LEARNING POINT
CONSIDERING ISSUES OF EQUITY AND EQUALITY

There is a considerable number of images on the internet that further illustrate what equity and equality 'look like'. This web page gives you access to some of them: www.google.co.uk/search?q=picture+of+equity+vs+equality&tbm=isch&source=univ&sa=X&ved=2ahUKEwi2l-rv7pnmAhUxkFwKHUonC0gQsAR-6BAgHEAE&biw=1252&bih=876 (accessed 26.10.2021).

Several images illustrate three boys, one tall, one of medium height, and one shorter, standing on the same size boxes, trying to look over a fence at the activities in the field beyond. This is an illustration of equality of opportunity, with the same size box assumed to fit all, but, of course, it does not give equal access to the view. The equity principle, on the other hand, means providing a larger box to fit the need of the shortest boy in relation to the height of the fence so that he can see over it.

If we assume that ensuring fairness in access to education means putting in the additional resource – the additional or special 'step' that is needed to look over the metaphorical 'fence' that is illustrated on the web pages above – we have, first, to assess the difficulty that is experienced, examine the height of the 'fence' and then make a judgement about what is required to address the need. In many of these illustrations, the problem is seen to be located within the individual. S/he is not tall enough to achieve a good view of what is going on.

Do you think there is an alternative explanation for the problem? What do you think? What about the height of the fence? Could something be done about this?

If we translate this issue into an educational context, difficulty in accessing the curriculum, what alternatives might there be in finding a solution?

Translated into the context of education, educational needs can be seen in relation to what a young person requires to be able to achieve the goals of the education system within which s/he is a student. Some of the problematic issues here are whether the education system within which the learner is expected to fit is itself suitable and appropriate for all young people, who should have the power of decision-making over what some learners 'need' to access the education on offer, and whether the resources some learners may need are available. For example, under the Labour government of the 1960s there was a child-centred approach 'strongly manifested in the Plowden Report (Central Advisory Council for Education, 1967) which largely endorsed emphasis on individualization (child-centredness) and learning by discovery'. The most significant effect of this approach was, in terms of special education, 'changing attitudes towards [. . .] pupils with special educational needs' (para 2.1). In England, this resulted in a range of legislation and policy documents, published later in the 1970s, that related specifically to the needs of individual 'handicapped' children.

In more recent years, the 1988 Education Act in England and Wales resulted in an increased focus on schools' accountability for the measured achievement of their students. The pressure on schools created by this development was reflected in special educational provision in a number of ways. Many schools became concerned to have the students whom they identified as under-achieving assessed for the purpose of accessing the special or additional resources, such as teaching assistants, that might assist them to achieve more highly. Between 1997 and 2003 there was a 99% increase in teaching assistants in English schools for this reason. Currently, in England, by the end of each key stage, pupils are expected to know, apply and understand the matters, skills and processes specified in the relevant programme of study (Department for Education, 2013a, p. 18). Necessarily, therefore, students' needs should be seen in relation to what they require to meet these targets.

Formal definitions of 'need' in UK educational contexts

In the UK, for the past 40 years, and until recently, there have been strong similarities in England, Wales and Northern Ireland in terms of education law related to special educational needs, including the definition of what constitutes a special learning or behavioural need as well as the assessment of the need and the kind of provision that is made. Revisions to legislation in Wales by the National Assembly for Wales, and by the Department for Education, for revisions in Northern Ireland, and legislation that was introduced in England in 2014, have increased the differences between them, however. Education law in Scotland is regulated by the Scottish Government in Edinburgh and continues to be different. We discuss law across the UK as it relates to the entitlements of children and young people who experience difficulties of various sorts, learning, emotional and behavioural, physical, sensory, and so on, in Chapter 4. In the discussion we raise issues of current formal conceptions of 'need' in educational contexts.

Conclusion

Across the UK, the Human Rights Act 1998 entitles all young people to education. However, this right relates to the education system that already exists. For learners who experience difficulties, there is a question about how to make what exists accessible to all in a way that is fair and reasonable. In other words, to assess what learners 'need' in this regard. The whole concept of 'need' in educational contexts can be very sensitive, however. On the one hand, the notion of fulfilling a 'need' can convey a sense of kindliness. On the other hand, as some writers (e.g. Salmon, 1995) comment, 'need' may be seen as 'weasel words' with connotations of helplessness and inadequacy; we cannot ignore issues of power related to who has the authority to make decisions about which learners 'need' what, and who should have an entitlement to additional resources. This includes power over decision-making related to the curriculum in the national context that itself may create barriers to some individuals' learning.

In your own context, what kinds of discourses and/or frames of reference are used to refer to learners who experience special or additional learning or support needs?

To what extent do you feel that labels enable us to understand and respond to the needs of individual learners? In the current author's view, there is no simple answer to this question. However, these days, with inclusion in schools and society in such high focus, the practical consequences of our answer to this question are very important for us all.

In Chapter 2 we turn to issues of teacher expectations and models of learning as important aspects of the frame of reference within which learners' needs are often understood, and provision is made.

Further reading

Needs in education

Griffith, W. S. (1978) Educational needs: Definition, assessment, and utilization. *The School Review*, 86(3), 382–394.

Hodkinson, A. (2019) *Key Issues in Special Educational Needs, Disability and Inclusion* (3rd edn). London: Sage.

International Bureau of Education (IBE) (n/d) *Basic Learning Needs*. Geneva: UNESCO. Available at: http://www.ibe.unesco.org/en/glossary-curriculum-terminology/b/basic-learning-needs

Noddings, N. (2005) Identifying and responding to needs in education. *Cambridge Journal of Education*, 35(2), 147–159.

Wedell, K. (2003) Concepts of special educational need. *Journal of Research in Special Education*, 3(2), 104–108.

Labelling

Arishi, A., Boyle, C., & Lauchlan, F. (2017) Inclusive education and the politics of difference: Considering the effectiveness of labelling in special education. *Educational and Child Psychology*, 34(4), 9–19.

Gibbs, S., & Elliott, J. (2015) The differential effects of labelling: How do 'dyslexia' and 'reading difficulties' affect teachers' beliefs. *European Journal of Special Needs Education*, 30(3), 323–337.

Human rights in education

Cole, M. (ed.) (2018) *Education, Equality and Human Rights* (4th edn). London: Routledge.

Jordan, L., & Goodey, C. (2002) *Human Rights and School Change: The Newham Story*. Bristol: Centre for Studies on Inclusive education. Available at: https://files.eric.ed.gov/fulltext/ED473539.pdf

2

UNDERSTANDINGS OF HUMAN LEARNING: INFLUENCE OF DISCOURSES

Major questions addressed in this chapter are:

- How can teachers' and others' expectations influence learning and behaviour?
- What theories of human learning lie at the root of approaches commonly employed to address perceived difficulties in learning and behaviour?
- What may be the strengths and limitations of each in devising ways to address difficulties in learning and behaviour most positively?

Key terms

Teacher expectations, motivation, behaviourism, Jean Piaget, Lev Vygotsky, Jerome Bruner, constructivism, social constructivism, attachment theory

Introduction

Teachers' expectations of the learners in their classrooms, their understanding of learning and behaviour and what may lie at the root of a learning or behaviour difficulty in an educational institution have a very strong influence on how they approach learners who experience difficulties and, in turn, how those learners respond. Across time, a range of social or psychological understandings have underpinned interventions. It is really important to recognise these in order to evaluate their likely appropriateness for use in supporting individuals' learning and progress in context. For this reason, a number of models of learning and behaviour will be introduced, discussed and critiqued. These will include behaviourism, constructivism and social constructivism, and attachment theory.

We begin this chapter by discussing seminal[1] research that investigates the association between expectations and achievement, and then move on to the models mentioned above.

Influences on achievement

Teacher expectations

There is a strong relationship between teachers' expectations and learners' achievement, self-esteem and development that has been well documented since the seminal work of Rosenthal and Jacobson (1968). In 1965 these authors conducted an experiment in Oak School, an elementary school in the USA, telling teachers that certain children could be expected to be 'growth spurters', based on the children's results on a fictitious assessment they called the *Harvard Test of Inflected Acquisition*. In fact, the children designated as 'spurters' were chosen at random. What Rosenthal and Jacobson hoped to investigate was the degree (if any) to which changes in teacher expectation produce changes in learners' achievement. At the end of one year Rosenthal and Jacobson concluded that 'one person's expectations of another's behavior may come to serve as a self-fulfilling prophecy' (1968, p. 20). When teachers expected that certain children would show greater intellectual development, those children did show greater intellectual development. For the basic year of the experiment, the self-fulfilling prophecy was in evidence primarily at the lower grade levels. Their findings therefore supported the idea of a self-fulfilling prophecy: if teachers label learners as high-flyers or unusually gifted, their attainment comes to reflect that label. Theoretically, the opposite would also be true, with negative labels. It has to be stated here, however, that later attempts to replicate Rosenthal and Jacobson's experiment yielded somewhat different results. For example, a self-fulfilling prophecy is not necessarily inevitable. Learners can also reject a label.

---

[1]In educational contexts, 'seminal' research is that which has provided new concepts/ideas and served as a basis for later developments.

LEARNING POINT
EXPECTATIONS OF LEARNERS WITH 'NEEDS'

In the current author's experience of teaching in eight different schools, it seems very clear that teacher expectations linked to prevailing discourses around 'needs' strongly affect teachers' own behaviour and the way in which we treat those with such needs. We might also ask ourselves whether our own presuppositions about the learning and behaviour of children identified as having 'special educational' or 'additional learning' or 'support' needs and/or a disability really enable us to understand and work with these children in the same way as we do their peers. These days, with inclusion in schools and society in such high focus, the practical consequences of our answer to this question are very important for us all.

What do you think about this issue?

'Attribution theory' of motivation

For those supporting young people who experience difficulties, it is really important to understand how what we might call learners' 'attributions' affect their motivation. Weiner's so-called 'attribution theory' of motivation (1979) describes how the way in which individuals interpret events influences motivation for learning as well as future learning behaviour. What those individuals see causing the outcomes of events are called attributions. An important consideration here is that, as Schunk and Zimmerman (2006) comment, individuals attribute causes to their own actions as well as the actions of others. Individual successes and failures in academic achievement are, most often, attributed to four factors: ability, effort, task difficulty and luck (Schunk & Zimmerman, 2006). Each factor is characterised by being either internal or external to the individual, stable or unstable over time, and controllable or uncontrollable. In terms of difficulties experienced in learning and/or behaviour, if learners believe, or can be persuaded to believe, that they have some control over the causes of their difficulties, they are much more likely to put effort into overcoming these difficulties (Demetriou, 2011).

LEARNING POINT
CONSIDERING WAYS TO CHANGE LEARNERS'
ATTRIBUTIONS OF FAILURE

Ability may be seen as internal, often unchangeable over time, but potentially controllable with effort and determination. If teachers can demonstrate to learners the degree to which they can some have control over their lack of achievement, for example their perceived lack of ability, they are 'much more likely to persist in their efforts at learning' (Demetriou, 2011, p. 17).

How might a teacher start to influence learners' attributions about their own ability?

What part might trust in the relationship between teacher and learner play in this process, do you think?

Views of learning

In the field of special educational, or additional learning and/or support needs, there is a crucial, though in some ways simplistic, distinction that we can make between two fundamentally different views of learning and the learner that are prevalent. Firstly, there is the view that all behaviour is learned and can be shaped by external influences, that knowledge can be transmitted or 'delivered', and that the learner can be seen 'as a rather passive recipient of pre-packaged knowledge' (Kozulin, 2003, p. 16), a container that can be filled by teachers. Then there is the view that the learner has active agency in learning in settings, schools and colleges, and is proactive from birth in interpreting and constructing the world.

Principles underpinning behaviourist views

The view that all behaviour is learned is most commonly reflected in the behaviourist model of learning. It is important to understand this model because it has so often underpinned interventions designed to address difficulties in learning and behaviour in educational institutions (Dwivedi & Gupta, 2000).

The behaviourist view is based on the principle that behaviour is learned through so-called 'conditioning': behaviour can be either stimulated by something, that is, by the antecedents, or else strengthened or weakened by its consequences. Early behaviourist theories (Watson, 1913) asserted that the human mind is like a 'tabula rasa',[2] a 'blank slate' at birth until impressions from external sources are inscribed on it. Even though later versions of behaviourism acknowledge the role of genes and biological components in behaviour, we still often hear it asserted that knowledge can be transmitted/delivered to learners.

Underlying behavioural principles is a basic concern with people's actions, not with assumptions about intentions or feelings. It tends to a view that the psychology of learning should be scientific: the only acceptable evidence is that which is observable and measurable. This has been the predominant model of learning for many years, particularly in the world of special or additional learning or support provision where individual education, learning or behaviour plans have often been drawn up with interventions designed to be 'done to' the child to shape learning and behaviour.

Most of the principles of behaviourism stemmed from research with animals in laboratories, for example Pavlov (1928) and Skinner (1938, 1953). There are two different forms of behaviourism that can be seen reflected in educational contexts: classical and operant, reflecting conditioning through either antecedents or consequences.

Classical conditioning: Pavlov

In the famous experiments that the Russian physiologist, Ivan Pavlov, conducted with his dogs, he first demonstrated how the presence of a bowl of dog food can act as a stimulus that triggers a dog's natural response to salivate. He noticed that the dogs started to associate his laboratory assistant with food and they started to salivate before the food arrived. This we might call a

---

[2] In Latin 'tabula rasa' literally means 'a scraped wax tablet'.

'learned' or 'conditioned' response. Pavlov then tried linking the sound of a bell to giving food to the dogs. Every time he gave food to the dogs, he rang the bell. After a while he tried ringing the bell without giving food to the dogs, and saw that there was an increase in salivation. The result of the experiment was a new conditioned response: salivation at the sound of the bell alone. Pavlov's theory developed into 'classical conditioning'. In other words, classical conditioning refers to learning that associates a stimulus that already results in a natural response with a new, conditioned stimulus that brings about the same response.

Translated into the context of education, if learners are behaving in a way that is unacceptable, from a behaviourist perspective it is important to investigate whether anything has happened that has stimulated this behaviour. If a stimulus, otherwise known as the 'antecedent', can be identified, the behaviour should alter when that stimulus is removed or modified. We discuss this issue further in Chapter 7.

Web activity WA2.1
Understanding Pavlov's work

If you are interested in exploring classical conditioning and Pavlov's work, you might choose to access the video material to which we have referred on the website.

Operant conditioning: Skinner

Classical conditioning is different from operant conditioning. In classical conditioning, behaviour is influenced by stimuli, as described above. In operant conditioning, behaviour is modified by its consequences, that is, by its effect. In straightforward terms, we might think of operant conditioning as a way of learning that occurs through rewards for desired, and punishment for undesirable, behaviour. In a famous series of tasks, Skinner (1938) studied operant conditioning by placing animals, for example rats, in a 'Skinner box'. The box contained a lever, and if the rats knocked it, immediately a food pellet would be released. If the rats repeated the behaviour, they would be rewarded with another food pellet. The rats quickly learned to go straight to the lever after being placed in the box. We might call this 'trial and error learning'. A reward, in this case food, strengthened the association between pressing the lever and finding food, and reinforced the behaviour. Consistency of reinforcement is important. If the association between the action and the response was then repeatedly broken by removing the reward, the rats' behaviour would gradually cease through 'extinction'.

Reinforcement of behaviour can be either positive or negative. Positive reinforcement strengthens behaviour by providing a consequence that the individual perceives as rewarding. The opposite of positive reinforcement is negative reinforcement. Where something unpleasant occurs as a result of an action, the removal of the unpleasant consequences can be experienced as rewarding and, thus, reinforces more acceptable action. Translated into human actions, undesirable behaviour can be discouraged through putting a stop to something unpleasant.

Behavioural principles have frequently been applied to attempts to modify interactions between teachers and learners in the context of settings/schools/colleges.

Web activity WA2.2
Understanding Skinner's work

If you are interested in exploring operant conditioning and Skinner's work, you might choose to access the video material to which we have referred on the website.

Behaviourist principles in practice in education

When behavioural principles are applied to modify undesirable behaviour in school settings, such behaviour is interpreted as having been learned as a result of either a stimulus, or some kind of reinforcement. To address this, the physical and social context (the setting conditions/ antecedents) in which the behaviour occurs and/or what happens afterwards to reinforce the behaviour – the consequences – can be changed to bring about improvement. This process may be called 'applied behavioural analysis' (ABA). There has been wide use in UK classrooms of the process of identifying and addressing the setting conditions/antecedents of the behaviour, and also identifying and applying reinforcers that are meaningful to learners so teachers can reward what they want their students to do again and ignore or punish what they want students to stop doing. Use of this model is often called 'behaviour management', where 'the antecedent conditions or reinforcing consequences of a behaviour are adjusted in order to moderate its frequency' (Dwivedi & Gupta, 2000, p. 76). The key here is consistency on the part of teachers and/or others responsible for the progress and behaviour of learners.

Critiques of behaviourism

Over time there has been a number of criticisms of the principles of behaviourism and behaviourist techniques for bringing about changes in behaviour. For example, one of the principles is that the only evidence that is valid is that which is directly observable. This approach might be able to explain natural reflexes and responses to stimuli. However, it ignores what one might think of as the inner workings of the mind and precludes the study of consciousness because this cannot be observed directly. Not all behaviour can be shaped, of course. Behavioural approaches often fail to take adequate account of the emotions. As an adult whom the current author interviewed in the education wing of a prison commented: 'I just wanted teachers to go away and leave me alone. Just leave me alone.' We might here follow Shyman (2016) and Cooper and Barbara (2011) in arguing that in ignoring consciousness we might see behaviourist approaches as dehumanising.

There is an ethical issue, too. Behavioural approaches might serve teachers' wishes to manage students rather than responding to individual learners' needs (Hanko, 1994) and interests. Overuse of praise might lead children into dependency. Besides, students may well see through this if it is not sincere. As Hanko (1994, p. 166) comments:

> emotional factors affect learning, especially if we see only their provocative or withdrawn facade which usually hides children in constant misery, loneliness, self-loathing and

fear. [...] teachers are frequently baffled by children who 'don't respond even to praise', 'spoil their work the moment I praise it', 'just shrug it off' and 'don't seem to care' [...] A praise-refusing student's determination not to be lured into the risks of failing yet again may be further reinforced.

These approaches tend to ignore the significance of behaviour within cultural and community contexts, together with the traditional values, in which behaviour is defined and understood (Glynn & Bishop, 1995; Gay, 2010). Where teachers do not understand the cultural norms of their students, they may 'mis-cue' in their application of behaviour management strategies. We might ask how many times we hear ourselves, and others, say to young people who have misbehaved: 'Look at me when you're talking to me' without our thinking about whether looking adults in the face is culturally acceptable in the young person's family's culture.

Further, behavioural approaches might also encourage students into unthinking conformity to authority. For example, in a notorious set of experiments, 'the electric shock experiments', Milgram, an American psychologist, demonstrated how ordinary people could be conditioned into giving severe electric shocks to their peers as punishment for failing tasks (Milgram, 1963, 1974).

Web activity WA2.3
Understanding Milgram's work

On the website we have uploaded references to video clips of Milgram's experiments so that you can see for yourself what they comprised and why they were later criticised as unethical.

Principles underpinning cognitive-behavioural models

In recent years, there has been a move towards understandings of learning that take more account of how individuals construct reality rather than assuming that all behaviour is directly learned. For example, cognitive-behavioural approaches developed out of behaviourist psychology to integrate human information-processing. Such approaches can employ perception, language, memory, and imagery, for example, to focus attention on 'the stream of automatic thoughts which accompany and guide [...] behaviour'. As they do so, for example in schools and colleges, learners 'can learn [how] to make choices about the appropriateness of these self-statements, and if necessary introduce new thoughts and ideas' (McLeod, 1998, p. 72).

Practical applications of cognitive-behavioural approaches

In Chapter 7, we discuss some of the cognitive-behavioural programmes that are designed to encourage meta-cognitive awareness, that is, awareness of one's own stream of thinking and feelings in order to be able to control emotions and/or regulate feelings associated with violence, disaffection or a sense of personal isolation (Meichenbaum & Turk, 1976; Shapiro & Cole, 1994).

Principles underpinning constructivist views

Skinner's work was seminal to advances in understanding learning from a behaviourist perspective. Since that time, however, there has been an increasing interest in the way individuals actively construct their understanding of the reality in which they live. There is an assumption here that the way in which young people view themselves in school has a strong influence on their learning and behaviour. It is less events themselves that cause 'the emotional and behavioural difficulties which people experience' but more 'the way they interpret and make sense of these events' (McLeod, 1998, pp. 71–72). As we discuss in Chapter 4, children have a legal right to be heard, not simply as a question of human rights, albeit this is very important. Teachers need to understand how children feel about, and make sense of, their own circumstances. Some learners in settings/schools/colleges might be 'highly anxious and continually under-value themselves', some can seem 'over-confident and extremely resilient', while others may know their own strengths and weaknesses. 'Students may be gregarious, or loners, or they may be lonely' (Pollard, 2002, pp. 97–98). Learning is highly dependent on both the context, what the learner makes of the situation, and the interaction between them (Greeno, 1998; Lave & Wenger, 1998). In terms of assessing progress and the barriers to this, adults in educational institutions have to be concerned all the time with the sense that learners are making of their worlds, their experiences, the way in which they understand tasks in classrooms, and so on. All of this requires careful observation and sensitive listening and reflection.

At the heart of the process of learning is the question of why any of us should make an effort to achieve a task if we do not see it as worthwhile compared to the effort that is required. This is especially so for learners who experience difficulties of some sort. It seems obvious that learners with special educational, or additional learning and/or support needs, like everybody else, come to decisions about what activities are worth investing in, and whether the benefits of any given learning situation outweigh the time, effort and (in some classrooms) the risk of being wrong and exposing themselves to public humiliation in being thought stupid. All have some power and control. Offering some degree of choice that can be accommodated within the setting/school/college day gives learners responsibility and acknowledges that they have preferences, dislikes and ideas.

Two of the foremost theorists in contributing to how we may see learning in education contexts from a constructivist view are Jean Piaget (1896–1980) and Lev Vygotsky (1896–1934). Another leading educationalist whose work in this area we also outline below and use in further chapters is Jerome Bruner.

Jean Piaget

Jean Piaget, a Swiss psychologist, was concerned with the development of a human thought processes and the way in which these thought processes influence our 'cognitions', in other words, how we understand and interact with the world. He was one of the theorists who contributed a lot to our understanding that the way that children think is different from the way adults think. Children's minds are not simply smaller versions of adults'. From his work with his children in his own family, Piaget (1954, 1964, 1969) came to see that children take an active role in the learning process, behaving rather like young scientists as they perform experiments, make observations and learn about the world. As they interact with the world around them, they continually build upon and add to their existing knowledge, and adapt previously held ideas to accommodate new information. His theory of cognitive development suggests that children move through four different stages of mental development and that these stages are universal:

- Sensorimotor (0–2 years). A baby has an inborn set of reflex movements and perceptual systems. During this initial phase of development, children use skills and abilities they were born with: looking, sucking, grasping and listening to learn about the environment. Learning is, in general, through trial and error and there is quick development of direct knowledge of the world as the child relates physical actions to perceived results of those actions. In the final part of this stage, children begin to develop symbols to represent events or objects in the world. This means that, as a result of direct experience of interaction with the environment around them, during this period children can begin to understand the world through what we might call 'mental operations' rather than purely through physical actions.
- Preoperational (2–7 years). The child begins to speak, develops the ability to represent events and objects mentally – the so-called 'semiotic function' – and to engage in symbolic play, for example using a broomstick as a horse. However, s/he cannot yet see others' points of view. This is a characteristic of 'egocentrism': an inability to understand that other people have different thoughts, feelings and views.
- Concrete operational (7–11 years). The child begins to use logical thought or rules, but can only apply logical thinking to real (concrete) objects. From this, we have the term 'concrete operational'. The child also starts to see things from the others' viewpoints, hence becomes less egocentric. S/he develops an understanding that number, area, volume, orientation and reversibility do not change when physical arrangements change. This is often called 'conservation'. S/he cannot yet think in the abstract or hypothetically.
- Formal operational (11+ years). The child begins to use abstract reasoning and to develop the ability to manipulate ideas mentally, without having to use concrete objects. For example, s/he develops an increasing aptitude for combining and classifying items, doing mathematical calculations, thinking creatively and imagining the outcome of particular actions.

We should acknowledge the importance of Piaget's work. His conclusions that learners learn by interactions in their own environment and reconstruct their understandings in light of experiences have made a significant contribution to primary schools' practice in particular. Also, in terms of designing strategies to address moderate learning difficulties, as we discuss in Chapter 8, it can be very useful to conceptualise learning as a continuum from the sensorimotor to the formal operational stage. It becomes very clear, then, that learners who are seen as working at the preoperational stage, for example, need learning activities from peers working at the formal operational stage.

Piaget's conclusions have, however, been criticised in a number of respects. His work implies that children go through stages of development, but actually development continues from birth throughout adulthood. Also, as Wood, Smith and Grossniklaus (2001) comment, he seems to have underestimated the ability of children at different ages. In addition, he appears not to have considered the variety of social or cultural contexts in which children are reared sufficiently. Further, some of his research methods have been questioned (Donaldson, 1984), leading some commentators to question some of his conclusions.

Web activity WA2.4
Understanding Piaget's work

On the website we have uploaded references to video clips of Piaget's work so that you can see for yourself how his investigations were conducted.

Lev Vygotsky

The social constructivist model of Lev Vygotsky was developed in the context of Soviet Russia, a very different national context from that of Piaget. Vygotsky began to work in psychology shortly after the Russian revolution, where Marxism replaced the rule of the czar. To understand the distinctiveness of Vygotsky's work (1962, 1978, 1981) it is important to be aware that the new philosophy of Marxism emphasised socialism and collectivism. Sharing and co-operation were encouraged, and the success of any individual was seen as reflecting the success of the culture. For Vygotsky, the individual's development occurs in interaction with his/her culture, hence thought, language and reasoning process were understood to develop through social interactions with others, especially the family.

We should not underestimate the importance he placed on the social context in which learning takes place. Vygotsky (1978, p. 57) proposed that there were two places, or 'planes', where the learning process occurs:

- the interpersonal (between people) plane in which individuals learn predominantly through interactions with others, both peers and, especially, more informed/expert others;
- the intrapersonal (within the person) plane, in which as s/he reflects on new learning and appropriates (literally 'takes to him/herself') new knowledge and skills.

Core to the Vygotskyan view of developmental processes is that concept formation is 'mediated'. The development of what Vygotsky called 'higher mental processes', in other words thinking, reasoning, and so on, depends on 'mediators' to mediate (make sense of) interactions between the individual and the environment. As Vygotsky (1962, p. 150) stated:

> direct teaching of concepts is impossible and fruitless. A teacher who tries to do this usually accomplishes nothing but empty verbalism, a parrotlike repetition of words by the child, simulating a knowledge of the corresponding concepts but actually covering up a vacuum.

Facts are not simply transferred to learners; rather, learners take the facts and appropriate their own meanings by means of these tools. Language, as Vygotsky (1962) suggested, is a tool that is very important to the sense-making process, and is acquired through interacting with a more knowledgeable mediator. In the process, mediators can mediate, for example guide, reward or model the use of 'cultural tools', particularly language, signs, texts, graphic organisers, and so on.

Social constructivist approaches in practice in education

Integral to the process of learning in a social context is the concept of the zone of proximal development (ZPD). Vygotsky (1978, p. 86) defined the ZPD as:

> the distance between the actual developmental level as determined by independent problem solving and the level of potential development as determined through problem solving under adult guidance or in collaboration with more capable peers.

The ZPD is, effectively, the next step in learning in terms of new knowledge and skills that learners cannot learn without interaction with more experienced or expert others. Wood, Bruner and Ross (1976) developed the concept of 'scaffolding' through the ZPD. This is structured support for new learning by a more informed/expert other that is based on his/her knowledge of the learner's current level of knowledge and understanding of a topic (Fani & Ghaemi, 2011) and the expert's knowledge of the topic in question. Assistance in the ZPD functions most effectively when it is tailored to the learner, adapted and eventually withdrawn in response to learner development (Lantolf & Aljaafreh, 1996). While learning in the ZPD requires scaffolding from more expert others, it is also about participating. However, an issue that is really important in relation to young people with difficulties in learning is that emotion is often implicated in the process. The experience of failure, particularly if it is a frequent occurrence, can be very upsetting (Wearmouth, Glynn & Berryman, 2005). Very importantly, learning and behaviour are mediated through the kind of relationship a learner has with a teacher. This relationship both develops over time and is influenced by the teacher's sense of a student's value and worth. An obvious implication here is that all learners, including those who experience difficulties, need a safe space for learning where they are not afraid either to make mistakes or ask for help. It is absolutely essential that they feel safe in talking about themselves as well as asking and answering questions (Bishop, Berryman & Wearmouth, 2014) and are not humiliated by the teacher's, or peers', reactions.

We discuss the very important issue of scaffolding further in Chapter 8 where we consider appropriate support for young people who experience difficulties in cognition and learning.

Jerome Bruner

Jerome Seymour Bruner (1915–2016) was a very well-known and influential psychologist in the field of education in the twentieth century. Below we outline two aspects of his work that are relevant in discussions of the conceptualisation of appropriate and relevant responses to the needs of learners who experience special educational, or additional learning or support, needs. These are Bruner's (1966) three modes of representation of reality, and his later (1996) work related to the importance to learning of the cultural context.

Three modes of representation

Piaget and Vygotsky both influenced Bruner's studies. Their work helped Bruner develop his theory of the way that cognition develops which he subsequently applied to the classroom. As cognitive growth occurs, learners interpret the world through three modes of representation: enactive, iconic and symbolic. Bruner maintained that these modes of representation follow in sequence, but, unlike Piaget, he argued that they are not age-dependent. They depend instead on the learner's familiarity with the subject matter, which is highly influenced by the environment. Like Piaget's model above, these modes move from the concrete 'learn by doing' to the abstract. Students must go through interpretations of all of them successively in order to connect new ideas and concepts if they are to generate their own understanding:

- In the enactive stage, students begin to learn through active manipulation: first doing, then understanding and knowing. In the very early years, for example, children learn to move through their own actions. At the enactive stage, they need the opportunity to 'play' with concrete materials to understand how things work. One implication here is that children whose sight, hearing, taste, touch, smell or physical movement are impaired will be less able to understand and know their world through 'doing' unless special efforts are made to make this possible.
- In the second stage, iconic, learners develop the ability to visualise concrete information. This means they can make mental images of physical objects and no longer need to manipulate them directly. Using this mode, children learn to understand the meaning of pictures and diagrams, and how to use numbers to carry out mathematical calculations without physically counting objects.
- The symbolic is the final stage in which students can use abstract ideas to represent the world. For example, students are able to evaluate, judge and think critically. The 'symbolic' mode is an abstract representation of something else. Abstract symbols are 'arbitrary'. This means that they do not necessarily resemble what they represent. We might take the example of spoken language. Commonly, unless a word is onomatopoeic its sound does not resemble reality.

Children's learning involves becoming proficient in each of these increasingly more complex modes, but they may experience difficulty at any point in their development. Effective teachers, Bruner maintains, must provide assistance and guidance through these three stages through 'scaffolding' to enable learners to build their understanding and, ultimately, to become autonomous:

> We teach a subject not to produce little libraries on that subject, but rather to get a student to think [...] for himself, to consider matters as a historian does, to take part in the process of knowledge-getting. Knowing is a process, not a product. (Bruner, 1966, p. 72)

Cultural context for learning

Bruner's later work, reflected in *The Culture of Education* (1996), was clearly influenced by Vygotsky, who placed such an emphasis on the importance of the social context for learning:

> Culture shapes the mind [...] it provides us with the toolkit by which we construct not only our worlds but our very conception of ourselves and our powers. (Bruner, 1996, p. x)

This orientation 'presupposes that human mental activity is neither solo nor conducted unassisted, even when it goes on "inside the head"' (1996, p. xi).

Attachment theory

What happens in our earliest years plays a crucial role in who we become as adults and how we live our lives, as the work of Owen (1824, 1841, 1857), Pestalozzi (1801/1894) and Froebel (1826/2005) indicate in their philanthropic and seminal work in establishing educational provision in the early years. One of the earliest theories of social development, so-called 'attachment theory' (Bowlby, 1944, 1952), contends that early relationships with caregivers play a major role in child development and continue to influence social relationships throughout life. This theory suggests that children are born with an innate need to form attachments that assist the child to survive by ensuring that s/he receives care and protection. Both children and caregivers engage in behaviours designed to ensure closeness. Children try to stay close and connected to their caregivers. In their turn, caregivers provide a secure base for children to explore their world.

Bowlby trained as a psychoanalyst and drew together two different traditions: child psychiatry and ethology (the study of animal behaviour). As a child psychiatrist he made the connection between the lack of consistent and caring relationships in early childhood and later development in his article 'Forty-four juvenile thieves: their characters and home-life' (Bowlby, 1944). Later, he was influenced by the work of the ethologist Lorenz, who had noted the significance of the bonding processes between mother and young of a species, which is called 'imprinting'. In his book *King Solomon's Ring* (1952), Lorenz described how signals he gave to a clutch of hatching ducklings persuaded them that he was their mother, so that they waddled after him in a line.

Central to Bowlby's work is the view that:

> children deprived of maternal care [...] may be seriously affected in their physical, intellectual, emotional and social development [...]. Bowlby asserts that 'prolonged separation of a child from his mother (or mother substitute) during the first five years of life stands foremost among the causes of delinquent character development' (Bowlby, 1944; Bowlby, 1952). (Holmes, 1993, p. 39)

Research confirms Bowlby's work on attachment theory, that:

- children who receive consistent support and care are more likely to develop a secure attachment style, while those who receive less reliable care may develop an ambivalent, avoidant or disorganised style. Consistent, loving, attentive behaviours by adults will typically result in children developing a secure attachment with those adults, whether their mother, other parent or caregivers;
- well-loved, emotionally secure children are more able to overcome problems, persist for longer, take risks in their learning and make secure long-term attachments as adults.

Support for a view of the devastating effects on their later social relationships of being reared in social isolation was indicated in the work of other ethologists, for example Harlow's famous study of rhesus monkeys (Harlow, 1962).

Web activity WA2.5
Understanding Harlow's experiments

On the website we have uploaded references to video clips of Harlow's experiments so that you can see for yourself what they comprised of and why they were later criticised as unethical.

In taking account of the relationship between the emotions and behaviour, Bowlby's theory of human social development has had considerable influence over educational provision for young children whose behaviour is of concern in settings and schools (Bowlby, 1952). Where experiences have been consistently impoverished and children have developed insecure attachments with their main carers or have been neglected or abused emotionally, physically, sexually or socially (and in some cases all of these), as we discuss in Chapter 7, there is the possibility for making secure attachments later with the care and attention of loving adults, for example in 'nurture groups' (Bennathan & Boxall, 2012).

Conclusion

A range of factors in settings, schools and colleges influence learning and behaviour. For example, research indicates that teacher expectations of learners and learners' expectations of themselves can have an impact on achievement and behaviour. Across time, a range of social or psychological understandings of learning and behaviour have underpinned interventions and also affected outcomes. Among these it is possible to distinguish between the view of the learner rather as a container to be filled by teachers and behaviour to be shaped and taught, or that the learner is proactive in interpreting and constructing the world, or that, from birth, children need to develop close attachment to primary caregivers without which they may not be able to overcome personal problems in later life, persist for longer, take risks in their learning and make secure long-term attachments as adults.

How do you understand the process of learning yourself? How do you think that the way you understand this process influences the way you teach – or might teach, if you are not in a position to teach others?

In Chapter 3 we turn to discussion of the historical context for the development of special provision in education as a backdrop against which current provision may be understood.

Further reading

Influence of teacher expectations

Alvidrez, J., & Weinstein, R. S. (1999) Early teacher perceptions and later student academic achievement. *Journal of Educational Psychology*, 91(4), 731–746.

Hinnant, J. B., O'Brien, M., & Ghazarian, S. R. (2009) The longitudinal relations of teacher expectations to achievement in the early school years. *Journal of Educational Psychology,* 101(3), 662–670.

Madon, S., Willard, J., Guyll, M., & Scherr, K. C. (2011) Self-fulfilling prophecies: Mechanisms, power, and links to social problems. *Social and Personality Psychology Compass,* 5(8), 578–590.

Rosenthal, R., & Jacobson, L. (1968) *Pygmalion in the Classroom.* New York: Holt, Rinehart and Winston.

Spitz, H. H. (1999) Beleaguered Pygmalion: A history of the controversy over claims that teacher expectancy raises intelligence. *Intelligence,* 27(3), 199–234.

Attribution theory

Burns, M. K. (2000) Examining special education labels through attribution theory: A potential source for learned helplessness. *Ethical Human Sciences and Services,* 2(2), 101–107.

Gaier, S. E. (2015) Understanding why students do what they do: Using attribution theory to help students succeed academically. *Research & Teaching in Developmental Education,* 31(2), 6–19.

Behaviourism, cognitivism and constructivism

Ertmer, P. A. & Newby, T. J. (2013) Behaviorism, cognitivism, constructivism: Comparing critical features from an instructional design perspective. *Performance Improvement Quarterly,* 26(2), 43–71.

Kirschner, P. A., & Hendrick, C. (2020) *How Learning Happens: Seminal Works in Educational Psychology and What They Mean in Practice.* London: Routledge.

Woollard, J. (2010) *Psychology for the Classroom: Behaviourism.* London: David Fulton.

Attachment theory

Holmes, J. (2014) *John Bowlby and Attachment Theory* (2nd edn). London: Routledge.

National Institute for Health and Care Excellence (NICE) (2020) *Attachment Difficulties in Children and Young People: Overview.* London: NICE. Available at: http://pathways.nice.org.uk/pathways/attachment-difficulties-in-children-and-youngpeople

3

A HISTORICAL BACKGROUND OF THE SPECIAL SECTOR IN EDUCATION

Major questions addressed in this chapter are:

- What kind of relationship is there between the national political context and contemporary policy and practices in education as they relate to those who experience difficulties?
- How did we reach the current position in relation to current policy and provision for learners identified as having difficulties in educational contexts?
- What should be, and has in the past been, done with children who make little or no progress and who were/ are thought to be holding others back?

Key terms

Rationale for special sector in education, disabilities of body and mind, special educational needs, Warnock Report (Department of Education and Science, 1978)

Introduction

In Chapters 1 and 2 we saw how preconceptions, labelling, and so on, as well as our own experiences, can influence the way in which we view and respond to learners who experience difficulties of various kind in settings, schools and colleges (Fulcher, 1989; Wearmouth, 2009, 2017). Chapter 3 begins with a discussion of the rationale for a special sector in education, followed by a summary of the historical context of educational provision for learners identified as 'different' from peers as a result of learning or physical difficulties or behaviour viewed as of concern in some way. It continues with a discussion of changes in thinking about learning, behaviour and children and young people's rights over time.

LEARNING POINT
RATIONALE FOR A 'SPECIAL' SECTOR IN THE EDUCATION SYSTEM

There are a number of different ways of looking at the rationale for the development of the special education sector. For example, some consider it was developed to:

- serve the economic and commercial interests of society, so that as many people as possible with difficulties should be productive and contribute to an industrial society. Certainly businessmen 'played a part in the founding of pioneer establishments for the deaf and for the blind, and [...] throughout the 19th century trade training took up much of the lives of the handicapped attending them' (Cole, 1990, p. 101); and/or
- address the needs of children in difficulty more effectively from an essentially benevolent position (Cole, 1989); and/or
- provide a deliberate means to exclude troublesome pupils, or pupils who required a lot of the teacher's time, from mainstream classes (Loxley & Thomas, 2007). For example, when a new national system of secondary schools was designed following the 1944 Education Act, it might be argued that the smooth running of those schools demanded the exclusion of some pupils, for instance those categorised as 'educationally subnormal'; and/or
- serve the vested interest of, for example, the medical profession and psychologists who benefit from the continued existence of special provision (Tomlinson, 1988).

As you read the sections below, you might wish to come back to these points and make up your own mind about the purpose of the special sector in education.

A historical overview of the development of the 'special' sector

To understand why special provision was developed in educational systems across the UK, it is important to look back at history and how the societal context at any one time influences national developments in education. Settings', schools' and colleges' curricula 'and educational institutions are products of the social system in which they were established' (Broadfoot, 2011, p. 9). This includes society's values, beliefs and political ideology (Wearmouth, 2009, 2017).

Education was not compulsory until the 1870 Forster Education Act in England and Wales, and the 1872 Education (Scotland) Act. It is interesting, therefore, that schools for blind and deaf children, founded by individuals or by charities, not by the government, had already been established well before education became compulsory in the UK (Department of Education and Science, 1978, chapter 2).

Prior to this, education in fee-paying grammar and so-called 'Public Schools', such as Eton and Harrow, was largely for the children of the wealthy. Children of poorer families might attend a network of Sunday Schools, 'voluntary' (mostly church) schools, and informal neighbourhood schools with low fees. However, a significant proportion of the poorest children had no access to education at all. A report from the Select Committee on Education of the Poorer Classes in England and Wales, in 1838, noted, for example:

> The kind of education given to the children of the working classes is lamentably deficient [...] it extends (bad as it is) to but a small proportion of those who ought to receive it. (Great Britain, Parliament, Select Committee on Education, 1838, vii–viii)

Lawson and Silver (1973, p. 235) comment that those who campaigned for mass education experienced vicious hostility to the very idea of educating the poor. For example, a philanthropist, Hannah More, and her sister, who by 1800 had been instrumental in setting up a number of Sunday schools, in which reading, the Bible and the catechism were taught to local children in the Cheddar area, met 'persistent and virulent opposition' (Lawson & Silver, 1973, p. 235) from farmers and church dignitaries. Farmers thought that education, even just learning to read, would damage agriculture. Clergy saw it as 'undermining the natural and necessary ignorance of the poor, and therefore the social order' (Lawson & Silver, 1973, p. 235). During the debate on the Parochial Schools Bill of 1807, Tory MP Davies Giddy is reported in *Hansard* as warning the Commons that:

> giving education to the labouring classes of the poor [...] would, in effect, be found to be prejudicial to their morals and happiness; it would teach them to despise their lot in life, instead of making them good servants in agriculture and other laborious employments to which their rank in society had destined them; instead of teaching them subordination, it would render them factious and refractory, as is evident in the manufacturing counties; it would enable them to read seditious pamphlets, vicious books and publications against Christianity; it would render them insolent to their superiors; and, in a few years, the result would be that the legislature would find it necessary to direct the strong arm of power towards them and to furnish the executive magistrates with more vigorous powers than were now in force. (Great Britain, Parliament, House of Commons, 13 June 1807, Vol. 9, Cols 798–799)

Early development of special education provision: focus on employability

Early special education provision began at the end of the eighteenth century, occurring at a time of rapid industrial expansion when there was no legal requirement to make education available to all children. In this age of insistent demand for child labour in factories in towns and cities, and on the land in the countryside, 'there could be no question of establishing a system of compulsory popular education' (Simon, 1974, p. 152).

In some areas 'Schools of industry' were set up to provide the poor with manual training and elementary instruction. Such a school opened at Kendal in the Lake District in 1799. The Board of Education (1926, pp. 3–4) comments that:

> the children were taught reading and writing, geography and religion. Thirty of the older girls were employed in knitting, sewing, spinning and housework, and 36 younger girls were employed in knitting only. The older boys were taught shoemaking, and the younger boys prepared machinery for carding wool. The older girls assisted in preparing breakfast, which was provided in the school at a small weekly charge. They were also taught laundry work. The staff consisted of one schoolmaster, two teachers of spinning and knitting, and one teacher for shoemaking.

Under the terms of the Factory Act of 1833, children from 9 to 13 years of age could work up to nine hours a day (www.nationalarchives.gov.uk/education/resources/1833-factory-act/, accessed 26.10.2021). It was not until 1893 that the minimum age of employment was raised to 10.

Web activity WA3.1
'Special' schools for the poorest children

On the website we have uploaded text and an activity related to what we might see as 'special' schools for the poorest children. You might wish to access the material and carry out the activity that is suggested.

The earliest institutions providing any kind of training for children who experienced difficulties of any kind, learning, sensory or physical, were therefore established in a societal context where child labour was the norm.

Schools for the blind

In relation to the special sector in education, schools for blind and deaf children were established first. These were founded by individual philanthropists or through charities (Department of Education and Science, 1978, chapter 2). Afterwards central government supplemented what was provided by voluntary agencies, and created a national framework for the provision of special education. Having said that, it was not until the Education (Handicapped Children) Act 1970 that all children were given entitlement to an appropriate education.

Early private foundations were designed with a focus on training in work skills, as well as moral improvement and the Christian religion (Oliphant, 2006): the Liverpool School of Instruction for the Indigent[1] Blind, founded in 1791, the London School for the Indigent Blind, 1800, and the Norwich Asylum and School for the Indigent Blind, 1805.

---

[1]That is, poor/destitute.

The first senior school for the blind was the College for the Blind Sons of Gentlemen founded at Worcester in 1866. Worcester College remained the only route for blind boys to achieve higher qualifications and entry into the professions until after the First World War. (The equivalent for girls was not established until 1921 in Chorleywood.)

Despite these developments, by 1870 there were still only a dozen or so institutions for the blind: most of these were training centres and only a small proportion of the blind benefited from them.

Schools for those with physical disabilities

The prospects of most children with disabilities were grim. In the Marylebone Cripples' Home and Industrial School for Girls, established in 1851, and the Kensington Training Home for Crippled Boys, founded in 1865, attempts were made to teach a trade. In the girls' school, for example:

> the girls were given lessons in reading and writing by ladies from the Home's committee. They were also given industrial training in the form of straw plaiting, straw hat making and needlework. (www.childrenshomes.org.uk/MaryleboneRefuge/?LMCL=Iq6cDY, accessed 26.10.2021)

Provision for the deaf

The first school for the deaf in Great Britain was Thomas Braidwood's Academy for the Deaf and Dumb that opened in Edinburgh in the early 1760s. More schools for the deaf followed: in Liverpool, Manchester, Exeter and Doncaster in the 1820s; at Aberystwyth in 1847; and in Edinburgh (Donaldson's Hospital) in 1851. The education they provided was limited, and despite the training they offered, many of their inmates subsequently failed to find employment and ended up begging, as the Warnock Report (Department of Education and Science, 1978, p. 9) notes ironically, although the curriculum was predominantly training.

Web activity WA3.2
Functions of early schools for the blind and the deaf

On the website we have uploaded text and an activity related to the nature of education and functions of early schools for the blind and deaf. You might wish to access the material and carry out the activity that is suggested.

Provision for the 'mentally defective'

Before the middle of the nineteenth century, so-called 'mentally defective' children who required custodial care were placed in workhouses and infirmaries. The first specific provision made for them was the Asylum for Idiots established at Highgate in 1847. Like the institutions for the blind and deaf, the Asylum took adults as well as children. This asylum had a philanthropic aim, as recorded in the National Archives. It was not simply to care for the 'Idiot and Imbecile', but 'to prepare him, as far as possible, for the duties and enjoyments of life' [Bye-laws 1857] (http://discovery.nationalarchives.gov.uk/details/rd/ed87972d-14f1-4b0c-ab59-d72bcdbee573, accessed 26.10.2021). However, the view that those with difficulties in learning could be educated did not last. It was replaced by:

> a eugenicist preoccupation with fears of national decline, because of what was seen to be a link between mental defectiveness and criminality (Thomson, 1998; Wright & Digby, 1996). Mental defectives were seen as genetically tainted; they should be both separated from society, and prevented from reproducing. (Hall, 2008, p. 1006)

By 1870 there were five asylums, only three of which claimed to provide education. Admission was generally by election or payment. It meant being certified as an 'idiot'. Parents had to agree to this, and many hated the label (Cole, 1989, p. 22). In the same year, the newly created Metropolitan Asylum Board established all-age asylums at Caterham, Leavesden and Hampstead. The children were later separated from the adults, and those who were considered to be educable followed a programme of simple manual work and formal teaching. The staff were untrained and classes were very large.

In Scotland, the first establishment for the education of 'imbeciles' was set up at Baldovan in Dundee in 1852. It later became Strathmartine Hospital. An institution for 'defectives' was founded later in Edinburgh, transferred to a site in Larbert in 1863, and later became the Royal Scottish National Hospital. The Lunacy (Scotland) Act of 1862 recognised the needs of the mentally handicapped and authorised the granting of licences to charitable institutions established for the care and training of imbecile children.

Growth of access to education

In the second half of the nineteenth century, for a number of reasons, both political and economic, pressure grew for a nationally-organised system of universal elementary education. This was to have an effect on the organisation of special education provision.

A Reform Act passed by parliament in 1867 increased the number of men who could vote in elections. It extended the vote to all householders and lodgers in boroughs who paid rent of £10 a year or more, as well as to agricultural landowners and tenants with very small amounts of land. Consequently, the electorate in England and Wales doubled from one to two million men. As a result of this Act, some politicians argued that the lower classes should be educated 'to qualify them for the power that has passed [...] into their hands', as a Liberal Party parliamentarian, Robert Lowe (1867, p. 31), stated in an address to the Philosophical Institute of Edinburgh at the time.

In addition, the expansion of industry during the industrial revolution led some manufacturers to call for a greater pool of educated individuals from which to 'select the higher grades of workers, foremen and managers' (Simon, 1974, p. 360).

Then there was the question of the social control of children in cities and towns. Those under 9 years of age could not legally be employed under the terms of the 1833 Factory Act, as noted above, and, in any case, fewer children were needed to work in factories once machinery became more complex. The outcome of this was that children with no organised occupation in urban and city areas were seen as potentially troublesome and in need of supervision.

Under the 1870 Forster Education Act in England and Wales, and the 1872 Education (Scotland) Act, school boards were given the responsibility to ensure that elementary education was provided in places where charitable provision was not sufficient. In 1880 a further Act finally made school attendance compulsory in England for children from 5 to 10 years of age. Children who had not reached the standard 'fixed by a byelaw in force in the district' (§4, p. 143) were required to attend to 13 years of age.

Developments post-1870

In 1862, prior to the introduction of compulsory schooling, the policy of payment by results was introduced into schools in England. National-level funding for individual schools, including teachers' salaries, now depended in part on the outcomes of examinations of pupils conducted by school inspectors. So in 1870, when large numbers of children who seemed to have poor intellectual ability came to school for the first time, the question was what to do with them now that they were compelled to attend. Their presence was often felt to be holding others back in the large classes that existed in public elementary schools. In 1886, a Bill for 'giving facilities for the care, education, and training of Idiots and Imbeciles' (Roberts, 1981, http://studymore.org.uk/7. HTM#1886) received Royal Assent and passed into law as the Idiots Act 1886. Cole (1989, p. 40) outlines evidence presented to the Sharpe Report (Education Department, 1898) of what might happen to children identified in mainstream schools as 'feeble-minded'. 'In London, before 1892, the feeble-minded over 11 years old had been mixed with 5-year-olds in Standard 1'. However, teachers were 'so concerned with getting their average children through the Standards and so conscious of HMI's [inspectors'] expectations that they would send the feeble-minded to play in a corner with a slate'. Payment by results lasted until 1898, when it was abandoned.

An 1889 Royal Commission advised compulsory education for blind children from age 5 to 16, and for the deaf from age 7 to 16. Deaf children, who, at the time, were considered slower to learn because of difficulties in communication, should be taught by teachers specially qualified to do so.[2] Legislation in Scotland came in 1890 with the Education of the Blind and Deaf Mute Children (Scotland) Act, and in England and Wales in 1893 with the Elementary Education (Blind and Deaf Children) Act.

That 1889 Royal Commission recommended what kind of educational provision should be made for three groups of children identified as experiencing varying degrees of learning difficulties: 'feeble-minded', 'imbeciles' and 'idiots'. Feeble-minded should be educated in 'auxiliary' schools away from other children, and imbeciles should be sent to institutions where education should concentrate on sensory and physical development and improved speech. 'Idiots' were not thought to be educable. These days we would consider the use of these labels for children unacceptable. However, in the context of nineteenth-century Britain there was a

---

[2] It is interesting to note that teachers in special schools for children with visual and auditory impairments still require specialist qualifications but those in some other kinds of special educational institutions do not.

big difference in status and respect given to various groups in society who were seen as less worthy than others. We only have to remember the words of Mrs Alexander (1818–1895), who was responsible for the following verse, usually now omitted, of the Christian hymn 'All things bright and beautiful', first published in 1848 in a collection of hymns to raise money for deaf mutes, to recognise this point:

The rich man in his castle,

The poor man at his gate,

God made them high and lowly,

And ordered their estate.

Web activity WA3.3
Understanding the history of 'All things bright and beautiful' in context

If you are interested in reading about the history of this hymn, you can access it at www.telegraph.co.uk/culture/music/3668059/The-story-behind-the-hymn.html (accessed 26.10.2021).

Developments in mainstream education to 1939

As already noted above, to understand the current form and organisation of special educational and/or additional learning support provision we have to be aware of the social, political and ideological contexts in which that provision develops (Wearmouth, 2009). Between 1870 and the beginning of the Second World War in 1939 a number of developments took place in the national education system. Further legislation extended compulsory attendance: to age 11 in 1893, to 12 in 1899, to 14 in 1918, and to 15 in 1936. The outcome of this expansion in secondary education was fragmentation and considerable variation in the system across the country. In some parts of the country there was still little provision for separate secondary schools before the Second World War. There were questions about whether a secondary system should be organised and, if so, how this should be done. As Gillard (2021) notes:

> In the first half of the nineteenth century, calls for mass education had been resisted by those who wanted to preserve class distinctions and who saw the education of working-class children as a dangerous development; in the first half of the twentieth century the provision of secondary education for all was similarly resisted but, since it was now less acceptable to use class as an excuse, spurious theories about 'innate intelligence' were put forward instead. (www.educationengland.org.uk/history/chapter08.html, accessed 26.10.2021)

Developments in special education

At the beginning of the twentieth century, the new discipline of psychology made formal identification and assessment of 'deficiencies' in children seem more legitimate in the context of the time. In 1913:

> the Central Association for Mental Welfare was founded, and London County Council appointed psychologist Cyril Burt to investigate cases of individual children who present problems of special difficulty and who might be referred for examination by teachers, school medical officers, or care committee workers, magistrates or parents, and to carry out, or make recommendations for, suitable treatment or training of such children (quoted in Underwood 1955: 8). (Gillard, 2021, www.educationengland.org.uk/history/chapter07.html, accessed 26.10.2021)

In 1913 also, a Mental Deficiency Act, passed in 1913, followed the three grades of 'mental defectives' identified by the 1889 Royal Commission, and added a fourth, 'moral defective'. In each case the condition had to be present 'from birth or from an early age'.

Web activity WA3.4
Considering early definitions of 'mentally defective'

The archive of the National Association for the Feebleminded (Kirby, 1914) contains a record of advice given to 'every public official and social worker' to memorise the definitions of the 'four classes of mental defectives' in relation to this Act so that 'the mentally defective may not pass unrecognized' and should not be 'submitted to inappropriate treatment'. We have uploaded this text on the website, together with a reflective activity. You might wish to access this material now.

This Act required local education authorities in England and Wales to identify which children aged 7 to 16 in their area were defective. Those certified as incapable of being taught in special schools were to pass to the care of local mental deficiency committees. Only three MPs voted against the Act. One of them, Josiah Wedgwood,[3] is cited in Woodhouse (1982, p. 130) as saying: 'It is a spirit of the Horrible Eugenic Society which is setting out to breed up the working class as though they were cattle.'

The duty to provide for 'educable' children was enacted a year later.

> It shall be the duty of the local education authority [...] to make suitable provision [...] for the education of children belonging to their area whose age exceeds seven years and who are ascertained to be mentally defective [...]. (Elementary Education (Defective and Epileptic Children) Act 1914, Ch 45, 1(1))

---

[3] You might be interested to know that Josiah Wedgwood was a descendent of the famous Wedgwood pottery family, with a reputation for championing the causes of underdogs.

In Scotland, the Mental Deficiency (Scotland) Act of 1913 required school boards to identify children in their area who were 'defective'. Those children deemed 'ineducable' became the responsibility of parish councils for placement in an institution.

In 1921 in England, an Education Act consolidated previous legislation. 'Defective' and epileptic children should be certified and then educated in special provision, of which there was a whole range made by both voluntary bodies and local education authorities (LEAs). The parents of children in any of the four 'defective' categories were required to see that their child attended a suitable special school from the age of 5 in the case of blind or deaf children, or 7 for other children, until the age of 16. Local education authorities had the duty to ensure the provision of such schools.

As Warnock (Department of Education and Science, 1978) comments, the statutory foundation of special provision continued broadly until the 1944 Act.

System change in education

In the latter half of the twentieth century there was considerable change in both the mainstream and special sectors. Prior to the Second World War, some areas of the country lacked provision for separate secondary schools and many learners continued to be educated in schools with all-through primary and secondary teaching. Reorganisation of schooling became a priority once the war was over.

Mainstream secondary school reorganisation

The 1938 Spens report *Secondary Education with Special Reference to Grammar Schools and Technical High Schools* (Board of Education, 1938) recommended three types of secondary school with the assumption that children could be divided into three groups: grammar schools for academically able children; technical schools for children with practical talents; and new 'modern' secondary schools for the others. In so doing, it was clearly influenced by an assumption from psychology that intelligence can reliably be tested and measured.

Towards the end of the Second World War, a coalition government sought to develop a common national framework for the education of a diverse student population and reorganised the education system through the 1944 Education Act in England and Wales 'in three progressive stages to be known as primary education, secondary education, and further education' (1944 Education Act, Part 11, § 7). Following the Spens recommendations, central government advised local education authorities to 'think in terms of three types' of state secondary schools in circular No. 73 (12 December 1945). A booklet, *The Nation's Schools*, published in 1945, described the purpose of the new 'modern' schools as providing for working-class children 'whose future employment will not demand any measure of technical skill or knowledge' (Ministry of Education, 1945, quoted in Benn & Chitty, 1996, p. 5). This booklet was soon withdrawn, but the policy remained the same and, two years later, was restated in *The New Secondary Education* (Wilkinson, 1947). This tripartite, grammar, technical and secondary modern, system was quickly adopted by many local education authorities and a system of selection based on the results of an examination at the age of 11. This was underpinned by an assumption that the 11+ examination could differentiate between 'types' of learners who should be educated in different types of secondary schools and that the educational hierarchy that developed was therefore fair.[4] In fact, the Act itself never mentioned the words 'tripartite', 'grammar schools' or 'secondary modern schools'. The only requirement was that education should be provided at three levels: primary, secondary and further. As the Parliamentary Secretary to the Board of Education, J. Chuter Ede, commented in a speech published in *The Times* of 14 April 1944:

> I do not know where people get the idea about three types of school, because I have gone through the Bill with a small toothcomb, and I can find only one school for senior pupils – and that is a secondary school. (quoted in Chitty & Dunford, 1999, p. 20)

Restructuring of special education

The organisation of special education at this time was also based on the assumption that different 'types' of learners could reliably be identified and categorised. Until this point the duty of local education authorities to ascertain which children required special educational treatment had been confined to 'defective' and epileptic children. However, the 1944 Education Act, Sections 33 and 34, and associated Regulations, extended this duty to all 'pupils who suffer from any disability of mind or body'. These days we might call this view of difficulties the 'medical' or 'deficit model'. In Scotland, the Education (Scotland) Act (1945) repeated much of the 1944 Education Act in England and Wales.

The Handicapped Students and School Health Service Regulations (1945) in England and Wales established a new framework of 11 categories of learners with difficulties: blind, partially sighted, deaf, partially deaf, delicate, diabetic, educationally subnormal, epileptic, physically handicapped and, for the first time, maladjusted and those with speech defects. Blind, deaf, epileptic, physically handicapped and aphasic children were required by the Regulations to be educated in special schools. Children with other disabilities were allowed to attend mainstream schools provided there was adequate provision (Department of Education and Science (DES), 1978, 2.46). Up to 2% would need education in a special school, as Warnock (DES, 1978, 2.48) noted:

> Detailed suggestions were made for provision. In large urban areas about 1–2 per cent of the school population would need to be educated in special schools (including 0.2 per cent in boarding schools) [...].

Increase in 'special' student population

Official guidance (Ministry of Education, 1946) estimated that the total number of children who might be expected to require special educational treatment, in both mainstream and special schools, would range from between 14% and 17% of the school population. Those politicians who were responsible for making decisions about provision for young people with difficulties in learning and/or behaviour assumed that most would be educated in mainstream schools. Damage to school premises in the Second World War and the new requirement to educate young people to age 15 required additional building and accommodation, however, and, in addition, trained teachers were in short supply. Further, secondary modern schools in particular often

---

[4]In Scotland the system was different. The 1918 Education (Scotland) Act had introduced the principle of universal free secondary education. Unlike the Education Act 1944 in England and Wales, following which the tripartite system was established, the Education (Scotland) Act 1945 consolidated what had already been established.

had large classes (DES, 1978, pp. 33–40). Provision in ordinary schools for those learners who experienced difficulties failed to develop as the planners expected. As Gillard (2021) comments:

> provision in ordinary schools failed to develop on the scale envisaged, partly because in the decade after the war LEAs were hard-pressed to maintain the fabric of the education service (*see* DES, 1978: 32–35). (www.educationengland.org.uk/history/chapter09.html, accessed 26.10.2021)

Special education came to be interpreted much more narrowly than originally anticipated.

During the following years, two groups continually expanded in numbers: learners identified as 'educationally sub-normal' (ESN) and as 'maladjusted' (DES, 1978). The number of children in ESN special schools nearly doubled between 1947 and 1955, from 12,060 to 22,639, with a further 12,000 children awaiting placement. The ESN category was not well-defined, however. In practice, this group of children consisted of:

> children of limited ability and children retarded by 'other conditions' such as irregular attendance, ill-health, lack of continuity in their education or unsatisfactory school conditions. These children would be those who for any reason were retarded by more than 20 per cent for their age and who were not so low-graded as to be ineducable or to be detrimental to the education of other children. They would amount to approximately 10 per cent of the school population. (DES, 1978, 2.48)

'Maladjusted', with its origins in the 1913 Mental Deficiency Act, which, as noted above, had created a category of moral imbeciles or defectives, was equally ill-defined. The concept was still relatively new when the Underwood Committee was set up in 1950 to enquire into 'maladjusted' children's medical, educational and social problems. The Committee referred to modes of behaviour outside the realm of the 'normal'. Its *Report* (Underwood, 1955, Chapter IV, para 96) lists six symptoms of 'maladjustment' requiring professional help from psychologists, child guidance clinics or doctors. They include four 'disorders', one category labelled 'psychotic' and one 'difficulties':

- nervous disorders, e.g. fears, depression, apathy, excitability;
- habit disorders, e.g. speech defects, sleep-walking, twitching and incontinence;
- behaviour disorders, e.g. defiance, aggression, jealousy and stealing;
- organic disorders, e.g. cerebral tumours;
- psychotic behaviour, e.g. delusions, bizarre behaviour;
- educational and vocational difficulties, e.g. inability to concentrate or keep jobs.

The overall definition read as follows: 'In our view, a child may be regarded as maladjusted who is developing in ways that have a bad effect on himself or his fellows and cannot, without help, be remedied by his parents, teachers and other adults in ordinary contact with him' (Underwood, 1955, Chapter IV, p. 22). It was 'a ragbag term describing any kind of behaviour that teachers and parents find disturbing' (Galloway & Goodwin, 1987, p. 32) and could be used to justify special provision. Between 1945 and 1960, the numbers of pupils classified as maladjusted rose from 0 to 1,742. By 1975, there were 13,000 pupils labelled as maladjusted (Furlong, 1985).

Education authorities in Scotland were empowered in 1945 to provide a child guidance service to advise teachers and families on appropriate methods of education and training (DES, 1978), and by 1966, 25 out of 35 education authorities had a child guidance service. In England, in the 20 years from 1950, the number of child guidance clinics increased from 162 in to 367. Accordingly, the Summerfield Working Party (DES, 1968) recommended doubling the numbers of educational psychologists, with new arrangements for training.

Web activity WA3.5
Considering the effects of identification as 'maladjusted'

On the website you will find text and an activity related to the experience of being identified as 'maladjusted'. You might choose to access this material now and carry out the activity.

Influence of growing global recognition of human rights

In the second part of the twentieth century there began a global move towards acknowledging human rights, which included both rights and entitlements in education.

Concerns about selection in mainstream

A growing concern for equality of opportunity in society at large led to criticism by some educationalists that the selective secondary system was divisive and functioned to sustain the position of some societal groups. As Douglas (1964) and Hargreaves (1967) found, for example, a disproportionate number of middle-class children were to be found in grammar schools. The majority of children – up to 86% in some local education authorities – failed the 11+ examination and were assigned to secondary schools where the quality of the education on offer might be sub-standard. Richmond (1978, p. 75), commenting on the findings of the Newsom Report (Central Advisory Council for Education, 1963), which had investigated the quality of education in secondary modern schools, wrote:

> It revealed that nearly 80% of Secondary Modern school buildings were seriously deficient, that the qualifications of Secondary Modern school teachers were often as 'below average' as their pupils were said to be, that the rapid turnover of staff vitiated the work of schools in the poorer districts – in short, that more than half the nation's children were getting a raw deal. [...] it urged the need for more intellectually demanding courses to counteract the aimless drift and low morale which characterised the work of many schools particularly among older pupils [...]

Richmond (1978) went on to conclude that Newsom indicated that the abilities of many children had been grossly underestimated and that they would be capable of better things, if given the chance.

Considerable doubt was increasingly thrown on the reliability and validity of the psychometric tests used in the 11+ examination and, therefore, the tripartite system of selection was not as fair as had been assumed (Clark et al., 1997).

In the secondary sector, beginning in the 1960s and increasingly in the 1970s, a growing number of comprehensive schools were opened. In contrast to the tripartite system where admission is restricted on the basis of the 11+ examination, a comprehensive school is a secondary school that does not select its intake on the basis of academic achievement or aptitude. Between 1965 and 1975, 'virtually all state secondary schools in Wales and Scotland went comprehensive. In England the figure was about 90 per cent' (Pring & Walford, 1996; www.timeshighereducation. com/news/comprehensive-schools-the-history/92186.article, accessed 26.10.2021).

Concerns arising in the special sector

In special education, and with particular regard to the ESN category, there was obvious overlap between the learning needs of students in mainstream and special schools (Wearmouth, 1986) that cast doubt on the validity of the process of identification. However, movement between school types was very difficult indeed. Further, there were around 32,000 children in institutions of various sorts together with an unknown number at home, who were categorised as ineducable and had no access to education.

Increasingly, again through the 1970s, special classes and 'remedial' provision were established in mainstream schools, and some children were integrated from special into mainstream. In terms of special provision, the Education (Handicapped Children) Act 1970 removed the power of health authorities to provide training for children who experienced the most serious difficulties in learning (deemed 'mentally handicapped') and required the staff and buildings of junior training centres to be transferred to the education service. In future they were to be regarded as 'severely educationally sub-normal' (ESN(S)), and entitled to education. In Scotland, the 1974 Act also gave education authorities responsibility for the education of children who previously had been viewed as 'ineducable and untrainable'.

Introduction of a new concept: 'Special educational needs'

In 1973, the Conservative government's education secretary, Margaret Thatcher, announced, together with the secretaries of state for Scotland and Wales, the appointment of a committee of enquiry into education in the special sector that was to be chaired by Mary Warnock. We can see from the introduction to this report that this enquiry very clearly reflects the aim of education as, at least in part, preparation for employment, and driven 'by a country's socio-economic goals' (Shuayb & O'Donnell, 2008, para 2). It was:

To review educational provision in England, Scotland and Wales for children and young people handicapped by disabilities of body or mind, taking account of the medical aspects of their needs, together with arrangements to prepare them for entry into employment; to consider the most effective use of resources for these purposes; and to make recommendations. (DES, 1978, p. 1)

The Warnock report of special educational provision in Great Britain (DES, 1978) replaced the 11 categories of 'disabilities of body or mind' established in the 1945 Regulations with a new concept, 'special educational needs'. A previous study by Rutter, Tizard and Whitmore (1970), enquiring into the incidence of difficulties in learning in the school population, was a forerunner to this report. The study reported teachers' perceptions that around 20% of their learners experienced some kind of difficulty. Hence Warnock's advice that teachers should plan on the expectation that one in five children would have 'special educational needs' at some time in their school career.[5] Approximately 2% of learners were anticipated by policy makers as likely to have difficulties requiring additional or extra provision or resources.[6] Legally, there are no official figures for this proportion. However, it can be useful to resource-providers, for example local authorities, to be able to estimate what proportion of their resources they may have to reserve for individual learners' educational needs.

The 1981 Education Act in England and Wales was based largely on the 1978 Warnock Report's recommendations to replace the 11 categories of 'handicap' with a new category, 'special educational needs', together with an understanding that learners' difficulties happen on a continuum. In the Act, Section 1, the definition of 'special educational needs' is set out as follows:

(1) For the purposes of this Act a child has 'special educational needs' if he has a learning difficulty which calls for special educational provision to be made for him.

(2) […] a child has a 'learning difficulty' if—

(a) he has a significantly greater difficulty in learning than the majority of children of his age; or

(b) he has a disability which either prevents or hinders him from making use of educational facilities of a kind generally provided in schools, within the area of the local authority concerned, for children of his age. (www.legislation.gov.uk/ukpga/1981/60/enacted, accessed 26.10.2021)

As we discuss in Chapter 4, the definition of special educational needs in this Act has remained largely constant in England and Northern Ireland ever since, although other terms are now used in Wales and Scotland.

Conclusion

We may well ask ourselves why decisions were ever taken to develop special provision in educational systems in the UK in the first place. To understand this, we really need to look back at history and how the societal context at any one time influences national developments in, as in this case, education. As Wearmouth (2009; Wearmouth et al., 2018) note, this includes society's values, beliefs and political ideology.

---

[5] It is noteworthy that, since that time, the figure of 20% has been used to estimate the number of children nationally who might experience difficulties at some point in their educational career.

[6] This figure of 2% is an arbitrary one, drawn from a count of students in special schools in 1944 (DES, 1978).

As Broadfoot (2011, p. 9) comments, schools' and colleges' curricula 'and even schools themselves are seen to be products of the social system in which they exist'. What evidence is there in the current chapter to support this view?

Since the Elementary Education Act 1870, when compulsory primary education was first introduced, there has been a question of the purpose that the special sector should serve, or, as currently, special educational/additional support/additional learning provision. We leave you with the following question: what do you think about this yourself?

In Chapter 4 we turn to the issue of legislation across the UK.

Further reading

Education for children with visual, hearing, physical and cognitive difficulties

Bartlett, P., & Weight, D. (eds) (1999) *Outside the Walls of the Rolph Asylum: The History of Care in the Community, 1750–2000*. London: Athlone Press.

Centre for Deaf Studies, University of Bristol (1997) *Chapter Two: Historical Fact in Deafness*. Bristol: Centre for Deaf Studies. Available at: www.bristol.ac.uk/Depts/DeafStudiesTeaching/dhcwww/chapter2.htm#6

Historic England (n/d) *Disability in Time and Place*, https://historicengland.org.uk/content/docs/research/disability-in-time-and-place-pdf/

Holonce, L. (2013) Victorian education for the blind: 'cheer them in their affliction'? *Wordpress*, 25 January, https://lesleyhulonce.wordpress.com/2013/01/25/victorian-education-for-the-blind-cheer-them-in-their-affliction/

Leaves Family History Research Services (2019) *The Victorian Deaf in England. Part 2. Education and Occupations*, https://leavesfamilyhistory.co.uk/blog/victorian-deaf_part_2/

Lees, C., & Ralph, S. (2004) Charitable provision for blind people and deaf people in late nineteenth century London. *Journal of Research in Special Educational Needs*, 4(3), 148–160.

Mangion, C. M. (2012) 'The business of life': Educating Catholic deaf children in late nineteenth-century England. *History of Education*, 41(5), 575–594.

Wright, D. (2001) *Mental Disability in Victorian England: The Earlswood Asylum 1847–1901*. Oxford: Oxford University Press.

Developments in the education system in Britain

Jones, K. (2016) *Education in Britain, 1944 to the Present* (2nd edn). Cambridge: Polity Press.

Richardson, R. (2016) *Grammar Schools: What are They and Why are They Controversial?* London: BBC. Available at: www.bbc.co.uk/news/education-34538222#:~:text=Grammar%20schools%20have%20existed%20since,the%20age%20of%2014%20free

Stephens, W. B. (1999) *Education in Britain, 1750–1914*. London: Palgrave Macmillan.

4

LEGAL ACCOUNTABILITIES IN EDUCATIONAL INSTITUTIONS

Major questions addressed in this chapter are:

- In the UK, what are the legal responsibilities of professionals who have a responsibility for learners with special educational, additional learning, or additional support, needs?
- What entitlements does the law give to learners and their families?
- What frames of reference are used to group together the range of difficulties commonly experienced by learners in educational institutions?
- How well does the law function to support learners with special educational, additional learning, or additional support, needs?

Key terms

Special educational needs, additional learning needs, additional support needs, disability, Code of Practice, Warnock Report, Human Rights legislation, reasonable adjustments, frame of reference

Introduction

As we have already discussed in Chapter 1, the fundamental rights to which learners in the education system are entitled are set out in the Human Rights Act 1998. The Act incorporates into domestic British law the rights set out in the European Convention on Human Rights (ECHR). Protocol 1, Article 2 (Council of Europe, 1952) protects learners' right to an effective education. It states: 'No person shall be denied a right to an education' (www.equalityhumanrights.com/en/human-rights-act/article-2-first-protocol-right-education, accessed 27.10.2021). The fact that courts have ruled that the right to education relates to the education system that already exists is very important for learners who experience difficulties. One implication is that settings, schools and colleges should make what exists accessible to all in a way that is fair and reasonable. The principle of equity that we also note in Chapter 1 implies that the special or additional support that some learners need to access the curriculum that is accessed by their peers should also be made available.

This chapter begins, chronologically, by considering how the principles of equity and equality in the education system relate to disability-equality legislation. It goes on to discuss legislation related to special educational needs and disability in England and Northern Ireland, the recently-introduced concept of additional learning needs in Wales, and additional support needs in Scotland.

Relationship between learning difficulties, disabilities and the law in the UK

Disability law applies to education as well as to other aspects of public life, most recently the Equality Act 2010. The same legislation operates across all the countries of the UK except for Northern Ireland, where policy is devolved to the Northern Ireland Assembly, and the relevant disability-equality legislation is the Disability Discrimination (Northern Ireland) Order 2006.

Disability-equality law across the UK

In the UK, the Equality Act 2010 imposes duties on schools, including private education, and local authorities, related to planned approaches to addressing discrimination and improving access. Settings, schools and colleges are expected to be proactive in anticipating and providing for the needs of disabled students.

Definitions of disability

LEARNING POINT
CONSIDERING THE TERM 'DISABLED'

Under the terms of the 2010 Equality Act, Section 6, a child or young person is 'disabled' if s/he has a physical or mental impairment which has a substantial and long-term adverse effect on his/her ability to carry out normal day-to-day activities. 'Substantial' is defined as more than minor or trivial, and 'long term' as lasting, or likely to last, more than one year.

Which 'normal day-to-day' activities would be included in a setting/school or college, do you think? What kind of mental impairments do you consider would be included? What, for example, about dyslexia or attention deficit/hyperactivity disorder? Would these count as disabilities in your view?

Not all children or young people in educational institutions with special educational, or additional support, needs will be disabled. Not all disabled children or young people will have special educational, or additional support, needs. Many, however, could be included under both legal definitions.

Educational institutions must prevent unlawful direct or indirect discrimination. For example, Paragraph 85 of the Equality Act 2010 states that an institution must not discriminate:

(2) (a) in the way it provides education for the pupil;
   (b) in the way it affords the pupil access to a benefit, facility or service;
   (c) by not providing education for the pupil;
   (d) by not affording the pupil access to a benefit, facility or service;

Children and young people with disabilities must not be treated less favourably than others. Since the original 1981 Education Act in England and Wales, stronger rights to a place in a mainstream school have made it unlawful for schools and local authorities (LAs) to discriminate against disabled learners, particularly in relation to admission arrangements. Paragraph 85 of the 2010 Equality Act, for example, also states that there must be no discrimination by an institution:

(1) (a) in the arrangements it makes for deciding who is offered admission as
       a pupil;
   (b) as to the terms on which it offers to admit the person as a pupil;
   (c) by not admitting the person as a pupil.

There is also a duty to make 'reasonable adjustments', to change current arrangements, including the provision of aids and services, if necessary to ensure a learner is not disadvantaged.

Families (and/or young people of a responsible age in Scotland) have the right of appeal to a tribunal if they feel there has been discrimination against a learner.

In Northern Ireland, the Disability Discrimination (Northern Ireland) Order 2006 extends previous law to bring public authorities within the purview of disability legislation and imposes a new requirement to promote positive attitudes towards disabled people and promote participation in public life (§49A).

Legislation in England, Wales and Northern Ireland

In England and Wales, the seminal piece of legislation concerned with children and young people who have difficulties or disabilities in education is usually seen as the 1981 Act. It introduced the new concept of 'special educational needs' and 'statements of special educational need', which set out an analysis of learners' difficulties and the resources, human and material, required to address them.

In 1993, an Education Act introduced a *Code of Practice for the Identification and Assessment of Special Educational Needs* (Department for Education, 1994) (see below), new procedures for assessing 'needs' and specifying resources in 'statements of special educational needs'. 'Independent' tribunals chaired by lawyers, following the model of industrial tribunals, were introduced that gave families legal remedies against decisions about assessment and provision for their children. The *Code of Practice* was designed to provide tribunals with a text to guide their decisions.

Law in England

The most recent legislation in England, the Children and Families Act 2014, has brought about a number of changes in the law relating to special educational needs. The new system now applies to young people from birth to 25 years provided they remain in education or training.[1] Age is important. In law, once a child becomes a young person, that is, s/he became 16 before the last day of the summer term (Section 83(2)), s/he can take decisions with regard to the Act on his/her own behalf, rather than the family. This is subject to a young person 'having capacity' to take a decision under the Mental Capacity Act 2005.

Definition of special educational needs in England

In England, the definition of 'special educational needs' has remained largely constant since the Warnock Report (Department of Education and Science, 1978).

LEARNING POINT
IMPLICATIONS OF THE TERM 'SPECIAL EDUCATIONAL NEEDS'

Read the outline below of the way the term 'special educational needs' (SEN) is defined in law in England. How straightforward do you find this way of defining learning difficulties? Note down any questions this definition raises for you.

Under the terms of current legislation, a child or young person has special educational needs if he or she has a learning difficulty or disability which calls for special educational provision to be made for him or her. (Children and Families Act 2014, Part 3, §20 (1))

That is, a young person only has 'special educational needs' when special provision is required in order to meet them: learning difficulties do not in themselves constitute such a need.

To understand the definition of SEN, we first need to know what is meant by 'learning difficulty'. A child or young person may be seen as having such a difficulty if s/he experiences:

(a)   significantly greater difficulty in learning than the majority of same-age peers, or

---

[1]This does not apply to students in higher education, however. Disability-equality law is seen as appropriate at higher education (HE) level.

(b) s/he has a disability which prevents him (or her) from making use of (educational) facilities 'of a kind generally provided for' same-age peers in mainstream educational institutions. (Children and Families Act 2014, Part 3, §20 (2))

In education law, a learning difficulty creates a need which is 'special' only if the provision required to address it is 'special'. A specific literacy difficulty which makes it hard for a student to engage in the same learning activities as others might mean that s/he might have a 'learning difficulty', for example. This much is fairly obvious. However, a student might also have a 'learning difficulty' if s/he has a physical disability that creates a barrier to moving around the school or classroom to participate in those activities with peers.

How clear is this definition, do you think?

Terminological ambiguity

Defining 'learning difficulty' raises a number of questions, for example:

- How can 'significantly greater difficulty in learning' be evaluated?
- How should we compare one learner to the majority? Any mistakes may leave some learners without additional support or resources that may be needed.
- How to gauge the extent to which the learning context has created the difficulty?
- What is meant by provision that is generally provided? Different schools have different facilities, for example.

Inevitably, the decision-making process is very variable across the country and will always leave room for inequality, however needs are identified.

The second part of the definition refers to a 'disability' as creating difficulties in learning. By law, then, if a learner with a visual impairment cannot access the same facilities as peers, s/he may be identified as having a learning difficulty.

'Areas' of need in England

Reasons why students might experience special or additional learning and/or support needs are conceptualised somewhat differently in the different countries of the UK. In England, the recommendation (Department for Education/Department of Health (DfE/DoH), 2015, §5.32) is that assessment and provision should focus on four broad 'areas of need', all seemingly 'within-the-person' definitions: communication and interaction, cognition and learning, social, emotional and mental health, and sensory and/or physical.

In terms of the first of the four areas of need in England, communication and interaction, the *Code of Practice* (DfE/DoH, 2015, §6.28) begins by making particular reference to receptive and expressive language acquisition:

Children and young people with speech, language and communication needs (SLCN) have difficulty in communicating with others. This may be because they have difficulty saying what they want to, understanding what is being said to them or they do not understand or use social rules of communication. The profile for every child with SLCN is different and their needs may change over time. They may have difficulty with one, some or all of the different aspects of speech, language or social communication at different times of their lives.

It goes on in the following paragraph (DfE/DoH, 2015, §6.29) to mention a specific syndrome, autistic spectrum disorder, that may be linked both to language difficulties and to cognition. This is still grouped under the subheading 'communication and interaction':

> Children and young people with ASD, including Asperger's Syndrome and Autism, are likely to have particular difficulties with social interaction. They may also experience difficulties with language, communication and imagination, which can impac*t on how they relate to others.*

Clearly there is a lot of overlap between the areas of need, therefore. In terms of communication and interaction, it is obvious that lack of facility with receptive and expressive language has important implications for cognition and learning, especially when we consider the extent to which thinking is dependent on language.

In relation to the next area, 'cognition and learning', the *Code* (DfE/DoH, 2015, §6.30) states:

> Learning difficulties cover a wide range of needs, including moderate learning difficulties (MLD), severe learning difficulties (SLD), where children are likely to need support in all areas of the curriculum and associated difficulties with mobility and communication, through to profound and multiple learning difficulties (PMLD), where children are likely to have severe and complex learning difficulties as well as a physical disability or sensory impairment.

Specific learning difficulties, encompassing 'a range of conditions such as dyslexia, dyscalculia and dyspraxia' (DfE/DoH, 2015, §6.31) are also included in this group.

In relation to the third area, the term 'emotional and behavioural difficulties' (EBD), first formally used by Warnock (Department of Education and Science, 1978), was later translated into 'social, emotional and behavioural difficulties' (SEBD), and then, as now in England, 'social, emotional and mental health' difficulties. The most recent *Code* (DfE/DoH, 2015, §6.32) defines this area as:

> a wide range of social and emotional difficulties which manifest themselves in many ways. These may include becoming withdrawn or isolated, as well as displaying challenging, disruptive or disturbing behaviour. These behaviours may reflect underlying mental health difficulties such as anxiety or depression, self-harming, substance misuse, eating disorders or physical symptoms that are medically unexplained.

Other sub-areas, described here as 'disorders', are also included here: 'attention deficit disorder, attention deficit hyperactive disorder or attachment disorder'. Schools and colleges are exhorted to manage the effect of any disruptive behaviour so it does not adversely affect other pupils (DfE/DoH, 2015, §6.33).

The final area, sensory and/or physical needs, is defined in terms of a disability 'which prevents or hinders them [i.e. learners] from making use of the educational facilities generally provided' (DfE/DoH, 2015, §6.34). These difficulties may include 'vision impairment (VI), hearing impairment (HI) or a multi-sensory impairment (MSI)' and/or 'a physical disability (PD) [that] requires additional ongoing support and equipment to access all the opportunities available to their peers'.

Learners' entitlements in England

A child or young person identified as having SEND is entitled to provision that supports him/her to achieve the 'best possible educational and other outcomes'. Local authorities (LAs) have a legal duty to identify all children and young people in their geographical area who have or may have SEN and/or disabilities. Statements of special education needs[2] have been replaced by Education Health and Care Plans (EHCs).

Regulation 12 of the Special Educational Needs and Disability Regulations 2014 is very specific about what an EHC Plan should contain. The LA has the legal duty to ensure that the educational provision is made. If the setting/school/college does not put the specified support in place, it is the LA's responsibility to make sure it does.

EHC Plans apply to further education but not to higher education. Where health provision has been specified in a Plan, the local health commissioning body – usually the Clinical Commissioning Group – has the duty to provide it.

Every LA is required to publish a 'Local Offer' (§30), a record of special services and provision it expects to be available both inside and outside its area. The Local Offer should make clear what special educational provision schools and colleges in its area should make from their existing budgets. LAs must also publish comments about the Local Offer from children, young people and their parents, and what they intend to do in reply (§30(6)).

When carrying out an EHC needs assessment or reviewing a plan for a young person, the LA must consider providing a personal budget (§48) for educational provision at a parent's request. This is notional money required to cover the special provision specified in the Plan. Head teachers or principals have a veto if they disagree with a direct payment for special provision in their institution.

Law in Wales

The legislative framework of the new system introduced in Wales is created by the Additional Learning Needs and Education Tribunal (Wales) Act 2018 ('the Act'), the ALN Code for Wales and regulations made under the Act. The Act replaces the terms 'special educational needs (SEN)' and 'learning difficulties and/or disabilities (LDD)' with the new term 'additional learning needs (ALN)'. A phased approach has been taken to introducing the ALN system, which is being implemented between September 2020 and July 2023 and which has been designed to support children and young people from birth; while they are in school; and, if they are over compulsory school age, while they are in further education. During this period, the ALN system will operate in parallel to the special educational needs (SEN) system, which will gradually be phased out.

---

[2]See below for an explanation of statutory assessment of special educational needs that previously might result in a Statement of SEN, but now may result in an EHC Plan.

LEARNING POINT
'ADDITIONAL LEARNING NEEDS' IN WALES

Read the text below relating to the term 'additional learning needs' (ALN) that is currently used in Wales. As you do so, you might like to compare ALN with SEN and consider similarities and differences.

In Wales, a new system was introduced through the Additional Learning Needs (ALN) and Education Tribunal (Wales) Act 2018. The definition which the Act uses for ALN is similar to the legal definition of SEN in England. If the child or young person (a) has a learning difficulty or disability, and (b) that learning difficulty or disability calls for Additional Learning Provision (ALP), then the child or young person is considered to have ALN.

Under section 2(2) of the Act, a child or young person[3] has a learning difficulty or disability 'if he/she:

- has a significantly greater difficulty in learning than the majority of others of the same age; or
- has a disability for the purposes of the Equality Act 2010 (c. 15) which prevents or hinders him or her from making use of facilities for education or training of a kind generally provided for others of the same age in mainstream maintained schools or mainstream institutions in the further education sector.'

Section 3 defines Additional Learning Provision (ALP) in the same terms as currently used for Special Educational Provision:

- for a person aged 3 or over, educational or training provision that is additional to, or different from, that made generally for others of the same age in mainstream maintained schools or colleges, or in nursery education;
- for a child aged under 3, educational provision of any kind.

Learners' entitlements in Wales

The new ALN system replaces existing support plans with a new statutory plan called an Individual Development Plan (IDP) to which all learners with ALN will be entitled, regardless of the severity or complexity of their learning difficulty or disability. The statutory status of the IDP will be the same irrespective of needs, with the same rights of appeal to the independent Education Tribunal for Wales for anyone with an IDP. This is clearly different from the situation in England, where EHC Plans are restricted to learners with the most complex needs. The Tribunal's decision will be legally binding on local authorities and further education institutions (FEIs). Importantly also, it will be able to require an NHS body to provide evidence with regard to health-related aspects of an appeal and recommend the exercise of a body's functions under the Act.

Views, wishes and feelings of children, their parents and young people will be considered at all stages of the IDP process. A one-page proposed mandatory IDP template will ensure that IDPs reflect the learner's needs and personality, including what is important to him/her. ALN will be identified, and IDPs will be prepared and maintained by the educational institution attended by the learner. Maintaining an IDP requires securing the additional learning provision included

---

[3] The Act uses the term 'child' to mean someone who is at or under compulsory school age and 'young person' as someone who is over compulsory school age but under 25.

in it, and reviewing the IDP as and when required to ensure the information and the provision described in it remains appropriate.

One of the core aims of the Act is to create a bilingual system of support for ALN.

The Additional Learning Needs Co-ordinator (ALNCo) is a statutory role which will replace the existing non-statutory SENCo role that exists in most maintained schools in Wales and similar non-statutory roles that are undertaken in FEIs in Wales. Section 60 of the Act requires FEIs and mainstream maintained schools, including maintained nurseries and pupil referral units, to have a designated ALNCo.

The ALN Act places a duty on all local health boards to designate an officer to have responsibility for co-ordinating the health board's functions in relation to children and young people with ALN. That person is known as the Designated Education Clinical Lead Officer (DECLO). The DECLO must be either a registered medical practitioner or a registered nurse or another health professional.

Law in Northern Ireland

In Northern Ireland, Part 11 of the Education Order (Northern Ireland) (1996) remains the basis of law related to special educational needs in the province. This Order was amended by the Special Educational Needs and Disability (Northern Ireland) Order (SENDO) 2005, Part II, Articles 3 to 12 and Schedule 1, which takes account, in particular, of disability legislation introduced across the UK in 2001. The Department of Education, Northern Ireland (DENI) provided statutory guidance for Education and Library Boards and schools in the *Code of Practice on the Identification and Assessment of Special Educational Needs* (DENI, 1998) and also the *Supplement to the Code of Practice* (DENI, 2005).

In Northern Ireland, the Special Educational Needs and Disability Act (Northern Ireland) 2016 received Royal Assent in March 2016. Implementation of the new SEN Framework was originally anticipated during 2020 but has been delayed. A revised *Code of Practice* is being developed at the time of writing this volume (August, 2021).

Definition of special educational needs in Northern Ireland

The definition of 'special educational needs' in Northern Ireland reflects that in England. A child has SEN if he or she has a learning difficulty which calls for special educational provision to be made for him or her (Education Order (Northern Ireland) 1996, Part 11, §3(1).

Learners' entitlements

The 2016 Act places new duties on Boards of Governors, the Education Authority (EA) and health and social services authorities, and sets out new entitlements for families and learners over compulsory school age:

- Boards of Governors will be required to ensure the appointment of a Learning Support Co-ordinator for each grant-aided school to co-ordinate provision for learners.
- The school will be required to complete and review a personal learning plan for each learner with SEN and ensure that this is transferred during transition from one grant-aided school to another.

- The EA will be required to take account of the views of the learners when deciding special educational provision, and organise an independent dispute avoidance and resolution service and mediation arrangements.
- There will be a need for increased co-operation between the EA and health and social services authorities to provide services to address a learner's SEN.

Law in Scotland

The situation is different in Scotland. Here, the Education (Additional Support for Learning) (Scotland) Act 2004 (as amended) established the concept of 'additional support needs'.

LEARNING POINT
DEFINITION OF ADDITIONAL SUPPORT NEEDS IN SCOTLAND

Read the text below. Compare the definition of 'additional support needs' in Scotland with what pertains in England. What differences and similarities can you identify?

Under this Act, a child or young person has such needs if 'for whatever reason', s/he is not likely to be able 'to benefit from school education provided or to be provided' for him/her 'without the provision of additional support' (Scottish Government, 2017, p. 18, §1). 'School education' here includes, in particular, 'such education that is directed to the development of the personality, talents and mental and physical abilities of the child or young person to their fullest potential' (p. 18, §3).

'Additional support' is defined as:

provision which is additional to, or otherwise different from, the educational provision made generally for children or, as the case may be, young persons of the same age in schools (other than special schools) under the management of the education authority for the area to which the child or young person belongs. (p. 206)

'Areas of need' in Scotland

In Scotland, the approach to conceptualising areas of need is rather different from other UK countries (Scottish Government, 2017, p. 11). Children or young people who may require additional support for a variety of reasons are those who:

- have motor or sensory impairments;
- have low birth weight;
- are being bullied;
- are children of parents in the Armed Forces;
- are particularly able or talented;
- have experienced a bereavement;

- are affected by the imprisonment of a family member;
- are interrupted learners;
- have a learning disability;
- have barriers to learning as a result of a health need, such as fetal alcohol spectrum disorder;
- are looked after by a local authority or have been adopted;
- have a learning difficulty, such as dyslexia;
- are living with parents who are abusing substances;
- are living with parents who have mental health problems;
- have English as an additional language;
- are not attending school regularly;
- have emotional or social difficulties;
- are on the child protection register;
- are refugees;
- are young carers.

In Scotland, a wide range of contextual factors broadly grouped into four overlapping areas are identified as potentially creating barriers that may lead to the need for additional support: 'learning environment; family circumstances; disability or health need; social and emotional factors' (Scottish Government, 2017, p. 23).

Learners' entitlements in Scotland

A 'co-ordinated support plan' is seen as needed if the child or young person has additional support needs arising from '(i) one or more complex factors', or '(ii) multiple factors', and if the needs 'are likely to continue for more than a year' (Scottish Government, 2017, p. 74, §3). There is a proviso that 'significant additional support' is required to address the needs. In this situation, a factor is defined as 'complex' 'if it has, or is likely to have, a significant adverse effect on the school education of the child or young person'.

The Act requires education authorities, together with health, social work and, in particular circumstances, Skills Development Scotland, to make provision for all learners with additional support needs, including those with complex or multiple additional support needs. Those with significant needs lasting more than one year may require a statutory co-ordinated support plan to meet their needs. This Act also sets out entitlements for families, and establishes mediation and dispute resolution for resolving differences for families and authorities, including the Additional Support Needs Tribunals (Scotland).

The legislation was amended by the Education (Additional Support for Learning) (Scotland) Act 2009. The amendments provided for a new national advocacy service for parents and young people. In addition, all looked-after children and young people are deemed automatically to have additional support needs unless the education authority decides otherwise.

Statutory guidance in the *Codes of Practice*

It is very important to be aware of the legal process that should be followed to maintain learners' entitlements to special or additional learning or support provision. In the years following the 1981 Education Act in England and Wales, a number of issues relating to identification and procedures for learners thought to 'have special educational needs' became apparent (Audit Commission and Her Majesty's Inspectorate, 1992). In 1994, the government published the first *Code of Practice for the Identification and Assessment of Special Educational Needs* (Department for Education, 1994), with the status of 'statutory guidance', for schools in England and Wales on interpreting the law for the purpose of providing appropriate support to those with difficulties in learning. The introduction of the *Code* gave the tribunals a shared text to guide their practice in hearing appeals about formal assessments. *Codes of Practice* with similar statutory status were published later to reflect the law in Northern Ireland and Scotland.

Since that time, further *Codes* have been produced, most recently in relation to the Education (Additional Support for Learning) (Scotland) Act 2004, revised in 2009, and the Children and Families Act 2014 in England. Draft *Codes* are currently in preparation to offer guidance in putting into effect legislation associated with the Special Educational Needs and Disability Act (Northern Ireland) 2016 and the Additional Learning Needs and Education Tribunal (Wales) Act 2018.

The content and implications of the most recent *Codes*[4] in countries in the UK are reviewed in chronological order of publication.

SEN and Disability Code of Practice 0 to 25 Years in England

In England, the *SEN and Disability Code of Practice 0 to 25 Years* (DfE/DoH, 2015) gives statutory advice to schools, further education colleges and other settings to identify learners who make less than expected progress, by making regular assessments of the progress of all pupils (§6.17). When a learner is identified as experiencing difficulties, there should be discussion early on with both the learner and the family so that a plan to address the difficulties can be considered and all can be clear about the learner's areas of strength and interests as well as difficulties, together with any concerns the parent(s) might have, and the next steps for the learner.

If a learner is identified as having SEN, settings/schools/colleges are expected to put 'SEN provision' in place through a graduated four-part cycle of assessment, planning, intervention and review (assess → plan → do → review). This approach employs more frequent reviews and interventions in successive cycles if they are needed to match provision to learners' needs. Where, following appropriate interventions and review, learners continue to make poor progress, the school should consider involving external specialists. At review meetings, the SENCo, class teacher, specialists and parents/family should agree the expected outcomes of further interventions and a date to review progress.

If the learner still does not make the hoped-for progress, the school or parents should consider requesting an Education, Health and Care needs assessment. They will have to provide evidence of the action taken by the school as part of its SEN provision.

Guidance about EHC Plans that is given in the 2015 *Code* is discussed in the section on statutory assessment below.

Supporting Children's Learning Code of Practice in Scotland

In Scotland, a revised *Supporting Children's Learning Code of Practice* was published in 2017 to explain (p. 6):

---

[4]That is, most recent at the time of writing (May, 2020).

the duties on education authorities and other agencies to support children's and young people's learning. It provides guidance on the [2009] Act's provisions as well as on the supporting framework of secondary legislation. [...] It also sets out arrangements for avoiding and resolving differences between families and education authorities.

Forms of additional support are categorised under three broad headings (p. 20): 'approaches to learning and teaching; support from personnel; provision of resources'.

The *Code* (§84) sets out a phased approach to addressing individual needs and a process of 'personal learning planning' (PLP):

All children with additional support needs should be engaged in personal learning planning and for many this process will be sufficient to address their additional support needs.

Personal learning planning (PLP) should be realistic and reflect both strengths and needs. Plans should be designed to result in goals related to the learner's own circumstances. The family, learner and school should be fully involved in the PLP process, and the learner should have the opportunity to discuss his/her progress with a member of staff regularly.

In Scotland, if learners require more detailed planning than through PLP, they may have an individualised educational programme (IEP). This details the learner's additional support needs, how these are to be met, the learning outcomes expected and the additional support that is needed. Relevant external agencies, health, social work, or voluntary, should be involved in developing the IEP, together with the learner and his/her family so that the plan is co-ordinated.

Draft *Code of Practice* in Northern Ireland

At the time of writing, in Northern Ireland the Department of Education is currently preparing a new draft *Code of Practice*. The development process includes engagement with stakeholders and a public consultation to identify reactions to the document. This new *Code* is intended to provide clear and practical guidance to schools, education authorities and others in the identification and assessment of children who have, or may have, SEN to ensure appropriate provision is given to support each child with SEN make progress in their education.

Draft *Additional Learning Needs Code of Practice in Wales*

In December 2018, the draft *Additional Learning Needs [ALN] Code* and a number of regulations which support the Additional Learning Needs and Education Tribunal (Wales) Act 2018 were published for consultation. The Welsh Government intended to lay the *Code* before the National Assembly for Wales for approval in 2020, with the intention of the *Code* being issued and published by the end of 2020. It was hoped that all subordinate legislation would also be in place by the end of 2020. However, these plans were delayed as a result of the Covid-19 pandemic (https://gov.wales/written-statement-implementation-additional-learning-needs-and-education-tribunal-wales-act-2018, accessed 22.03.2021). The current, as of March 2022, draft *Additional Learning Needs [ALN] Code* is described as a 'Draft Code laid before and for approval by resolution of Senedd Cymru under section 5(2) of the Additional Learning Needs and Education Tribunal (Wales) Act 2018' (Welsh Government, 2021, p. i).

One of the principles of this *ALN Code* is to lay out the new system and encourage inclusive education where children and young people are supported to participate fully in mainstream education, wherever feasible, and a whole-setting approach is taken to meet the needs of learners with ALN.

The draft *Code* states (§20.16):

> Where progress continues to be less than expected and the application of differentiated teaching or standard targeted interventions have failed to address the attainment gap between the child or young person and their peers, this would usually indicate to the school, FEI or local authority that the child or young person may have ALN. Alternatively, it might be obvious from the outset that the extent of the concern or nature of a pre-identified disability is such that it is clear that differentiated teaching or standard targeted interventions will not be sufficient.

The draft *Code* describes the Individual Development Plan as a flexible document that will vary in length and complexity depending on the different needs of learners and the way in which an individual learner's needs develop and change over time. The proposed mandatory IDP template will include a one-page profile to ensure that IDPs reflect the child's or young person's needs and personality, including what is important to and for them, as required by the 2018 Act. The *Code*, chapter 23, outlines the required content for an IDP: the child or young person's ALN and the ALP that is called for by their ALN. Services will be required to consider whether a child or young person needs ALP in Welsh; this duty will be an ongoing one, rather than a one-off decision. If they do, this must be documented in the IDP and 'all reasonable steps' must be taken to secure the provision in Welsh.

The role of the ALNCo is described as the individual who, at a strategic level within a school or further education institution, ensures the needs of all learners with ALN within the education setting are met. As with the role of SENCo in England, in Wales the ALNCo should therefore be a member of the senior leadership team or have a clear line of communication to the senior leadership team. Regulation 27(a) of the Additional Learning Needs (Wales) Regulations 2021 prescribes the qualifications and experience required to be an ALNCo as those of a school teacher, unless the individual was already in place as a special educational needs co-ordinator prior to January, 2021.

Statutory assessment in the UK

In all four countries in the UK there is provision for statutory assessment of young people's educational needs. Chapter 9 specifies the processes and the requirements of the final legal document of entitlement to the identified resources.

Challenges in meeting legal accountabilities

We conclude this chapter by outlining some of the challenges for local authorities, settings, schools and colleges in conforming to legal requirements.

In addressing the needs of young people who experience difficulties of various kinds, it is obvious that some approaches can be incorporated into regular class teaching, but that others will need additional resourcing. It also has time implications and the will to privilege some young people's learning needs over others.

Findings from House of Commons Select Committee report (2019)

Funding has become a major issue in some areas of the UK. A House of Commons Select Committee report, published in October 2019 (Great Britain, Parliament, House of Commons, 2019), was highly critical of a number of aspects of current SEND policy and provision in England (https://publications.parliament.uk/pa/cm201919/cmselect/cmeduc/20/2003.htm, accessed 08.02.2020). It considered that:

> Let down by failures of implementation, the 2014 reforms have resulted in confusion and at times unlawful practice, bureaucratic nightmares, buck-passing and a lack of accountability, strained resources and adversarial experiences.

It stated that implementation of the 2014 Act was hindered 'by poor administration and a challenging funding environment in which local authorities and schools have lacked the ability to make transformative change'. The provision available does not match children's needs and the resources at hand. 'The significant funding shortfall is a serious contributory factor to the failure on the part of all involved to deliver on the SEND reforms.'

Ensuring that the provisions mandated by the Act are implemented requires a rigorous accountability mechanism, and this has been lacking with those 'required, or enabled, to "police" the system […] limited in part by an apparent unwillingness to grapple with unlawful practice'. The report recommends 'a more rigorous inspection framework with clear consequences for failure', stating that 'The distance between young people's lived experience, their families' struggles and Ministers' desks is just too far'.

Parents and carers have to 'wade through a treacle of bureaucracy, full of conflict, missed appointments and despair'.

Although the role of health and social care providers was reported as crucial, the meshing of the systems had not taken place, leading to the Education, Health and Care Plan being no more than a Statement by another name. The report also identified serious gaps in therapy provision across the country. The report concludes:

> The Department for Education has an approach which is piecemeal, creating reactive, sticking-plaster policies, when what is needed is serious effort to ensure that issues are fully grappled with, and the 2014 Act works properly, as was intended.

Academisation of schools

Academies have powers to decide their own admission policy and, hence, control student intake. Some researchers have questioned the degree to which the academisation of schools and the frame of reference that views education as a commodity in the school marketplace (Heilbronn, 2016) may be associated with overt or covert policy intentions not to include learners whose entitlements to special provision are costly to schools.

> Complex and unfair admissions processes are a longstanding problem in England […]
> While this problem is not new to the school system, there is a danger that the growth

of academies has made the situation worse. This is because schools are more likely to manipulate admissions when they act as their own admissions authority and administer the system themselves. [...] the growth in the number of schools acting as their own admissions authority does appear to have increased the risk of bad practice in this area. (Muir & Clifton, 2014, p. 6)

The Academies Commission (2013), for example, found that some academies manipulated admissions rather than exercising strong leadership to achieve school improvement. Black et al. (2019, p. 3) note anecdotal evidence of Academies being less willing to offer places to pupils with significant levels of special needs (SENs) 'by deploying covert selection'. The Institute for Public Policy Research (IPPR) (2014; Galton & MacBeath, 2015), in an in-depth study of a range of contemporary English schools, reported the increased pressure on school leaders to avoid 'reputational damage' (IPPR, 2014, p. 21) and maintain their competitive status by not taking in pupils who may harm their academic credibility through poor academic results. They also reported anecdotal evidence from some head teachers that neighbouring Academies seemed to be 'cherry picking wealthier pupils' and 'excluding the neediest' (p. 49). Exclusion data may also suggest that Academy schools are more likely to exclude students permanently. This may be explained in terms of some students requiring more costly support than other students, which detracts from schools' examination performance results.

Problems with the previous Welsh SEN system were pinpointed in the National Assembly for Wales White Paper, 2014. This outlined three main issues that justified reforming the existing legislative framework for SEN:

- replacing the term 'SEN' with 'ALN' that was argued to be less stigmatising;
- the divide between learners who required a statement of SEN and those who did not was unclear. Lack of clear guidance and inconsistencies in criteria and approach across Wales created a perception of unfairness among families that the current system provided legal status to provision listed on a statement of SEN but did not for others with needs but no statement. This has led to a desire by the National Assembly for Wales to provide statutory protection to all learners with SEN;
- the existing system was too complex, making flexible approaches to providing appropriately to meet needs difficult.

Whether the new system for Additional Learning Needs that replaces the previous approaches to Special Educational Needs succeeds in overcoming these problems remains to be seen at the time of writing this volume.

Web activity WA4.1
Accountability in law for providing effective support

If you are interested in disputes at law associated with a perceived lack of local authority and school support for a special educational need and the long-term consequences of this, you might choose to access the activity we have uploaded on the website that relates to a dispute taken to law over provision for a dyslexic learner.

Conclusion

Across the UK the Human Rights Act 1998 incorporates into domestic British law the rights set out in the European Convention on Human Rights (ECHR). Protocol 1, Article 2 (Council of Europe, 1952) protects learners' entitlement to an effective education. One implication is that settings, schools and colleges should make the education that exists accessible to all in a way that is fair and reasonable. Under the principle of equity this means that special or additional support that some learners need in order to access the curriculum should be made available.

The definition of the 'need' that such support should address varies across the four countries. In England, the definition of 'special educational needs' has remained largely constant since the Warnock Report (Department of Education and Science, 1978), and is reflected in Northern Ireland. In Wales, the Additional Learning Needs and Education Tribunal (Wales) Act 2018 has introduced the concept of additional learning needs that, as in England, appears to take a largely within-person view of need. In Scotland, the Education (Additional Support for Learning) (Scotland) Act 2004 (as amended) established the concept of 'additional support needs' with a frame of reference that conceptualises need as both related to the context in which difficulties arise, and also issues within the individual.

In some contexts, local and national, concerns continue to be raised around, for example, funding issues, bureaucracy and perceptions of fairness in relation to the allocation of resources.

Further reading

Warnock Report

Norwich, B. (2019) From the Warnock Report (1978) to an Education Framework Commission: A novel contemporary approach to educational policy making for pupils with special educational needs/disabilities. *Frontiers in Education*, 4, article 72. Available at: www.frontiersin.org/articles/10.3389/feduc.2019.00072/full

Webster, R. (2018) Why the Warnock report still matters today. *Times Education Supplement*, www.tes.com/news/why-warnock-report-still-matters-today

Legislation

Castro, S., & Palikara, O. (2016) Mind the gap: The new special educational needs and disability legislation in England. *Frontiers in Education*, 4(1), doi.org/10.3389/feduc.2016.00004

Enquire (2020) *Additional Support for Learning: A Guide for Parents and Carers*. Edinburgh: Children in Scotland/Scottish Government. Available at: https://enquire.org.uk/3175/wp-content/uploads/2020/02/asl-guide-parents-carers.pdf

Welsh Government (2020) *Additional Learning Needs (ALN) Transformation Programme*. Cardiff: Welsh Government. Available at: https://gov.wales/sites/default/files/publications/2020-09/additional-learning-needs-aln-transformation-programme-guide.pdf

Websites

Independent Parental Special Educational Advice: www.ipsea.org.uk/
Council for Disabled Children: https://councilfordisabledchildren.org.uk/about

5

DIFFICULTIES IN COMMUNICATION AND INTERACTION

Major questions addressed in this chapter are:

- What particular needs are experienced by learners with difficulty in the acquisition of speech, language and communication?
- What kind of approaches can be effective in addressing these needs?
- How can we understand autistic spectrum disorders?
- How can we address the needs of learners who experience autistic spectrum disorders and ensure that they are included in settings, schools and colleges?

Key terms

Speech difficulties, pragmatic language impairment, autistic spectrum disorders, Picture Exchange Communication System (PECS), Treatment and Education of Autistic and related Communication Handicapped Children programme (TEACCH), Alternative and Augmentative Communication (AAC)

Introduction

Difficulties in communication and interaction, in particular in speech and language, are acknowledged as important – and relatively common – areas of need across the UK. The Department for Education (DfE) (2019) publication *Statistical First Release (SFR): Special Educational Needs in England*, for example, compiled through data from the census in schools in January 2019, indicated that speech, language and communication needs constituted 23% of primary types of need. The proportion of those who experienced SEND and were identified as autistic was higher, at 29%. Assuming that there are similar proportions of young people with similar needs across the UK, it behoves all of us, therefore, to consider the needs of these learners very carefully in order to enhance their future life chances. This is especially so since speech, language, communication and cognition so clearly overlap in terms of skill sets. In terms of communication and interaction, it is obvious that lack of facility with receptive and expressive language has important implications for cognition and learning, especially when we consider the extent to which thinking is dependent on language.

Significance of language development in teaching and learning

At any level in the education system learners need to be able to use language competently in order to access the curriculum. In the classroom, teachers teach and learners learn primarily through spoken language. Language development is critical to thinking and learning (Goswami & Bryant, 2007), and, in most circumstances, to making friends and becoming a contributing member of the learning community in settings, schools and colleges. Verbal reasoning is the foundation of many elements of education: reasoning, investigation, problem-solving and inferring meaning. The acquisition of language and emotional development occur at the same time in children and have a reciprocal effect on each other (Cross, 2004). In the early stages of education, children learn to play and interact through language, negotiate their roles, organise their activities, and make their thinking known to others, including whether they are or unhappy with a situation.

It is obvious, therefore, that the experience of difficulties in language acquisition and communication can have a serious impact on a learner. It is really important that the frustration and anti-social behaviour that can result from a child's inability to understand spoken or written language, or to express him/herself intelligibly, is understood as such and addressed as a language and communication need and not simply as poor behaviour.

Range of speech, language and communication needs

Children with speech, language and communication needs may have problems with receptive aspects of language, or with expressive language, or with language delay, or with what we might call 'pragmatic language'.

Receptive language difficulties

Some learners may not understand the teacher when s/he tells the class what they need to do or explains a new concept, because they do not understand the words and/or the way that the grammar of the spoken language works (Bishop & Adams, 1992). They may struggle to remember information given verbally, making it difficult for them to follow more than one instruction at a time. Having a vocabulary relevant to topics and activities in classrooms is essential to make good progress in learning and achievement.

Expressive language difficulties

Class and group talk and discussion is really important to enhance learning through what some researchers call 'inter-thinking' (Littleton & Mercer, 2013). It is really difficult for learners to make themselves understood if they struggle to acquire an age-appropriate vocabulary, construct sentences using correct grammatical rules, and use the right words in the correct order. All this can be very frustrating and have a negative impact on how these learners see themselves and are seen by peers.

Some learners with language and communication needs may not be able to differentiate the speech sounds in words that are important for beginning reading and spelling (Carroll & Snowling, 2004). For example, they may be unable to identify which sounds come at the beginning and end of words. They may not be able to break up words into syllables.

Language delay

Some children have speech and language skills that are poorly developed. This is often called 'language delay'. Language acquisition follows the usual or expected pattern but at a slower rate. Speech may be unclear, vocabulary smaller, sentences shorter, and learners may be able to understand only simple instructions.

Pragmatic language difficulties

So-called 'pragmatic language' means, broadly, appropriate use of language in a social context. Those who experience difficulty in this area may not know the difference between appropriate ways to speak to adults and to peers. They may not understand jokes, sarcasm or metaphorical language, and may well take phrases often used in schools, for example 'fold your arms', at face value.

Children having other difficulties, such as moderate or profound difficulties in learning, autistic spectrum disorders and hearing impairment, may also have significant communication difficulties.

Addressing speech, language and communication difficulties

Given the prevalence of speech, language and communication difficulties, and their importance in learning and social engagement, there is an important issue regarding what may be done to support learners.

LEARNING POINT
RESPONDING TO THE LANGUAGE LEARNING NEEDS OF A YOUNG PERSON WITH RECEPTIVE AND EXPRESSIVE LANGUAGE DIFFICULTIES

Lennie, a 15-year-old in a comprehensive upper school, experienced difficulties in both receptive and expressive language. The current author took him and a group of his peers on a residential school trip to Hadrian's Wall and to York. She also took her young, very voluble son on the trip. From time to time, Lennie would say: 'Miss, can you stop your son talking? He's doing my head in?' The author's son spoke quickly and had not yet developed the skill to monitor other people's comprehension of what he was saying, either through their facial expressions or any other way. At one point also, as they were passing across the open moorland in County Durham, Lennie leant over, waved out the window and said: 'What's all this?', and then, more loudly, with a note of desperation in his voice: 'Miss, WHAT'S THIS?' At first the author did not know what he was referring to until Lennie said, 'What's it **for**?'. She then realised that he meant the moorland itself. He had never seen such open countryside and had no words to talk about it.

Think about a young person who experiences difficulties in language comprehension and use. You might think, for example, about a young person like Lennie. What practical strategies do you think you could use in classrooms to support the learning needs of a young man like him – in other words, his comprehension of spoken language and his ability to express himself intelligibly?

Hayden and Jordan (2015) have some suggestions about ways to develop attention and listening skills, and language skills more generally. Among these are that teachers should:

- when talking to students, pause to give them time to think about what has been said, and then pause to give them time to respond;
- point out and explain new vocabulary, and find opportunities to repeat the new terms in different contexts;
- when giving instructions make sure that they are clear, short, and given in the order in which they need to be followed, and above all, ensure that students are attending;
- where appropriate to the age and stage of learning, use visual cues to remind learners of new vocabulary, and display these cues around classroom walls;
- explain abstract words by linking them to concrete words that learners already know and understand.

How useful do you find these suggestions?

Addressing pragmatic language impairment

So much of the teaching and learning in settings, schools and colleges depends on spoken and written forms of language, hence difficulties with pragmatic language may well create challenges in the classroom (Adams & Lloyd, 2007).

LEARNING POINT
ADDRESSING THE NEEDS OF LEARNERS WITH PRAGMATIC LANGUAGE IMPAIRMENT IN SETTINGS, SCHOOLS AND COLLEGES

Have a look at the list below of common barriers to learning experienced by young people with pragmatic language impairment (PLI). For each one, note down what you think would begin to address needs at an age and stage of learning with which you are familiar:

- over-literal interpretation of language (Leinonen, Letts & Smith, 2000);
- difficulty in acquiring conversational skills in terms of turn-taking and sustaining the topic of a conversation (Bishop & Norbury, 2002);
- insensitivity to listeners, and a tendency to talk endlessly about their own interests;
- problems understanding narrative and telling stories in a logical order (Norbury & Bishop, 2003);
- comprehension difficulties despite correct use of the formal grammatical structure of spoken or written language (Rapin & Allen, 1998).

Now have a look at the text below and consider how far the elements of the intervention that is outlined here addresses each of the points above.

Adams and Lloyd (2007, pp. 229–230) describe a highly structured classroom intervention to address PLI. This intervention employs 'modelling and individual practice' to demonstrate and reinforce new skills, role-play to practise specific pragmatic skills in conversations with peers and be supported by adults 'to make both immediate and hidden meanings of language and communication explicit', as well as the pragmatics of grammatical structure. In terms of the steps in this intervention, first, good practice was established 'in interacting at an appropriate social and language level with the child'. The complexity of the language in the classroom was modified. This was achieved by, typically, a classroom assistant translating language 'into short meaningful utterances' and using a visual demonstration at the same time. Following this, the children were taught 'the vocabulary of social situations' and how to interpret others' emotions. Changes to routines were added in small steps and discussed before they were put into effect. A focus was placed on supporting children to understand 'social and verbal inferences, metaphors and hidden meaning in language'. Teaching the pragmatics of language focused on 'explicit exercises and classroom support in exchange structure, turn-taking, topic management, conversational skills, building sequences, cohesion and coherence in narrative and discourse'.

PLI is one of the difficulties often experienced by autistic children, as we discuss in Chapter 6 on 'Difficulties in cognition and learning'.

Ways to overcome profound barriers to communication through the use of Alternative and Augmentative Communication

Some young people with very serious difficulties in communication may benefit from a form of communication that replaces standard means of communication such as speech and that is called Alternative and Augmentative Communication (AAC). The term AAC typically refers to an area where the focus is impairments in communication. An AAC system is a combination of strategies, techniques, symbols and aids that increase the user's ability to communicate effectively with those around them. This is often used where young people experience particular difficulties in verbal communication to complement and/or enhance standard means of communication.

AAC systems can fall into two categories, unaided and aided communication:

- Unaided communication does not require any special equipment, and can include sign and/or body language, such as gestures, facial expressions, and so on.
- Aided communication means an external device is needed to communicate, for example objects, drawings, charts, voice output systems, symbols, and so on. Aided AAC systems are sometimes categorised into low- and high-tech systems. Low tech describes alternative and augmentative communication strategies which use equipment that is not electronic, for example communication boards and books, the Picture Exchange Communication System (PECS), picture-based AAC systems other than PECS. High tech comprises all electronic communication aids including mobile devices, for example cell phones and tablets, and speech-generating devices.

Below we discuss four of these systems: the Picture Exchange Communication System (PECS), the use of objects of reference, Widgit symbol systems and 'Talking Mats'.

The Picture Exchange Communication System

The Picture Exchange Communication System (PECS) is one form of AAC in which an adult teaches a child to exchange a picture of something for an item s/he wants, for example a picture of a biscuit for a biscuit. PECS (Bondy & Frost, 1994) is key to a number of specialist approaches such as the TEACCH programme. (See below for a discussion of this programme in relation to autistic learners.) The teaching protocol is based on applied behaviour analysis, which is discussed in Skinner's (1957) book, *Verbal Behavior*. PECS is based on the view that learners who cannot talk or write can be taught to communicate using pictures. Prompting and reinforcement strategies are used with the expectation that they will lead to self-directed (i.e. autonomous) communication. The adult first teaches the child to exchange a picture of an item s/he wants. For example, if the child wants a drink, s/he will give a picture of 'drink' to the adult, who will then immediately give him/her a drink. The adult will then teach the child progressively more difficult skills, such as using pictures to make whole sentences. PECS was originally designed to help non-verbal autistic children to communicate, but it has also been used with adolescents and adults with a wide range of difficulties in communication, cognition and motor movement.

Web activity WA5.1
Considering the use of PECS

You will find reference to a website and a suggested activity related to PECS on the website. You might choose to access this now.

Objects of reference

'Objects of reference' is a term given to physical objects that can represent things about which people communicate, for example events, activities, ideas and people. These physical objects can also lead to the use of more abstract modes of communication, for example words, signs and symbols. A particular object of reference may be chosen because of its multi-sensory properties that can give the individual a clue about what it represents, for example a bar of soap to signify a bath, or a seat buckle for a car journey. For consistency purposes, the same item should be used for the same event (Park, 1997). The contexts in which different objects of reference have a meaning are obviously different for different learners.

Widgit symbol systems

There are other pictorial means of supporting communication, such as symbol-based language programs, that have been developed over many years. Widgit Software is one organisation that has produced an array of software that uses pictorial symbols to support the development of communication skills.

Web activity WA5.2
Considering the use of Widgit symbols

You will find reference to a website for Widgit symbols and a suggested activity on the website for this book. You might choose to access this now.

'Talking Mats'

Visual approaches to supplement spoken language can often be valuable (Lee, 2008). A further example of a symbol-based program is 'Talking Mats', an interactive resource that uses three sets of picture communication symbols – topics, options and a visual scale – and a physical space, the 'mat', on which to display them. This mat might be a physical mat or it might be a digital space, for example a tablet, smart board or computer screen. The topic comprises whatever the learner wishes to discuss, with pictures symbolising this. Options relate to each topic, for example what the learner feels about something. The visual scale at the top of the mat enables learners to indicate what they feel about each topic and option. When a topic is chosen, the learner is given the options one at a time and asked what they feel about each one. They can then place the symbol under the appropriate visual scale symbol (www.talkingmats.com/about-talking-mats/#howit-works, accessed 27.10.2021).

Understanding 'autism'

LEARNING POINT
PRIOR KNOWLEDGE ABOUT AUTISM

In Chapter 2, we discussed the issue of the frames of reference through which we make prior judgements about people or events. Before reading the section below, you might like to note down what you already know about autism, for example:

- what kind of behaviour is often associated with it;
- how, in your experience, people may react to such behaviour when they know nothing about whether a learner is autistic or not.

Nature of autistic spectrum disorders

The National Autistic Society (NAS) (2021, www.autism.org.uk/advice-and-guidance/what-is-autism) makes its position on autism very clear, stating that 'Autism is a lifelong developmental disability which affects how people communicate and interact with the world'. However, the exact causes of autism are still not known, although there is evidence that genetic factors are implicated (National Autistic Society in the UK, 2019, www.autism.org.uk/advice-and-guidance/what-is-autism/the-causes-of-autism, accessed 27.10.2021).

It is highly likely that all of us in education – and, in fact, in society generally – will meet or already know individuals who experience an autistic spectrum disorder (ASD). At a national level, according to the National Autistic Society, there are around 700,000 autistic people, including both adults and children, or more than one in 100, in the UK today (NAS, 2021). In terms of gender differences, the proportion of males rather than females diagnosed with autism varies across studies, but in general shows a greater proportion of males. A study by Werling and Geschwind (2014), for example, concluded that ASD affects females less frequently than males. The outcome of a recent meta-analysis of studies of the prevalence of autism also concludes that the proportion is around 3:1 (Loomes, Hull & Mandy, 2017). There is some debate around the accuracy of these figures, however. They may, for example, relate to diagnostic gender bias, with current autism profiles and criteria based upon male characteristics, which do not take account of the female autism phenotype (Bargiela, Steward & Mandy, 2016).

History of autism as a 'condition'

The term 'autism' has been in use in relation to a range of difficulties experienced by children for around 80 years. Leo Kanner was an Austrian-American psychiatrist who was born in Austria, educated in Germany and later established a psychiatric clinic at the Johns Hopkins Medical School in Baltimore, Maryland, in the USA. Based on his observation of 11 children with similar behaviour, Kanner (1943) identified a common profile that seemed to centre on excessive focus on the self. Several years before Leo Kanner's 1943 paper on autism, Hans Asperger (1944/1991) used the term 'autistic psychopaths' to describe a group of children with distinct psychological characteristics.

Web activity WA5.3
Understanding the history of identification of ASD

If you are interested in reading a summary of the history of ASD as a condition, you might choose to access the material we have uploaded on the website.

Categorising autistic behaviours

It is possible to group autistic behaviours in a number of ways. Wing and Gould (1979), for example, identified what they called a 'triad of impairments' in around 15 in 10,000 children. This triad covers difficulty in regard to:

- social interaction, for example social relationships, and apparent indifference to other people, and/or aloofness;
- both verbal and non-verbal social communication; and
- imagination.

In addition, there is resistance to change in routine and repetitive behaviour patterns. Each area implies particular barriers to learning. Lack of social understanding and relating clearly affect interactions with other children and adults. A child who lacks social understanding is unlikely to understand unwritten social rules, recognise others' feelings or seek comfort from others.

Although Wing and Gould (1979) classified autistic behaviours into a 'triad of impairments', since that time, the *Diagnostic and Statistical Manual of Mental Disorders*, 5th edition (DSM-5) of the American Psychiatric Association (APA, 2013) has combined the first two descriptions of difficulties into one and has added an additional element: an unusual way of responding to sensory stimuli (Frederickson & Cline, 2015, p. 283). This dyad comprises difficulties in:

- social communication and social interaction;
- restricted, repetitive patterns of behaviour, interests or activities, including sensory difficulties.

While behaviours labelled 'autistic' and 'Aspergers' share similar characteristics, there is some difference in emphasis. Three-quarters of the autistic population have difficulties in learning, some at a severe level. Asperger syndrome tends not to be associated with these levels of learning difficulties. Measured levels of intelligence are often average or above (National Autistic Society, 2021). Delay in speech and language development is not likely.

A few autistic individuals may have very well-developed abilities in one particular area generally related to memory, for example rapid calculation, artistic ability, map making or musical ability. However, it is not true that all autistic people are geniuses. So-called 'savant' abilities, that is abilities far in excess of the average, are rare.

LEARNING POINT
PERSONAL NARRATIVES OF EXPERIENCE

Sometimes autistic children may appear to behave 'strangely' or inappropriately. Rather than simply dismissing behaviour as bizarre, it is really important to understand that there is meaning underlying behaviour. Misconceptions can lead to some autistic people feeling isolated and alone. In extreme cases, it can also lead to abuse and bullying. A number of publications have been written by writers reflecting on their own experiences of being autistic and it can be very illuminating to pay close attention to what they say. Below, we have summarised extracts from two such accounts.

Case study 1

As we have already noted, 'aloneness' is characteristic of autism. Grandin (1996) recalls not wishing to be hugged by others. Her senses were over-stimulated when she was touched and she was overwhelmed by this. She always wanted to share in activities with other children but did not know how to, and she felt she never fitted in. She recollects trying to work out how to behave from watching others.

Over-sensitivity to sound is another common experience. Grandin (1996) described her hearing as like a microphone in a hearing aid, permanently at the full volume position. She had two choices: either to turn the microphone off altogether, or turn it on and be swamped with sound.

Case study 2

Higashida (2013, p. 47) describes what it feels like to be alone so much of the time when others do not understand and say: 'Ah, don't worry about him – he'd rather been on his own.' He comments:

How many times have we heard this? I can't believe that anyone born as a human being really wants to be left all on their own, not really. No, for people with autism, what we're anxious about is that we're causing trouble for the rest of you, or even getting on your nerves. This is why it's hard for us to stay around other people.

Learners on the autistic spectrum are likely to find it difficult to understand what gestures, facial expressions or tone of voice mean. Sustaining eye contact can be difficult during a conversation. Higashida (2013, p. 43) comments: 'True we don't look at people's eyes very much. [...] I've been told again and again, but I still can't do it.' He goes on to explain what trying to make eye contact feels like to him:

> To me, making eye contact with someone I'm talking to feels a bit creepy, so I tend to avoid it.

> Then, where exactly am I looking? [...] What we're actually looking at is the other person's voice. [...] we're trying to listen to the other person with all our sense organs. When we're fully focused on working out what the heck it is you're saying, our sense of sight sort of zones out.

To what extent do you agree that personal narratives are a really important way to enable us to understand other people's behaviour and how we might respond appropriately?

Over-sensitivity to stimuli is a factor in another account of autism (Barron, 1992). This includes a description of a boy's reaction to the texture of food and needing to touch and feel it before it went into his mouth. Food had to be of one type. Bread, for example, could not be made into sandwiches with fillings, otherwise it provoked vomiting.

Identification of autism

It is not the case that all of us are 'a bit' autistic. To be autistic, individuals must consistently display behaviours in all aspects of the condition. Liking routines, having a good memory or lacking confidence and being shy does not mean that a person is 'a bit' autistic. Having said this, it is really important for all of us always to remember that autistic individuals should be respected as human beings, first and foremost. Children with autism are part of a distinctive group with common characteristics that are different from those of their peers. This implies not assuming a model of behaviour to which every child should be expected to conform. In his personal account of the experience of autism, Higashida (2013, p. 16) emphasises the importance of not assuming that there is one 'normal' model of behaviour:

> [...] even a straightforward activity like shopping can be really challenging if I'm tackling it on my own. During my miserable, helpless, frustrating days, I've started imagining what it would be like if everyone was autistic. If autism was regarded simply as a personality type, things would be so much easier and happier for us than they are now. For sure there are bad times when we cause a lot of hassle for other people, but what we really want is to be able to look towards a brighter future.

Co-ordination between health agencies and other key services, such as education, social care and the voluntary sector, is important. The National Institute for Health and Care Excellence (NICE, 2011) advises that a local autism multidisciplinary group (the autism team) should include, in its core membership, a paediatrician and/or child and adolescent psychiatrist, a speech and language therapist, and a clinical and/or educational psychologist. Multi-agency staff should also work in partnership with the child or young person with autism and their family or carers.

Once a concern about possible autistic tendencies has been raised, a member of the core autism team should advise on whether a referral should be made for a formal assessment.

'There are no biological markers in the identification of autism', as Klin et al. (2000, p. 163) comment. This means that, typically, autism in young people is identified through a profile of symptoms and characteristics of autistic behaviour.

In Chapter 9, we discuss formal assessment tools for identifying autism.

Approaches to addressing difficulties associated with autism

When considering the needs of autistic learners in general terms, it is useful to return to the *Code of Practice* in England (Department of Education/Department of Health, 2015, §6.27) that concurs with what has been outlined above in relation to behaviour commonly associated with autism. The *Code* suggests that 'young people with an Autistic Spectrum Disorder (ASD) may have needs across all areas, including particular sensory requirements'. They 'are likely to have particular difficulties with social interaction. They may also experience difficulties with language, communication and imagination which can impact on how they relate to others' (DfE/DoH, 2015, §6.29).

What is needed in educational institutions to support autistic learners at any age and stage is an approach that combines structure with support that acknowledges individuality and the importance of establishing positive relationships peer to peer and learner to teacher/other adults.

Among the core principles of 'good practice in autism education' in a report by the Autism Education Trust/Centre for Research in Autistic Education (CRAE) (2011, p. 44) are to:

Embed specialist, evidence-informed approaches in quality-first teaching practice to remove barriers for students on the autism spectrum

[…]

Build and consolidate autism expertise at a consistently high level by maintaining an on-going programme of training and CPD on autism for all staff

so that staff can:

Use innovative and individualised methods of adapting the curriculum, utilising students' strengths and interests, to make it accessible and rewarding for students with autism.

In schools or colleges, and from the current author's personal experience and discussion with special educational needs co-ordinators (SENCos) and learning support managers (Wearmouth & Butler, 2020), it can be very useful to have an agreed safe and quiet sanctuary, for example the library, for autistic learners to go to when they feel anxiety building or are overloaded by sensory stimuli. This may not be the same place for all autistic students and may need to be negotiated individually. It is really important that stigma is not attached to this place. Use of the agreed quiet location and the benefit of it to individual learners should be monitored regularly because it is also important that autistic learners have the opportunity to interact socially with their peers.

Class teachers and lecturers have the responsibility for ensuring that all the learners in their classrooms make progress. In classrooms, teachers can address learning and behavioural needs associated with autism in a number of ways. For example, a teacher can pay close attention to clarity and order, reduce extraneous and unnecessary material in order that children know where their attention needs to be directed, and maintain a predictable physical environment with very predictable and regular routines, ensuring that everything is kept in the same place. Children might be taught agreed signals to be quiet or to call for attention. Teachers might provide specific low-arousal work areas free from visual distractions. Headphones might be made available to reduce sound. They might also provide a visual timetable with clear symbols to represent the various activities for the day, and a simple visual timer with, for example, an arrow that is moved across a simple timeline to show how much time has passed and how much is left.

The future quality of life for young people with ASD may well depend on how far they can learn to understand and interact with others rather than solely on the academic skills and qualifications they may have gained (Jordan & Powell, 1995). In order to develop greater understanding of personal emotions, children might be taught in a very deliberate, overt and structured way to name their feelings and relate these to their own experiences, predict how they are likely to feel at particular times and in particular circumstances, and recognise the signs of extreme emotions, such as anger. A visual gauge showing graduated degrees of anger in different shades of colour can often be helpful here.

Students might also be taught, again very deliberately and in small steps, to identify and name others' feelings and link these to possible causes, and identify appropriate responses to others' emotions. They might, for example, keep a feelings diary in which they record times when they feel happy, sad or frightened, and what they can do about this. Teachers might use art, drama and social stories to identify the different kinds of emotions and/or explore their physical aspects and/or talk through situations that need to be resolved. Above all, it is really important to get to know the student really well and to understand his/her individuality, strengths, weakness, likes and dislikes, and so on.

LEARNING POINT
USEFULNESS OF VISUAL SUPPORTS

The National Autistic Society (2021) outlines a range of visual supports for autistic learners on its website (www.autism.org.uk/about/strategies/visual-supports.aspx, accessed 27.10.2021). You should access this website now.

Please note down your responses to the following questions:

- What kind(s) of supports might be the most useful for learners in your context?
- How might they be used effectively, both at school and at home?

Specialist approaches

The current national climate emphasises learning targets and measured improvements in students' progress. As befits this context, many of the more specialist approaches for children with autism rely on training or teacher direction, and less on intuitive responding, for example the Treatment and Education of Autistic and related Communication Handicapped Children programme (TEACCH) (Mesibov, Shea & Schopler, 2004), and the Lovaas method (Lovaas, 1987).

TEACCH approach

The TEACCH programme, developed by Eric Schopler in the 1970s (Schopler, Reichler & Lansing, 1980; Schopler, 1997), takes account of the individuality of the person with autism as they are and 'the culture of autism', and then builds a programme around each learner's skill level, interests and needs to support their development (Mesibov, 2015) (www.autismuk.com/training/what-is-teech/, accessed 08.09.2019). Important to any TEACCH approach is the development of communication skills and the opportunity for the individual to follow his/her own social and leisure interests.

As a result of 'the TEACCH research and experience that structure fits the "culture of autism" more effectively than any other techniques we have observed' (Mesibov, 2015), structured teaching is an important priority in the programme. '[...] a TEACCH-influenced classroom places a large emphasis on physically structuring the room to facilitate learning interactions' (Sheehy, 2004, p. 347). Structure is important in the physical environment, schedules of activities, clear, explicit expectations, use of visual representations, for example in timetables, and 'precision teaching'. This latter involves dividing up new skills and more appropriate behaviours into a hierarchy of small steps that can be taught one after the other with specific goals. Progress can be charted through the steps that have been achieved. In summary, the TEACCH approach, then, is designed to include a focus on individual strengths and interests with structured teaching. Families are often encouraged to collaborate with professionals in continuing the approach in the home.

Lovaas approach

The Lovaas approach, on the other hand, is a form of applied behaviour analysis (ABA) (Lovaas, 1987) based on the work of Skinner (1938). It is built on behavioural methods such as reducing identified tasks into small, discrete 'teachable' steps, reinforcing appropriate behaviours associated with each step, and using highly structured, intensive teaching strategies. (See Chapter 2 for a discussion of ABA.) ABA is used to reduce stereotypical autistic behaviours, such as repetitive body movement, through 'extinction' and the learning of socially-acceptable alternatives to such behaviours.

Alternative and Augmentative Communication

Alternative and Augmentative Communication (AAC) may well be used to support young people who experience considerable difficulties in verbal communication. AAC systems can be very useful for autistic learners who experience particular difficulties in verbal communication, because they are designed to complement and/or enhance standard means of communication and can replace speech.

In a recent publication (Smith, 2019, p. 194), Martha, the mother of an autistic child, N, described how she and her husband taught N to communicate with them at home, using the Picture Exchange Communication System (PECS) (see above for discussion of PECS) and other strategies. The hardest thing for the parents was how long every aspect of development in his ability to communicate took. They started with teaching him the purpose of communication. Up till then, he had not seen the purpose of it because his mother had done everything for him:

> We had to start from object exchange, hand over hand at the beginning. I placed a raisin in a magnetic picture frame on the fridge and tried to entice him to take it and exchange it with me for an actual raisin. No chance. Days passed. As a last ditch effort, I swapped it for a picture of a chocolate biscuit. Bingo. Before long he would bring the picture to me, I would say 'biscuit please', swap it for a biscuit and he would scuttle off with his prize.
>
> Communication suddenly had a point; there was something in it for him. Within weeks this had become embedded and he started to branch out, bringing me a cup when he wanted a drink or the small plastic banana from his toy food collection.

Establishing daily routines in autistic learners' lives can provide predictability and so reduce anxiety about what is happening around them. A development on the use of single pictures is that of visual scheduling, that is a visual timetable of events that are to take place during the day. In an educational setting, children and young people can have individual timetables where each lesson has its own card featuring pictures, words, or both, which the student can place by their workstation in the classroom or carry around with them. They will then have a visual order of events that they can refer to during the day for reassurance. If the timetable is made with a Velcro backing, students can remove all the cards at the end of the day to signify that the timetable for that particular day has finished and that it is time to go home.

Providing visual schedules enables learners to see clearly what is happening and when. From his own experience, Dumortier (2004) comments that many of his problems could be avoided by prior planning. Schedules were very important to him and he needed to know well in advance what was going to happen, how it would happen, who would be involved, and so on. Any change of plan, including either being late or being early, could lead to feelings of frustration, powerlessness, anger and anxiety.

LEARNING POINT
IMPORTANCE OF UNDERSTANDING ASD AND WAYS TO SUPPORT LEARNING NEEDS

Many of us believe that it is crucial to know something about autism spectrum disorder (ASD), how we might understand individual autistic learners from their earliest years in educational institutions, and some of the ways in which we might support them if they experience difficulties in learning and/or social behaviour.

To what extent do you agree with this viewpoint?

The following summary of a report from a survey on parents' and young people's experiences of the English education system (Reid & Ayris, 2011) spells out why it is so important.

(Continued)

Reid and Ayris found that a quarter of autistic children were not happy at school, and one in five did not feel safe. Seventeen per cent had been suspended from school and, of these, nearly one half had been suspended three or more times. Nearly one half considered that teachers did not know enough about autism. Many parents had to fight the system to make it work. Nearly 70% reported it had not been easy to get the educational support their child needed. Nearly one half said they had waited over a year to get the right support for their child, and over one quarter more than two years. Nearly 20% of parents had to go to tribunal to ensure appropriate support for their children. Autistic children do not grow out of autism. Autistic children become autistic adults. Autism is lifelong. In the UK only 16% of autistic adults are in full-time paid employment. Only 32% are in some kind of paid work.

Appropriate support for older autistic learners

The Social Care Institute for Excellence (SCIE) (2017, www.scie.org.uk/autism/transition/adult-services) comments that 'the transition from children's to adults' social care can be particularly difficult for people with autism' and notes a number of issues that can be particularly problematic. For example, 'school provides a structure that many people with autism like, and feel the lack of when they leave'. For many, it can be problematic to cope with change, and thinking about the range of new options can be hard. Life as an adult and the expectations this carries can bring new challenges. Further, 'there is limited provision of further education options, especially for those who display challenging behaviour'.

LEARNING POINT
IMPROVING THE TRANSITION PROCESS FOR AUTISTIC LEARNERS

If you are interested in issues of transition between phases of education for autistic learners, please access the SCIE (2017) website at www.scie.org.uk/autism/transition/adult-services (accessed 27.10.2021).

Now reflect on the following questions:

- The CSIE outlines suggested improvements in transition for autistic learners when they leave school. Which of these do you think relates to all learners of any age and stage at transition?
- Which relates specifically to autistic learners' post-compulsory education?

Conclusion

In summary, as Lindsay, Dockrell and Strand (2008, p. 825) comment in a longitudinal study of the reciprocal effects of difficulties in language acquisition and use, behaviour and relationships with peers in schools:

Language difficulties impacted on children's literacy development and so put them at greater risk of BESD [behaviour, social and emotional difficulties] at school. Their peer relationships were also related to language development, especially pragmatic abilities. Together these findings suggest a complex set of relationships and indicate the importance of addressing all three factors when considering the development of children with developmental difficulties, namely within-child factors, the context and development over time.

Lee (2008, p. 18) takes account of these factors in her recommendation that good practice is to support learners in 'communication supportive' environments. This includes eliciting learners' views of their strengths and difficulties, as required in legislation across the UK.

As you reflect back on what we have discussed in this chapter, what, in your view, are the most important considerations to be taken into account in addressing the particular needs of learners who experience difficulty in the acquisition of speech, language and communication?

Further reading

Speech and language

Nash, S., & Hackney Speech and Language Therapy Service for Children (eds) (2013) *Speech and Language Activities*. Buckingham: Hinton House Publishers.

Specific language impairment

Norbury, C. F. (2014) Practitioner Review: Social (pragmatic) communication disorder conceptualization, evidence and clinical implications. *Journal of Child Psychology and Psychiatry*, 55(3), 204–216.

O'Handley, R. D., Radley, K. C., & Lum, J. D. K. (2016) Promoting social communication in a child with 'specific language impairment'. *Communication Disorders Quarterly*, 37(4), 199–210.

Autism

Bellini, S., Peters, J. K., Benner, L., & Hopf, A. (2007) A meta-analysis of school-based social skills interventions for children with autism spectrum disorders. *Remedial and Special Education*, 28(3), 153–162.

Bondy, A., & Frost, L. (2011) *Topics in Autism: A Picture's Worth. PECS and Other Visual Communication Strategies in Autism* (2nd edn). *Bethesda, MD:* Woodbine House.

Mesibov, G. B., Shea, V., & Schopler, E. (2004) *The TEACCH Approach to Autism Spectrum Disorders*. New York: Springer.

Timmins, S. (2017) *Successful Social Stories for School and College Students with Autism*. London: Jessica Kingsley.

Wong, C., Odom, S. L., Hume, K. A., Cox, A. W., Fettig, A., Kucharczyk, S., Brock, M. E., Plavnick, J. B., Fleury, V. P., & Schultz, T. R. (2014) Evidence-based practices for children, youth, and young adults with autism spectrum disorder: A comprehensive review. *Journal of Autism and Developmental Disorders*, 45, 1951–1966.

Websites

The following websites also contain a wealth of information about autism:

Action Medical Research for Children: https://action.org.uk/search?search=autism
Autism Alliance: www.autism-alliance.org.uk/
Mencap: www.mencap.org.uk/
National Autistic Society: www.autism.org.uk/

6

DIFFICULTIES IN COGNITION AND LEARNING

Major questions addressed in this chapter are:

- What do we mean by 'cognition'?
- What might be considered the primary needs of young people who experience difficulties in the area of cognition and learning?
- How might we understand such needs?
- What can we do to ensure that young people who experience difficulties in cognition and learning can access the curriculum most effectively and be included in the education system?

Key terms

Cognitive difficulties, precision teaching, Bloom's Hierarchy, constructivist learning theories, profound and multiple learning difficulties, specific learning difficulties, dyslexia

Introduction

The term 'cognition' is derived from the Latin 'cognoscere', to get to know. Strictly speaking, therefore, 'cognition' is the process of acquiring knowledge and understanding through thought, experience and the senses. In other words, it relates to the processing of information and includes a range of functions, for example memory, problem-solving, reasoning, comprehension and production of language, and perception.

'Cognitive' difficulties can be defined in a number of ways. If we take the example of the definition in England, in the section entitled 'Cognition and learning', the *Code of Practice* (Department for Education/Department of Health, 2015, §6.30–6.31) describes such difficulties as covering:

> a wide range of needs, including moderate learning difficulties (MLD), severe learning difficulties (SLD) [...] profound and multiple learning difficulties (PMLD) [...] and specific learning difficulties (SpLD) [that] affect one or more specific aspects of learning. This encompasses a range of conditions such as dyslexia, dyscalculia and dyspraxia.

This chapter opens by discussing what is implied by the term 'moderate learning difficulties', continues by considering severe, profound and multiple learning difficulties, and goes on the review issues around specific learning difficulties, including dyslexia, dyspraxia and dyscalculia. Threaded through the text is discussion of ways in which we can address some of the barriers to learning that may be experienced by learners.

Moderate learning difficulties

A term that is in frequent use, 'moderate learning difficulties' (MLD), relates to slower cognitive development, or difficulty in the acquisition of cognitive skills. This might be any or all of problem-solving, language, memory, attention and thinking. The document *Statistical First Release (SFR): Special Educational Needs in England* for January 2019, published by the Department for Education, indicated that young people who experienced MLD constituted 20% of the total number identified with special educational needs. The term 'MLD' is not entirely straightforward, however.

In the American Psychiatric Association's *Diagnostic and Statistical Manual of Mental Disorders* (DSM-5) (APA, 2013, p. 31), such learning difficulties are termed 'intellectual developmental disorder' and are characterized by:

> deficits in general mental abilities, such as reasoning, problem solving, planning, abstract thinking, judgment, academic learning, and learning from experience.

In schools and colleges, the progress of young people who experience MLD will be, as Hayes and Whittaker (2016) comment, well below expected levels in all or most areas of the curriculum: acquisition of literacy and numeracy skills, conceptual understanding, speech and language acquisition, confidence and self-efficacy ('I can do'), concentration and attention levels, and development of social skills. It is important to stress again, however, that while learners may have a very general difficulty in learning, they are also individuals with their own needs, strengths and interests, not simply a member of a homogeneous group labelled 'MLD' students

(Fletcher-Campbell, 2005), Once a learner's difficulty in a particular area of functioning has been recognised, provision needs to be made in relation to individual learners' particular needs, not to the assumed needs of a group labelled 'MLD'.

Addressing moderate difficulties in learning

If we interpret MLD as difficulties in cognition, we might take three examples: comprehension of text, memory and social skills.

Difficulties in comprehension

To understand a text, learners need to be able to cope with the conceptual level in the first place. If students are interested in, and have prior knowledge of, topics they are reading about, they are more likely to be able to grasp the meaning of more difficult text, especially if new concepts are expanded and explained step by step. There are implications here for teachers to get to know their learners very well. It is also important to be able to judge the difficulty implicated in sentence length and complexity, word length and familiarity (Lunzer & Gardner, 1979).

It can be very helpful to scaffold reading comprehension by adding visual aids, for example pictures, and inserting subheadings and summaries into the text. Learners can be taught to scan the text before reading in depth, focus on pictures, diagrams, captions and subheadings, and identify and underline key passages. The amount read can be shortened to a page-by-page or even a paragraph-by-paragraph reading, so that learners with comprehension difficulties have less to remember at one time. The amount of text to be read before questions are asked can be lengthened as learners grow in confidence. Groups of learners can be encouraged to extend their understanding by sharing the reading of a text and then discussing the main points. Careful attention to learner groupings is important here so that no one is afraid to ask questions or show that they do not understand aspects of the text.

Often learners need to gain more experience in reading in order. One very effective way to increase word identification, knowledge of letter/sound combinations and use of contextual information and inference (Duke & Pearson, 2002) for learners who experience difficulties is following the text with the eyes while listening to a recording (which has to be word-perfect), 'Paired Reading' (Topping, 2001) or 'reading buddies'.

We consider the issue of reading comprehension further in Chapter 10.

Difficulties with short-term memory

Poor memory can be one of the difficulties experienced by some learners. Many of those with short-term memory difficulties have problems absorbing and remembering information, or carrying out instructions in a busy classroom. They may find it difficult to copy from the blackboard because they are unable to remember what they have seen and translate it to the paper on the desk. In considering why this might be the case, it could be that they did not grasp the new concepts, information or instructions properly in the first place, or have not been able to link this to what they already knew. Or perhaps they have not made the distinction between newly introduced concepts and previous knowledge, so that the newly-acquired information is confused with the old. Memory can be accessed through recognition or through recall. Recognition is usually more straightforward than recall.

Memory difficulties may often be improved with training. Teachers and/or families might use a multi-sensory mode of learning through oral, visual, auditory and kinaesthetic modes, encourage learners to think up their own mnemonic (memory cues) and visualisation techniques and, if possible, repeat aloud and rehearse items to be remembered. If appropriate, and to reinforce the input stimuli, teachers might make a deliberate effort to enable learners to see, hear, say and, if possible, touch the materials to be learned. This may help to consolidate the new information for use and transfer to other areas of the curriculum. Verbal instructions should be clear and concise and, if relevant, be prefaced with a warning to ensure that learners are ready to attend and listen. In the classroom, teachers might encourage learners to repeat back key points and/or talk through tasks in their own voice to help to direct their attention, and supplement auditory verbal material with visual cues such as pictorial reminders, and practical demonstrations (Wearmouth, 2009, p. 48).

In terms of memory span, teachers and families might gradually increase the number of items to be remembered and the length of time between presenting the list and asking for recall. As memory span improves, an activity might be introduced between presentation and recollection. They might also try gradually to increase sequences and the complexity of instructions, beginning with one or two only and at a simple level.

Difficulties in social interaction

Many learners who experience MLD find it difficult to understand social rules. If so, they should be taught them explicitly. Social stories with pictures to illustrate their meaning, and/or story boards, can be created that make key social skills very clear. For example, in relation to behaviour in the playground:

> I like to play with my friends out in the playground → Sometimes I like to walk around →
> I will not push or hurt anyone when I'm walking around → I will talk to my friends → If
> I do this I will keep my friends. (Wearmouth, 1986)

Story boards or flow diagrams can also be very useful to teach the consequences of actions, and cause and effect.

LEARNING POINT
USING STORY BOARDS AND FLOW DIAGRAMS TO TEACH THE CONSEQUENCES OF ACTIONS

Now please think about a young person who experiences MLD. Imagine, or remember, a situation where his/her actions have had dangerous consequences. Create a story board, using simple line diagrams, to show him/her how his/her actions have led to these consequences and what s/he might have done differently.

You will find a whole series of examples of social stories/story boards at: www.google.com/search?q=social+stories+examples&tbm=isch&chips=q:social+stories+examples,g_1:conversation:e0nh18EFlel%3D&us-g=AI4_-kQ2TKvRoAoqGoejGiAtF9sdTe4FnA&sa=X&ved=2ahUKEwjC68WJnvnnAhXHQEEAHRzKCQ4Q-gloDKAR6BAgJEAs&biw=1366&bih=625#imgrc=r2akr0Ej6p6hdM (accessed 28.10.2021). You might like to access these now for future reference.

Applications of learning theories

There is no single model of learning that we can use as a framework for designing programmes or interventions for young people who experience moderate difficulties in learning. Below we refer back to two of the models discussed in Chapter 2 that can be used to underpin effective curricula in this area – behaviourism and constructivism.

Applications of behaviourist learning theories

As discussed in Chapter 2, behaviourist theories of learning assume that all behaviour is learned. One way to approach the learning of new knowledge and skills is to conceptualise the new area of knowledge or skill as a hierarchy built up of a sequence of stages, and then teach each stage until the learner has mastered it. Only then should the teacher move on to teaching the next stage. The stages can be smaller or bigger, depending on the student's current learning and progress, and the particular area of study.

Precision teaching

So-called 'precision teaching' consists, first, of conceptualising the new topic as a hierarchy of very small steps, starting from the baseline of the learner's current level of understanding or skill to a final end point. Once the teacher has worked out the hierarchy, each small step can be taught to mastery level in the predefined sequence, with one stage building on from the one below. The learning of each step can be reinforced through different types of reward, whatever is reasonable and meaningful to the learner.

Web activity WA6.1
Using precision teaching

On the website we have uploaded a link to a guide to precision teaching and an activity to accompany this. You might choose to access this now.

Examples of hierarchical frameworks

Two examples of hierarchical frameworks that are sometimes used to support the conceptualising of structured approaches to teaching knowledge and skills for learners with MLD, and often more serious degrees of difficulty in learning, are Bloom's *Taxonomy* (Bloom & Krathwohl, 1956) and Haring's 'Learning Hierarchy' (Haring et al., 1978).

Bloom's *Taxonomy* of learning

Bloom's *Taxonomy* was first created in 1956 (Bloom & Krathwohl, 1956, www.bloomstaxonomy. org/Blooms%20Taxonomy%20questions.pdf, accessed 28.10.2021). Three categories of areas of learning in education were identified: cognitive – mental skills (knowledge); affective – growth of feelings/emotions (attitude – self); psychomotor – manual or physical skills. Each category was divided into subdivisions, starting from the simplest to the most complex behaviour, with an assumption that the simplest had to be mastered before moving on to the more complex. The hierarchy was revised in the 1990s to substitute verbs for nouns, for example 'remembering' is substituted for 'knowledge' (Anderson et al., 2001).

In terms of the 'cognitive' category, Bloom's hierarchy (revised) is a framework of six levels of thinking that can be very useful for teachers in designing tasks, preparing questions for discussion with students, and providing feedback on students' work. In the bullet points below, the first term is from the original *Taxonomy*, and the second from the revised version:

- Level I Knowledge/Remembering: the lowest level that requires recall only of basic facts and concepts;
- Level II Comprehension/Understanding: that is evidenced by describing, comparing, interpreting and organizing of facts;
- Level III Application/Applying: problem solving in new contexts by applying new techniques, knowledge, and rules;
- Level IV Analysis/Analyzing: investigating information and identifying causes by making inferences and supporting generalizations with evidence;
- Level V Synthesis/Creating[1]: compiling and combining information in a new way and/or a new pattern;
- Level VI Evaluation/Evaluating: this is the highest level and requires defending opinions and views through making judgments about the validity of ideas in relation to set criteria.

Web activity WA6.2
Considering how to use Bloom's *Taxonomy* as a framework to differentiate teaching

We have uploaded an example of the use of Bloom's *Taxonomy* on the website, together with an activity related to it. You might choose to access this now.

Stages in Haring's 'Learning Hierarchy'

Haring's 'Learning Hierarchy' consists of four stages in increasing levels of complexity (Haring et al., 1978). The Hierarchy is a tool that can serve as 'a dynamic interface between instructional activity and learner competence' (Burns, VanDerHeyden & Boice, 2008, p. 1153) by supporting teachers to choose appropriate approaches based on the learner's current stage of learning':

1. **Acquisition**: the initial stage of learning is to complete the target skill correctly but with no assumption of accuracy or fluency in the skill. When learners are at the acquisition stage, teachers or other adults might demonstrate and model an approach that will lead to

---

[1] In the revised hierarchy, 'Creating' has been reordered as Level VI and 'Evaluating' as Level V.

acquiring that skill, for example demonstrating a way to solve a mathematics problem, and praise and encourage the effort that learners have made.

2. **Fluency**: the next stage is where the learner can complete the target skill accurately but slowly, and is not yet fluent in its use. At the fluency stage, teachers or other adults might structure learning activities so that learners have the opportunity to respond and participate, give learners frequent opportunities to repeat the newly-acquired skill and practise the skill in context to solve problems. They might also give learners feedback on the fluency and accuracy of what they have achieved, and praise and encourage them for increased fluency.

3. **Generalisation**: the third stage is where the learner is accurate and fluent in using the target skill but uses it in a limited way, and not in a range of situations or settings. Or the learner may confuse 'similar' skills with the target skill. At the generalisation stage, teachers or other adults might structure academic tasks to ensure that learners use the new skill regularly in tasks, encourage, praise and reward learners for using new skills in different contexts, and give learners practice items to ensure that they can correctly discriminate between similar skills.

4. **Adaptation**: at the fourth stage, the learner uses the skill accurately and fluently and in a range of situations or settings. However, s/he cannot adapt the skill to fit new task demands or situations at this point. The goal is to identify and adapt elements of previously learned skills to new demands or contexts. At the adaptation stage, teachers or other adults might help learners to identify the essential element(s) of new skills that they can modify to address unfamiliar tasks and situations. For example, as Haring et al. (1978) comment, fractions, ratios and percentages relate to the 'big idea' of the part in relation to the whole. They might also ensure learners have opportunities to practise the target new skills, with minor modifications, in new contexts, offer formative feedback, and reward effort and success.

Constructivist understandings of learning

As also noted in Chapter 2, constructivist understandings take a rather different view of the learning process. Instead of the passive view of learners, constructivist understandings assume their active agency in interpreting and constructing personal understandings of the world.

Piaget's staged theory of learning

In Chapter 2 we discussed the work of Jean Piaget (1954, 1964, 1969), who identified four universal stages of learning – sensorimotor (0–2 years), preoperational (2–7 years), concrete operational (7–11 years) and formal operational (11+ years) – from his observations of his own children. Over time there have been a number of criticisms of this work. However, despite the criticisms, Piaget's conclusions that learners construct knowledge by interacting with their environment, and that they re-construct their thoughts in the light of new experiences, have made a strong contribution to practice in Early Years settings and primary schools particularly. Thinking about learning as a continuum from the sensorimotor to the formal operational stage can be very helpful in considering how to structure activities and tasks suitable for young people who experience difficulties in learning. Just to give one example, it is obvious that some learners will need to use concrete materials for much longer than others if they are to acquire new concepts and skills. To assume that all young people can engage in abstract reasoning from the age of 11 and manipulate ideas in their heads is likely to be damaging to young people with difficulties in learning.

Bruner's 'modes of representation'

As also discussed previously, a different way to understand learners' progress in developing conceptual understanding of the world is through Bruner's (1966) three modes of representation: 'enactive', where we 'do' and then we understand and know; 'iconic', where we understand reality through visual representations of the real thing; and 'symbolic', where we understand and can use abstract representations of reality. Bruner's model also offers a very useful framework for planning differentiated activities to meet learning objectives for a range of learners in classrooms.

Like Piaget's model, young people's learning is seen as becoming more proficient in each of the increasingly complex modes from the concrete 'learn by doing' to the abstract. Having said that, learning does not occur in discrete stages. It is continuous. Children may face barriers to learning and progress at any point in development. Those with difficulties in cognition are very likely to need representation of reality more through concrete objects if necessary, using an enactive mode to learn by doing.

Vygotsky's social constructivist understandings

As we discussed in Chapter 2, the zone of proximal development (ZPD) is a core concept in the model of learning proposed by Lev Vygotsky (1978).

LEARNING POINT
APPLICATIONS OF SOCIAL CONSTRUCTIVIST
UNDERSTANDINGS OF LEARNING

Read the following summary of a social constructivist understanding of learning and its application. Consider whether, and how, you might put the list of implications into practice in a classroom setting for the benefit of learners who experience cognitive difficulties.

The zone of proximal development is, effectively, the next step in learning in terms of the range of skills and knowledge that learners cannot yet learn on their own but can learn when supported by more informed and experienced others.

A more informed/expert other may provide structured support for, might 'scaffold', new learning (Wood, Bruner & Ross, 1976) through the ZPD based on his/her knowledge of the subject material or the particular skill and what might come next in the sequence of learning, and the learner's current level of knowledge and understanding of the subject. Learners need scaffolding but not so much that it encourages over-dependency.

This is really important in relation to learners who experience difficulties. Emotions can be very powerful in supporting, or inhibiting, learning. Success can be pleasant and/or exciting. Failure, especially when it happens often, can be upsetting (Wearmouth, Glynn & Berryman, 2005). Getting the balance right is really important. Without active participation and the sense of being a contributing member of the classroom, learners will not feel included and they will fail to learn properly (Wearmouth, 1999). Very importantly, learning and behaviour are influenced by the kind of relationship a learner has with a teacher. The relationship both develops through time and is influenced by the teacher's perception of a learner's value and worth.

Some of the implications of this view of the learning process are that all learners, including those who experience difficulties, need

- time for focused talk between themselves and the more informed other(s), most often the teacher(s), in a safe space where they will not be afraid to ask questions and be wrong without feeling humiliated by the teacher's, or peers', reactions. It is absolutely essential that they feel safe in talking about themselves as well as asking and answering questions (Bishop et al., 2014);
- a safe space also for interaction between themselves and peers to enable 'interthinking' (Littleton & Mercer, 2013) around new learning to clarify and consolidate their understanding;
- respectful relationships between and among learners and adults in the learning environment.

Learning from real life

Case study: Provision to meet the needs of learners with cognitive difficulties

The school environment/curriculum can present a range of barriers to participation and learning for learners who experience cognitive difficulties. 'George', for example, an ex-student of the current author, had been identified as experiencing such difficulties almost from the beginning of his school career. He had been assessed as requiring a statement of need, and then an EHC Plan, from the early years of his education. He had been educated in mixed-attainment mainstream classes, including in his secondary school, since the age of 5.

George experienced difficulties in understanding and acquiring basic concepts and skills in reading, writing and numeracy. His communication skills were limited, as was his ability to think logically. His long- and short-term memory were poor, and this meant he had a problem remembering both what lessons had been about, and what to bring to school for practical lessons such as P.E. and cookery. He lacked the self-belief to develop the skills he did have. Every lunchtime he would come to the learning support room to be with adults rather than try to engage with peers outside. In his secondary school, a teaching assistant spent around 12 hours per week supporting George in his mixed-attainment classes, but this was more a 'bolt-on' than the result of careful pre-planning.

(Continued)

His overall developmental delay had resulted in attainments significantly below expected levels in most areas of the curriculum. When he reached his teenage years, he found it difficult to mix with his peer group because he had nothing of interest to say to them. He could often be frustrated by his inability to understand what was going on in the hustle and bustle of a busy school day and the speed of his peers' conversations. By the age of 16, he was still very needy, with an over-reliance on adult support from his TA, and very lonely.

As a result of difficulties in learning, communicating and thinking logically, young people may well display behaviour that is seen as anti-social and challenging if their needs are not fully recognised and understood. George was a prime candidate to be used by less well-meaning peers for nefarious purposes, because he rarely thought about the possible consequences to himself of anti-social actions. One day, for example, persuaded by two other students, he stole some laptops from a class where he was being taught word-processing. He tried to sell them openly on the street in the local town without realising that this would inevitably be reported – which it was – and he was caught 'red-handed'.

George survived his secondary education – just!

You might like to consider what school life felt like to him.

In retrospect, and in his mainstream classes, especially in the secondary school, a much more clearly defined approach to appropriate differentiation, in other words adaptation of learning activities, should have been planned for him. This should have included individual learning outcomes matched to his own prior learning and designed to build on what he already knew, understood and could do but with sufficient challenge so that he could make progress. As it was, the tasks he was expected to complete were often not achievable. Such tasks could have been broken down into small steps to identify gaps in his prior learning and point to future new learning. He often found that the teacher moved on too quickly, before he had a chance to reflect on what he knew. He would have benefited more from opportunities to handle concrete objects and to see pictures and diagrams than from continuous teacher talk. He really needed multiple examples of new concepts, carefully devised 'scaffolding' from a teacher, TA or peer, with that scaffolding withdrawn as he became more confident with the task or concept at hand, and lots of opportunities (certainly more than most of his peers) to practise newly-learnt skills and knowledge.

Differentiation and curriculum adaptation is an important approach to consider to meet the needs of a young man like George.

LEARNING POINT
DIFFERENTIATION AND CURRICULUM ADAPTATION TO MEET THE NEED OF LEARNERS WITH MLD

A very useful handout on differentiated activities designed to meet the identified needs of learners with MLD has been prepared at the Institute of Education in London (now part of University College, London) and is available at: http://dera.ioe.ac.uk/13820/2/handouts3.pdf (accessed 28.10.2021).

You might like to access this material now. Consider how you might use these materials to conceptualise differentiated activities for one or more learners you know with MLD.

Profound and multiple barriers to learning

Learners with profound and multiple learning disabilities (PMLD) may be identified as having a range of what we might call 'conditions'. They may, for example, be identified as having autism or Down's syndrome, Rett syndrome, tuberous sclerosis, Batten's disease, or another disorder. Learning is likely to be very slow. One common factor is difficulty in communication. Many people with PMLD 'rely on facial expressions, vocal sounds, body language and behaviour to communicate'. Some people may only 'use a small range of formal communication, such as speech, symbols or signs' (Mencap, undated, p. 4). Many may find it hard to understand others, and it is therefore very important for those supporting people with PMLD to 'spend time getting to know their means of communication and finding effective ways to interact with them' (p. 4). For a long time, as we saw in Chapter 3, there was an assumption that learners with profound difficulties in learning could not learn. However, more recently, there has been an acknowledgement that they can learn throughout their lives if appropriate support is made available.

Addressing profound and multiple difficulties

In Chapter 5 (pp. 63–68) we discussed a number of ways to encourage the development of communication skills for learners who experience difficulties. Below we discuss an approach – 'Intensive Interaction' – that was specifically designed to encourage interaction and communication with, and by, learners with PMLD.

Intensive Interaction

Approaches to addressing communication difficulties have often been based on applied behaviour analysis and assumed that acts of communication can be broken down into small steps that can be taught separately. Intensive Interaction, in contrast, adopts a different – and holistic – approach based on the model of 'natural' interactions between caregivers and infants (Nind, 1999). Rather than a closely structured, predetermined programme, Intensive Interaction is designed to support practitioners to adopt a holistic, nurturing framework for communication (Yoder, 1990). The adult begins by trying to 'connect' with the learner by, for example, modifying his/her facial expressions, body language, including vocal and gaze behaviours to fit those of the learner, thus responding to the learner as if his/her behaviour has 'intentional and communicative significance' (Nind, 1999, p. 97).

Web activity WA6.3
Understanding Intensive Interaction

You will find links to two articles describing the origins and use of Intensive Interaction uploaded on the website, and an activity. You might choose to access this material now.

Specific difficulties in learning

We might take our definition of what constitute 'specific learning difficulties' from *The International Classification of Diseases, ICD-11* (World Health Organization, 2019). In this document, 'developmental learning disorder' is an umbrella term that refers to a difficulty with particular aspects of learning irrespective of overall ability level. The most recent definition (WHO, 2019, 6A03, https://icd.who.int/browse11/l-m/en#/http://id.who.int/icd/entity/2099676649, accessed 06.01.2020) states that such a disorder:

> is characterized by significant and persistent difficulties in learning academic skills, which may include reading, writing, or arithmetic. The individual's performance in the affected academic skill(s) is markedly below what would be expected for chronological age and general level of intellectual functioning, and results in significant impairment in the individual's academic or occupational functioning. Developmental learning disorder first manifests when academic skills are taught during the early school years. Developmental learning disorder is not due to a disorder of intellectual development, sensory impairment (vision or hearing), neurological or motor disorder, lack of availability of education, lack of proficiency in the language of academic instruction, or psychosocial adversity.

In the USA, the *Diagnostic and Statistical Manual of Mental Disorders*, 5th edition (DSM-5) (APA, 2013, p. 68) offers a definition of what it terms 'specific learning disorder', which is:

> [...] a neurodevelopmental disorder with a biological origin that is the basis for abnormalities at a cognitive level that are associated with the behavioral signs of the disorder. The biological origin includes an interaction of genetic, epigenetic, and environmental factors, which affect the brain's ability to perceive or process verbal or nonverbal information efficiently and accurately.

According to this definition, such a 'disorder' relates to the brain's ability to process information.

Further, the learning difficulty may be restricted to one academic skill or area, for example reading single words, retrieving or calculating number facts. An individual may experience one of these, or they can co-exist as part of a wider profile. These learning difficulties are persistent, despite the provision of extra help at home or school. The DSM-5 goes on to note that, in relation to literacy:

> *Dyslexia* is an alternative term used to refer to a pattern of learning difficulties characterized by problems with accurate or fluent word recognition, poor decoding, and poor spelling abilities. (315.00 [F81.0])

As applied to numeracy:

> *Dyscalculia* is an alternative term used to refer to a pattern of difficulties characterized by problems processing numerical information, learning arithmetic facts, and performing accurate or fluent calculations. If dyscalculia is used to specify this particular pattern of

mathematic difficulties, it is important also to specify any additional difficulties that are present, such as difficulties with math reasoning or word reasoning accuracy. (315.2 [F81.81])

Effect of specific learning difficulties across ages and sectors

Specific learning 'disorder', as it is termed in the USA, is lifelong, but its effect on the individual learner depends on the range and severity of the individual's learning difficulties, the available support systems and intervention, and so on. Even so, problems with reading fluency and comprehension, spelling, written expression, and numeracy skills in everyday life typically persist into adulthood (APA, 2013):

- In the Early Years, young children with SpLD may have trouble breaking down spoken words into syllables, for example 'grand-ma', recognising words that rhyme, for example hat, mat and sat, and connecting individual letters with sounds. They may commonly experience difficulties with phonological awareness, working memory, rapid serial naming, rhyming or counting, or the fine motor skills required for writing, pronouncing words correctly, and remembering names of letters, numbers or days of the week, recognising letters in their own names, and learning to count.
- Typically, children continue to experience difficulty at the infant stage: learning letter–sound correspondence, spelling, decoding of words, or number facts. Reading aloud is often slow and laboured. Some struggle to understand the amount that the sign for a number represents.
- In Years 1–3, children may continue to find problems with recognising and manipulating phonemes,[2] sequencing numbers and letters, reading common one-syllable words, recognising common irregularly-spelt words, remembering number facts, and adding, subtracting, multiplying and dividing. They may well find ways to avoid tasks that require these skills.
- In later junior years children may confuse words sounding alike, have problems remembering dates and names and completing work or tests on time. Accuracy in spelling and writing may still be very poor.
- Teenagers may have mastered decoding of words, but reading may still be laboured. They may continue to have problems in reading comprehension and writing, including spelling, and have poor mathematical skills.
- Adults' reading may still be laboured, they may need to reread text to understand it, may continue to make numerous spelling mistakes and, consequently, may avoid activities that require reading or writing. Throughout life it is common to experience somatic complaints or panic attacks.

Addressing difficulties associated with dyslexia

Putting the learner at the centre means taking an informed view of what will be most effective, and suit the needs, interests and strengths of the particular learner at which point in time. Teaching

---

[2]A phoneme is the smallest identifiable unit of sound in a language. For example, the word 'when' has three phonemes: /wh/, /e/ and /n/. The word 'went' has four phonemes: /w/, /e/, /n/ and /t/.

approaches for dyslexic students can be grouped into those that are designed to enable the child to overcome the difficulties that are experienced as far as possible – almost to train the personal information-processing system to become more organised in a deliberately systematic and focused way (the current author's personal reflections) – and those that enable the child to cope.

Multi-sensory approaches

For many children with dyslexic-type difficulties, adopting a multi-sensory approach to teaching and learning can be very powerful. This means harnessing several senses simultaneously to support the processing of information and, hence, learning. The principles of multi-sensory teaching which apply to literacy work also apply to the mathematics field, for example introducing new mathematical concepts and processes using concrete materials, diagrams, pictures and verbal explanation. Progress should be carefully monitored at each stage, checking that a particular concept has been thoroughly mastered and understood before moving on to the next step.

Pavey (2016, p. 20) offers an example of a multi-sensory approach to teaching sounds and letters:

[...] a child who is struggling to remember a letter shape or a sound might remember it better by drawing it, modelling it in clay or some other material. Scribing it in the playground by writing with a 'squirty' bottle. Matching it to a physical movement, handling it, or drawing or modelling a picture or object to remind themselves of it [...] a child who is experiencing possible dyslexia may need a lot of help of this kind, over a long time, and perhaps involving several small steps, plus recall and rehearsal.

Responses in the early years

If we really wished to put dyslexic learners at the centre, we would ensure that identification and intervention would begin in the early years before disillusionment and disengagement with schooling has begun. As Wearmouth et al. (2018) comment, observation is a very important aspect of identifying any particular cause for concern in children's learning in the early years. Observations can provide information about how a child behaves and may be informal and unstructured, or structured and systematic. Purposeful listening to a child's reading provides a useful opportunity to assess and monitor the acquisition of reading. Informally, a teacher might 'start to wonder about' possible difficulties a young child experiences in literacy development if s/he displays any or all of: lack of interest in printed materials; reluctance to engage in, or slowness in completing, literacy-based activities; poor memory word games; difficulty in recognising rhyme or repeating rhythmic patterns (Pavey, 2016). Persistence over time may suggest possible dyslexia. Pavey (2016) describes 'putting in a step' when a young child struggles to learn a letter or sound. Effectively, this is precision teaching. It means identifying the child's current level of skill, knowledge and/or understanding, having a clear view of what the learning target is, and working out very small steps in between them that the child can achieve in sequence.

A number of educators, for example Pavey (2016) and Reid (2017), note how important it can be for children with dyslexic-type difficulties to continue building foundational skills to support literacy learning, beginning in the early years and continuing past the point where formal teaching of literacy has begun. Activities might include a focus on:

- precision in listening, through identifying voices and sounds, counting and repeating beats and rhythms, and repeating songs and rhymes;
- the articulation of speech sounds, through, for example, exaggerating the opening of mouths for fun in singing, talking and reciting;
- developing a sense of rhythm through clapping syllables in words in, for example, games where one group might clap one pattern while, simultaneously, another group claps a different pattern;
- remembering new words or the sequence of story narratives through drawing, painting and modelling in a discrete area of the classroom where required resources are available;
- using new words in expressive language through retelling stories, seeing who can use a new word during the school day, and so on;
- visual discrimination through shape-matching and sorting activities while the child verbalises the way in which s/he is setting about finding the solution;
- sequencing and organisation, through using construction toys, setting out the order of toys by shape, colour, size, and so on, making story boards of familiar activities in arranging the elements in the logical sequence, for example feeding a pet;
- fine motor skills, for example making a game of tying shoe laces supported by think-alouds to add to the multi-sensory aspect of the activity;
- memory, through developing personally meaningful mnemonics, techniques to enable individuals to memorise something. Objects or letters that look similar should not be taught together, otherwise there is the probability that they will forever be confused. Instead, one should be taught first.

Where there is left–right confusion, it is the experience of the current author that one side should be taught and repeated over and over before there is any attempt to teach the other side. If both are taught together there is a danger that children will forever be confused about which is which. Use of mnemonics can reinforce memory for the first side that is taught.

Many of these strategies are effective practice in the early years but may need to be used for a longer period with some dyslexic children.

Importance of listening

Articles 12 and 13 of the United Nations *Convention on the Rights of the Child* (United Nations, 1989) state that children have a right to receive and impart information, to express an opinion and to have that opinion taken into account in any matters affecting them from the early years. Their views should be given due weight according to their age, maturity and capability.

Numbers of researchers have commented on the damaging effect the experience of dyslexia has on young people's confidence and happiness. Riddick (2010), for example, notes the way in which all the mothers of dyslexic children in her study commented on how bright and happy their children had been before going to school, and the anxieties and concerns that they expressed. For example, one mother said:

> It got to the stage where I heard myself saying as my little boy cried himself to sleep at night, it's not long now (to the end of term). [...] He started wetting the bed, and came home shaking if he had a spelling test to revise for the following day. (Riddick, 2010, p. 52)

Across the UK, there is a legal requirement for young people to participate in decision-making about the special educational provision that is made for them. In England, for example, the *Code of Practice* (DfE/DoH, 2015) states:

> 1.3 Local authorities must ensure that children [...] and young people are involved in discussions and decisions about their individual support [...].

> 1.4 [...] providers, schools and colleges should also take steps to ensure that young people and parents are actively supported in contributing to needs assessments, developing and reviewing EHC plans.

Participants' own views should be sought not only because there is a legal requirement to do so, however. Students' narratives of experience can form the basis for identifying barriers to literacy learning and conceptualising ways forward.

In eliciting the views of those who experience learning difficulties, it is clear that the conditions should support learners to express what they want to say. Ideally, they would be allowed to choose the adult with whom they would like to work in this area. This should be somebody whom they trust. It should also happen at a time when learners are in an appropriate frame of mind and not, for example, if they are angry, upset, hungry or tired (Hayes & Whittaker, 2016).

You will find more advice about encouraging literacy acquisition in Chapter 10.

Addressing barriers to mathematics learning

Much of the teaching and assessment of mathematics takes place through symbolic representation, that is, through written text and pictures (Rogers, 2007). We discuss this issue further in Chapter 11. For now, we simply summarise below what researchers suggest about teaching learners who experience difficulties in the primary years.

LEARNING POINT
ADDRESSING DIFFICULTIES EXPERIENCED BY PRIMARY-AGED PUPILS IN MATHEMATICS

Riddick, Wolfe and Lumsdon (2002, p. 50) offer a number of suggestions about teaching primary-aged pupils with specific difficulties in mathematics:

- make sure they understand basic symbols, e.g. = , +, −, etc.;
- make sure they understand basic number language, e.g. subtract, multiply, etc.;
- repeat learning and revision of number facts;
- teach child to estimate a sensible answer;
- teach child to check their answer against the set question;
- be alert for reversals which lead to child making a wrong calculation;
- practise counting forwards and backwards in sequences, e.g. in ones, then twos, etc.;

- use pattern methods to teach number bonds;
- teach multiplication using table squares;
- use squared paper to aid correct setting out of calculations;
- give a sample strip with digits in correct orientation for checking reversals;
- use multi-sensory teaching; rehearse what has just been learnt with oral revision at the end of the lesson;
- teach using logic rather than just rules so conceptual ability can be utilised.

Conclusion

In summary, for any young people who experience difficulty in cognition and learning, it is really important to ensure that they have the opportunity, and feel confident, to ask for help if they need it, without feeling stupid or humiliated. Before any learner can begin a task, s/he needs to understand what it is that s/he has been asked to do, what previous information will assist, and what the end product might look like. If a learner is experiencing difficulties, it is worthwhile considering whether s/he has a problem at any of these points and adjusting support as appropriate (Hayes & Whittaker, 2016).

In order to enable learners with MLD to have a greater chance of remembering something, it is helpful for teachers to:

- have a clear grasp of what the learners can do. This understanding should be informed by assessment of learning levels and supported by an individual learning/education plan, pupil profile or other record;
- identify topics or concepts that are likely to be more difficult for the learner, using a range of modes to present the material, and repeating if necessary to ensure sufficient opportunities for learning;
- review progress through the assess–plan–do–review (or similar) cycle to ensure that teaching approaches are effective.

Learners with MLD benefit when new skills and knowledge are introduced in a way that enables them to:

- link to other skills and knowledge they already have;
- experience themselves through action, having access to tactile resources, role play, and so on;
- see through visual representations, for example pictures, photographs and clear diagrams;
- understand it and its importance;
- have repeated access to the information.

A major principle underpinning effective pedagogy for learners who experience moderate learning difficulties or specific difficulties in learning is to adopt a multi-sensory approach to teaching. As you think about the material that has been included in this chapter, why do you consider such an approach to be so important?

Further reading

Dyslexia

Reid, G. (2019) *Dyslexia and Inclusion: Classroom Approaches for Assessment, Teaching and Learning* (3rd edn). London: Routledge.

Riddick, B., Wolfe, J., & Lumsdon, D. (2016) *Dyslexia: A Practical Guide for Teachers and Parents* (Resource Materials for Teachers). London: David Fulton.

Learning difficulties in schools

Lewis, A., & Norwich, B. (2004) *Special Teaching for Special Children? Pedagogies for Inclusion.* Maidenhead: Open University Press.

Moray Educational Psychology Service (2013) *Precision Teaching: What is it?* Available at: www.moray.gov.uk/downloads/file88660.pdf

Tilstone, C., Lacey, P., Porter, J., & Robertson, C. (2016) *Pupils with Learning Difficulties in Mainstream Schools.* London: David Fulton.

Ylonen, A., & Norwich, B. (2012) Using Lesson Study to develop teaching approaches for secondary school pupils with moderate learning difficulties: Teachers' concepts, attitudes and pedagogic strategies. *European Journal of Special Needs Education*, 27(3), 301–317.

Piaget and Vygotsky

Bruner, J. (1997) Celebrating divergence: Piaget and Vygotsky. *Human Development*, 40(2), 63–73.

Wadsworth, B. J. (1996) *Piaget's Theory of Cognitive and Affective Development: Foundations of Constructivism* (5th edn). London: Longman.

7

SOCIAL, EMOTIONAL AND MENTAL HEALTH DIFFICULTIES AND ASSOCIATED BEHAVIOURAL ISSUES

Major questions addressed in this chapter are:

- How can learners' social, emotional and mental health difficulties be explained?
- What can be done about behaviour associated with these difficulties in the context of schools and in liaison with families?
- What do we know about settings, schools, colleges and classrooms within them that are effective in including learners who experience social, emotional and mental health difficulties?

Key terms

Social, emotional and mental health difficulties, counselling, attachment difficulties, attention deficit/hyperactivity disorder (AD/HD), bullying in educational establishments

Introduction

There is considerable evidence that young people's overall level of well-being influences their behaviour and engagement in school and their ability to make good academic progress. A study in the UK (Gutman & Vorhaus, 2012) found that pupil well-being at age 7 is a good predictor of later academic progression and engagement in school. There are a number of in-school factors that can influence learners' mental health and well-being. For example, the physical and social environment, including interpersonal relationships, in which staff and pupils spend a high proportion of every weekday may have profound effects on their physical, emotional and mental health as well as affecting their attainment.

The chapter opens with an outline of the kinds of difficulties, for example 'depression, anxiety disorders, self-harm and eating disorders' (Department of Health (DoH), 2011, §59), for which external specialist support such as the Child and Adolescent Mental Health Services (CAMHS) might be sought for a young person, and the kind of 'talking' therapies' that might be used. It goes on to discuss issues of problematic attachment, and some of the ways that may be employed to address behaviour that is often associated with this. Subsequently, there is discussion of attention deficit/hyperactivity disorder (AD/HD) and approaches to tackle this. Finally, there is consideration of ways in which educational institutions can be proactive in creating environments that acknowledge and provide for the needs of learners who experience these difficulties, as well as their peers.

Serious mental health issues

The issue of mental health and, with it, emotional and behaviour concerns, has been a matter of disquiet nationally for some time. In 2011, for example, the government set out 'a strategy for people of all ages [...] to encompass infants, children, young people, working-age adults and older people' (1.3) entitled *No Health without Mental Health: A Cross-government Mental Health Outcomes Strategy for People of All Ages* (DoH, 2011).[1] This document highlighted the prevalence of mental health issues in the population as a whole, and the significance of taking the issue seriously from an early age:

> [...] around half of people with lifetime mental health problems experience their first symptoms by the age of 14. By promoting good mental health and intervening early, particularly in the crucial childhood and teenage years, we can help to prevent mental illness from developing and mitigate its effects when it does. (DoH, 2011, Foreword)

It noted that the majority of referrals to specialist Child and Adolescent Mental Health Services (CAMHS) were the result of 'depression, anxiety disorders, self-harm and eating disorders, together with conduct disorders' (§59). Further,

> One in ten children aged between 5 and 16 years has a mental health problem, and many continue to have mental health problems into adulthood (Green et al., 2005) [...] Self-harming in young people is not uncommon (10–13% of 15–16-year-olds have self-harmed (Hawton et al., 2002). (DoH, 2011, p. 8)

---

[1]Technically this document related solely to England.

Below we outline ways that might be employed to support young people who experience mental health issues: referral to a CAMHS team and examples of counselling therapies that might be employed.

Referral to the Child and Adolescent Mental Health Services

We cannot stress strongly enough how important it is to make a referral to the local specialist services, such as the Child and Adolescent Mental Health Services (CAMHS), when there is a serious concern about a learner's mental health difficulties, for example depression, obsessive-compulsive disorder, extreme anxiety and eating problems. Any one team of CAMHS might include:

- child and adolescent psychiatrists: medically qualified doctors who specialise in working with young people and their families;
- child psychotherapists: professionals trained in therapies designed to help young people to deal with emotional and mental health problems;
- clinical psychologists: professionals qualified in assessing and supporting learners' psychological and emotional functioning;
- family therapists: therapists who focus on the family 'systems' and emphasise family relationships to help them understand and manage the difficulties in their lives;
- social workers: professionals trained to help socially-disadvantaged children and families who need additional support through social welfare, or need to be kept safe;
- other professionals: educational psychologists and speech and language therapists.

Uses of counselling

Counselling is a process often seen as taking place 'at a physical, bodily level and through language, and in the thoughts, feelings and memories of each participant' (McLeod, 1998, p. xvii) simultaneously. 'Counselling' and 'psychotherapy' are umbrella terms that cover a range of talking therapies (McLaughlin et al., 2013, p. 3).

Effectiveness of 'talking therapies'

Careful account should be taken of students' own sense-making and ways in which young people's behaviour relates to the way that they make sense of their worlds, even if this may be experienced by teachers and families as uncomfortable at times. A systematic review of the effectiveness of counselling and psychotherapies for children and young people (McLaughlin et al., 2013) set out to address the question: 'Is counselling and psychotherapy effective for children and young people?' The review concluded that:

> Cognitive behavioural therapies (CBT) were found to be effective for anxiety and behavioural and conduct problems. There is less evidence of the effectiveness of CBT for children as opposed to adolescents, and for depression as opposed to anxiety. (p. 5)

The report noted the growth in the incidence of play therapy:

> As a therapeutic intervention, play therapy is highly effective for a variety of presenting problems, particularly anxiety and behaviour/conduct problems; for a range of young populations, but particularly primary-aged children; and in a number of settings, particularly clinics and schools. (p. 5)

Below we review both CBT, 'solution-focused brief therapy', mindfulness, and play therapy.

Cognitive-behavioural therapy

Cognitive-behavioural therapy (CBT) is a family of relatively structured and directive therapeutic interventions that aim to produce change by directly influencing a client's thinking or actions. It focuses on the way individuals process information. Such an approach can incorporate the use of perception, language, problem-solving, memory, decision-making and imagery, for example in the school situation, to enable students to begin to pay attention to 'the stream of automatic thoughts which accompany and guide their behaviour'. In doing so, 'they can learn to make choices about the appropriateness of these self-statements, and if necessary, introduce new thoughts and ideas' (McLeod, 1998, p. 72). Interventions that deliberately focus on developing meta-cognitive awareness – awareness of one's own thinking, feelings and emotions – in order to be able to regulate emotions and/or cope with feelings such as violence, bullying, disaffection or isolation (Meichenbaum & Turk, 1976; Shapiro & Cole, 1994) can be categorised as cognitive-behavioural.

de Shazer's 'Solution-focused brief therapy'

'Solution-focused brief therapy' (SFBT) (de Shazer, 1985) is a cognitive-behavioural approach that is used in some situations to focus on solutions rather than problems, as its name suggests. The main aim is to encourage a learner to imagine how s/he would like things to be different, and what this would take. A well-known technique here is the 'miracle question' (de Shazer, 1988). A paraphrase of this might be: 'If a miracle happened one night while you were asleep, and the problem that brought you here was resolved but you didn't know this, how would you know that the miracle had taken place – what would be different?' As de Shazer et al. (2007, p. 40) comment: 'ultimately the miracle question is not so much about figuring out what would be a "dream come true" [...] as it is about discovering [...] and replicating the effects of it.'

In schools and colleges, learners are first invited to work out how to reach a positive outcome. Then they are supported to use their responses to learn ways of behaving that are more socially appropriate and/or achieve higher academic standards. Important here are the 'scaling questions', where learners are asked, on a scale of 1 to 10, worst to best, what the worst things have been and where they are currently; where they need to be, what would support them to move up one point, and how they might keep themselves there.

Mindfulness

'Mindfulness' is a simple technique that emphasises paying attention to the present moment in an accepting, non-judgemental manner. In many countries across the world, it has emerged as a popular mainstream practice and, increasingly, is taught from the level of executives in corporations to children both at home and in school. At each developmental stage, mindfulness can be an effective technique for promoting happiness and decreasing anxiety. Gotink et al. (2016) concluded from a systematic literature review that stress reduction based on mindfulness techniques can induce changes in the brain that are similar to traditional long-term meditation practice.

Mindfulness practices can be integrated into all classroom levels from pre-school to high school (Lyons & DeLange, 2016).

Part of the reason why mindfulness is so effective for children can be explained by the way the brain develops. While our brains are constantly developing throughout our lives, connections in the prefrontal circuits are created at their fastest rate during childhood. Mindfulness, which promotes skills that are controlled in the prefrontal cortex, like focus and cognitive control, can therefore have a particular impact on the development of skills, including self-regulation, judgement and patience during childhood. The way we represent reality to ourselves, what we might call 'mental representations', and our understandings develop over time as we reflect on our experiences, are guided by others, and as we acquire new information. 'Self-regulation' in settings/schools/colleges can be seen as the process of learners 'acquiring beliefs and theories about their abilities and competencies, the structure and difficulty of learning tasks, and the way to regulate effort and strategy use to accomplish goals' (Schunk & Zimmerman, 2003, p. 66).

There is some evidence from developmental psychology and cognitive neuroscience that mindfulness training in children and adolescents has the potential to improve students' brain functioning and lead to changes in brain structure that facilitate academic success. In particular, it seems that mindfulness practice improves various aspects of self-regulation that are central to academic achievement.

Play Therapy

So-called 'Play Therapy' – therapy through play – has its origins in child psychotherapy. It is strongly associated also with both attachment theory and the humanistic tradition. There is an assumption that child's play is a natural medium of self-expression and a core means of communication (Pidgeon et al., 2015), through which children transmit their emotions, thoughts and perceptions. Primarily, Play Therapy is non-verbal. Children aged 2–12 are encouraged to play with, for example, toys, sand, puppets, clay, art, dance and music, and hence transmit their difficulties and feelings (Pigeon et al., 2015). 'Play Therapy' is based on a relationship between therapist and child. This relationship needs to be stable and secure so that the child can feel safe enough to explore and grow. To join the child in finding meaning in his/her world (Mountain, 2016), British Play Therapy is non-directive and currently defined as:

> the dynamic process between child and Play Therapist in which the child explores at his or her own pace and with his or her own agenda those issues, past and current, conscious and unconscious, that are affecting the child's life in the present. (www.bapt.info/play-therapy/history-play-therapy/, accessed 19.03.2021)

Play Therapy may also be directive with the therapist structuring the play activities.

Those who support Play Therapy claim that it is effective in supporting learners who experience psychosocial and behavioural difficulties, including depression, grief and loss, trauma, abuse, ADHD, anxiety and stress of various kinds.

Issues of attachment

In recent years there has been a growing understanding of the extent to which the nature of a child's early attachment affects the way in which s/he behaves in relationships and inter-actions with other people into adulthood. Relationships, learner to teacher and learner to learner, are a really important factor in learning in settings, schools and colleges. It is crucial that teachers and other adults consider how to engage those with attachment difficulties in their education:

> In schools [...] we can help these children to learn adaptive, healthy responses, supporting them to think differently and to take control over their physical states, feelings and behaviours. (Bombèr, 2007, p. 9)

As the National Research Council (US) Division of Behavioral and Social Sciences and Education (2001, p. 27) notes: 'Human relationships, and the effect of relationships on relationships, are the building blocks of healthy development.' Babies are born with a predisposition to learn and huge potential for brain growth. In the early years, attachment develops through interactions between the young child and the primary caregiver. The stress level on a baby or small child induced through neglect, abuse, trauma or loss can limit brain growth, making a child who is affected in this way at risk of vulnerabilities in the development of emotional and cognitive abilities. The outcome may be attachment difficulties.

Every young person needs to feel safe and secure to make progress in all aspects of develop-ment. Parents' and carers' actions teach children a lot about how much they are valued. Children who are emotionally, physically or sexually abused, are neglected or who witness domestic vio-lence are likely to be fearful and have high levels of stress hormones in their bodies. Toxic stress can result from strong, frequent or prolonged activation of the body's stress response systems where there is no adult to support and protect the child (Felitti, Anda & Nordenberg, 1998; Asok et al., 2013). A young child may be forced to adapt behaviour to suit that of the caregiver. If the parent is abusive or neglectful, for example, the child's behaviour is likely to reflect the need to survive in very difficult circumstances, for example by becoming overly passive, or screaming and shouting, or constantly looking for ways to adapt to the adult's moods. Adaptive responses can translate into specific styles of relating to other people. Three attachment styles that we might classify as 'difficult' are: avoidant, ambivalent and disorganised. These are important in consider-ing appropriate responses in educational institutions. Even when the young person is in a safe environment, his/her behaviour that was learned in order to survive can remain inappropriate and sometimes challenging, and prevent him/her from engaging in healthy relationships with peers and teachers:

- 'Avoidant' attachment behaviour is often a response to depression or abuse: 'James', for example, whose father was physically abusive, went out of his way to avoid contact with staff in his secondary school, and had no positive relationships with his peers at all. Like some other learners with an avoidant style, he seemed to want to make himself more in control by being almost obsessively tidy. One of his teachers reported to the current author that he had had a sudden outburst of anger, slammed his fist on the desk in the middle of a lesson, and sworn loudly at his peers. It seemed to be the outcome of a build-up of stress and anger in this otherwise withdrawn young man (Wearmouth, 2004a).

- 'Ambivalent' attachment behaviour reflects adaptation to the behaviour of an inconsistent caregiver. It can result in excessive attention-seeking.
- 'Disorganised' attachment behaviour usually results from severe neglect and chaotic, abusive, frightening backgrounds. It is unpredictable and difficult to manage, physically and emotionally. After 'John's' mother died, his father came home drunk every day, dragged 'John' and his sister to woman after woman in a series of short-lived relationships, and was very physically abusive. 'John' and his sister quickly became fearful and very anxious. Finally, he resolved the situation for himself by going on a car-thieving spree and ending up in a youth offenders' institution.

Bombèr (2007, p. 39) offers some very important advice to staff in settings/schools/colleges in her reminder that, for many young people, their behaviour is a major means of communicating distress and that educational institutions should ensure that child welfare is high on their agenda:

> Please note that if a child is currently at risk, then their behaviour needs to be viewed as a communication expressing the danger they are in. Action needs to be taken. View their behaviour as a 'cry for help', and ensure you log concerns and follow your area's Child Protection guidelines.

Addressing attachment issues in schools

Approaches to behavioural issues associated with children's attachment issues may be conceptualised in a number of ways. For example, for groups of young children entering school for the first time, some schools have instituted so-called 'nurture groups'. For individuals, even though the outcome of a young person's experience of insecure attachment can be highly problematic in settings/schools/colleges, it is possible to draw to some extent on the kind of therapeutic approaches that have been found effective in separate therapy rooms, as Bombèr (2007), for example, suggests.

Nurture groups

Some infant and lower schools attempt to create features of adequate parenting within school for those young children identified as having attachment issues, through nurture groups. Such groups were developed originally in the Inner London Education Authority in 1970–1971 by Marjorie Boxall, an educational psychologist. More recently, such groups have been established in some local authorities. Boxall (2002) argues that the outcome of inadequate early care for young children from families struggling with poverty, difficult relationships and harsh living conditions may well be personality and behaviour difficulties. The underlying intention of the nurture group is to recreate the experience of a normally-developing child from babyhood, and provide a predictable, reliable environment, after which children can go on to interact in regular settings (Bennathan, 2000).

Web activity WA7.1
Considering nurture groups in action

We have uploaded a reference to materials and an activity related to nurture groups on the website. You might like to access this now.

Responses to individual needs

Bombèr (2007) suggests that the way in which staff relate to individuals with attachment issues and the language that is used are very important considerations. In Chapter 2, we described behaviour modification as a deliberate strategy to shape behaviour. This approach is not appropriate for a young person with early experience of loss and trauma. If behaviour is interpreted as communication, and the young person is in distress, then responses in settings/schools/colleges should begin from this understanding.

> # LEARNING POINT
> # SUPPORTING LEARNERS WITH ATTACHMENT DIFFICULTIES IN SCHOOLS
>
> Read the text below and consider the feasibility of following Bombèr's (2007) advice about supporting a child with serious attachment issues in a school.
>
> Assuming that the advice of external professionals is that a child should remain in an educational institution with support, one way to address emotional needs of the sort discussed above could be, as Bombèr (2007, p. 52) suggests, to 'allocate someone to the child to spend time getting to know him [sic], finding his strengths and interests and building on these. If the child does not have a positive sense of who he is individually, or that he is valued for himself, he is not going to be able to access what is on offer or contribute in a healthy way to the bigger group.'
>
> Effective learning depends on emotional development (Greenhalgh, 1994). Containing and regulating emotional states and the behaviour that accompanies this is something a caregiver would do in the early years. An identified key adult might take this role in a setting/school/college. A positive, consistent relationship of trust with a key person in school/college can facilitate brain growth and emotional development, and reduce stress hormones such as cortisol in the child's system (Bombèr, 2007). All of us need to go through the stage of dependency on trusted others before we learn to become autonomous. Some young people with attachment issues would benefit from a planned approach to 'relative dependency' on a reliable adult so that they have another opportunity to learn:
>
>> [...] people need to have a satisfying experience of dependency before they can become truly independent and largely self-regulating. Yet this feels counter-intuitive to many adults, who respond to the insecure with a punitive attitude, as if becoming more mature and self-regulating were a matter of will-power. (Gerhardt, 2004, p. 65)

The main role of a trusted key person is to provide consistency of support and ensure that the young person knows that s/he is at the forefront of thinking. Attune to the learner's behaviour, collate examples of the young person's success in school/college and act as an advocate for him/her. Engaging in 'think alouds' to scaffold the learning of more socially-acceptable behaviour, for example knowing when it is acceptable to talk, differentiating between different kinds of relationships, 'reading the minds' of peers and/or teachers through body language and other forms of communication, and so on.

The ability to inspire trust and dependability is crucial. Greenhalgh (1994, p. 53) discusses the issue of projection from young people who are distressed as a result of loss and/or trauma:

> One of the reasons that working with children experiencing emotional and behavioural difficulties is so disturbing is that such intense and painful feelings are somehow pushed into the staff (as well as other children). Sometimes it might feel as if it is difficult to know where the feelings are coming from, and the intensity of them might lead one to question one's own competence and professional worth.

In this situation the emotional stability of the key adult is a really important consideration, as is his/her availability. And, of course, it is vital that a key person has a support network in settings/schools/colleges and a safe place to discuss concerns.

Funding this role is another matter and will depend on the way that an institution either allocates resources or prioritises applications to the local authority.

What attributes do you think would be needed in a 'key person' in the role of assistant for a child with attachment difficulties if inclusion in a school is to be effective?

Attention Deficit/Hyperactivity Disorder (AD/HD)

Attention deficit/hyperactivity disorder (ADHD) is a neurodevelopmental disorder characterised by inattention and/or hyperactivity-impulsivity (American Psychiatric Association, 2013). Approximately 5–7% of all children meet diagnostic criteria for ADHD (Polanczyk et al., 2007; Willcutt, 2012), implying that, on average, every classroom will contain a child with ADHD. Within the classroom, learners with ADHD are more inattentive (off-task) and disruptive than typically-developing peers (Kofler, Rapport & Alderson, 2008). They often struggle to sustain attention to tasks and instructions, frequently talk to classmates at inappropriate times, and may call out and leave their seat without permission. As a consequence, learners with ADHD are at risk of academic difficulties, including underachievement and suspension or expulsion from school or college (Barkley, 2015). They may also disrupt the learning of classmates and may provoke anti-social behaviour in return.

Effective responses to AD/HD

A meta-analytic review (Gaastra et al., 2017) indicates that classroom interventions can reduce off-task and disruptive classroom behaviour in children with symptoms of ADHD. The most effective were antecedent-based, consequence-based and self-regulation interventions, or a combination of all of them. Antecedent- and consequence-based approaches are based on behaviourist principles. They involve identifying the antecedents: what stimulates or provokes the unwanted behaviour. Or they involve the consequences, with a focus on encouraging the learner's desired behaviours by consistently rewarding them and/or using negative consequences (such as removal of specific privileges) to discourage their unwanted behaviours. Goal(s) are agreed with the learner and rewards and/or consequences that are meaningful to the individual are awarded, depending on progress towards his/her goals. It is really important that parents and families are informed about the positives as well as the negatives of their child's behaviour and achievement, so a daily report card to take home to share with their parent or carer can be really effective. This approach may be better suited to younger learners in settings or schools, rather than older learners in further education settings (Richardson et al., 2015).

Coaching learners in cognitive-behavioural self-regulation techniques involves working with the individual to develop meaningful ways to monitor personal behaviour on an ongoing basis and to make positive changes as a result. This includes helping the learner to identify triggers that result in problem behaviour, ways to address these, and training for the learner to be able 'self-instruct' him/herself to achieve more desirable behaviour. The quality of the relationship between learners and providers (typically teachers) is potentially critical to effectiveness. Teachers known to have a positive relationship with the target learners can be more effective than when there is no previous relationship or a negative relationship between the provider and pupil (Richardson et al., 2015).

Case study: Trialling the use of 'Stop, Think, Do'

'Peter' was a special educational needs co-ordinator (SENCo) in a secondary school. He was responsible for negotiating individual plans for addressing problematic behaviour, as well as individual learning plans. At one point, he had a lot of concerns about a young man whose behaviour had been troubling for a considerable period of time. In discussion with the school's educational psychologist, he decided to trial the use of a cognitive-behavioural self-regulation intervention that has become popular, particularly in schools in Australia: 'Stop, Think, Do' (www.stopthinkdo.com/prog_core.php, accessed 28.10.2021). Peter was advised that, following this programme, in the first instance when the young man's misbehaviour was unacceptable or anti-social, he should use visual, sound or tactile signals to remind him to stop what he was doing, consider his behaviour, and think about how to control his behaviour. Peter taught him to use self-talk phrases: 'What will happen if I don't stop doing this?' and 'What could I do to help myself behave better/concentrate more?' Then he encouraged the young man to put a plan into action to improve his behaviour and concentration, by concentrating on what the teacher had to say and/or making more effort to complete the task in hand.

This intervention was originally designed to improve learners' social skills, but Peter found that it also improved his pupil's motivation for learning.

To what extent would it be feasible for you to try out this programme with one or more young people whose behaviour and/or motivation is of concern to you?

The most common treatment for children with ADHD is stimulant medication (DuPaul & Stoner, 2014). The use of psycho-stimulants relies on a theory of biochemical imbalance in the brain:

> The medication stimulates areas of the brain regulating arousal and alertness and can result in immediate short-term improvements in concentration and impulse control. The precise mechanism is poorly understood and the specific locus of action within the central nervous system remains speculative. (British Psychological Society, 1996, pp. 50–51)

Of the most commonly used stimulants, methylphenidate (Ritalin) is most widely administered, usually in the form of tablets to be taken at regular intervals.

Although pharmacological interventions enhance on-task behaviour and academic achievement in children with ADHD (Prasad et al., 2013), pharmacological interventions are limited by several factors, including possible side effects, lack of evidence of long-term effects and compliance problems (Smith et al., 2000). Because of these significant limitations, there is a need for non-pharmacological interventions, including school-based interventions.

Responsibility for administering chemical psycho-stimulants

Over time, a number of concerns have been expressed about the use of such psycho-stimulants relating to the effects and side effects of the drugs and the ethics of how effectively to monitor the day-to-day classroom learning and behavioural outcomes of the medication that is prescribed. As the British Psychological Society (BPS) (1996, pp. 51–52) comments, such concerns relate to the so-called 'zombie effect' noted by some researchers and 'illustrate the practical issues of managing medication at home and at school', as well as the ethical risks in relying on medication alone to bring about behaviour change at school, without providing appropriate learning tasks and activities that can create positive reinforcement of more socially-acceptable behaviour.

LEARNING POINT
STATUTORY GUIDANCE ABOUT
ADMINISTERING MEDICATION

Questions about where the responsibility lies for administering medication to learners in schools and colleges may be a matter of concern. It is therefore really important that we are all aware of statutory guidance in this regard.

In England, statutory guidance (Supporting Pupils at School with Medical Conditions: Statutory Guidance for Governing Bodies of Maintained Schools and Proprietors of Academies in England, Department for Education, 2014a, §19) makes it clear that any member of school staff may be asked to support learners with medical conditions and they should take into account the needs of pupils with medical conditions that they teach. This includes administering medicines. They cannot be required to do so, however. If they do so, they should be trained appropriately.

Guidance is also available for schools in Scotland, Northern Ireland and Wales at: www.medicalconditionsatschool.org.uk/documents/Legal-Situation-In-Schools.pdf (accessed 10.05.2020).

Physical confrontation and aggression

There are times when learners may be aggressive, out of control and a danger to themselves and others. Dealing with incidents of extreme behaviour can be far more challenging and stressful for a teacher or others than dealing with, for example, mild disruption.

Dealing with physical confrontation

It is important to minimise the risk of physical confrontation in the first place, rather than having to deal with it at the time. As Dunckley (1999, p. 16) notes, learners who are 'in an agitated state' need 'guidance and direction to increase their sense of security [...] where possible and appropriate, give a choice, time for the student to respond, then, after an appropriate time, follow through with consequences.' To manage a dangerous situation, it seems sensible for teachers to use physical restraint only as a last resort, and there are formal guidelines on this issue in educational institutions across the UK.

Web activity WA7.2
Application of formal advice on the use of reasonable force

On the website we have uploaded references to formal guidance on reasonable force for educational institutions across the UK, together with an activity. You might choose to access this material now.

Bullying behaviour

Bullying behaviour is a focus of concern in many schools and colleges. The Department for Education (2018) reports that, in the year ending March 2018, around 17% of children aged 10–15 in England were bullied in a way that frightened or upset them. Some groups were significantly more likely to report having been bullied: younger children (aged 10–12), those of white ethnic backgrounds, those with a long-term illness or disability (9%), those needing extra help at school, those living in the most deprived areas, those who had truanted or been suspended or excluded from school in the past year, those living in one-adult households or rented accommodation, and those living outside London. The most common types of bullying that were reported were verbal (89%) and physical (60%). Around 7% had experienced cyberbullying, and 59% reported they had been bullied by the same people. Most respondents (around three-quarters) felt their school had dealt with bullying either 'very' or 'quite' well.

Addressing bullying behaviour

In a research project designed to identify effective anti-bullying practices, commissioned by the Department for Education in England (DfE, 2018), all the schools surveyed agreed that a whole-school approach to combating bullying was important. Among the components of the approaches common to the schools were:

- values embedded throughout the school that were visible and underpinned everything the school did, for example a focus on kind behaviour in primary schools, and 'values, such as Democracy, Equality, Respect, Resilience, Tolerance and Understanding' in secondary schools;
- a clear definition of what constitutes bullying in their anti-bullying policies, and a system of sanctions;
- anti-bullying policies that are regularly reviewed and updated;
- training and support for all staff, including non-teaching support staff and senior leadership, to ensure they model expected behaviour and can deal effectively with incidents of bullying.

All schools focused on reducing the number of bullying incidents. This might be by:

- addressing prejudice and increasing awareness and understanding for others, including challenging racist language and instilling a common understanding of the way in which pejorative names can cause distress to others;
- teaching pupils to self-regulate their behaviour;
- training pupils to provide support for peers in a strategic buddy system;
- encouraging pupils to take an active role in anti-bullying sessions in schools and contribute to behaviour and anti-bullying policies;
- responding to incidents quickly, including providing a range of ways for pupils to report incidents, for example providing 'bully boxes', a bully email address on computers, and anonymous pupil questionnaires.

Cyberbullying was often targeted separately within the school.

Cyberbullying

Secrecy and the anonymity of the bully(ies) are major factors in explaining cyberbullying, the sense of power of the perpetrator and, often, the fear or anxiety of the victim.

Addressing cyberbullying

Childnet International and the Department for Children, Schools and Families have issued guidance to schools about how to address cyberbullying: *Let's Fight it Together: What We Can All Do to Prevent Cyberbullying* (Childnet International and the Department for Children, Schools and Families, 2007/2008, available at http://old.digizen.org/downloads/Let'sFightItTogether-guide.pdf, accessed 09.06.2020). Some of the strategies to be discussed with learners that they suggest include:

- Respect for others: Be careful what is said online and what images are sent. Ask permission before photographing someone.

- Forethought: Think carefully before posting information on a website. Information could stay online for ever. Do not give your mobile phone numbers to others in a public domain.
- Maintain the confidentiality of passwords: Do not disclose these to anyone, and change them regularly.
- Block bullies: Websites and services often allow individuals to block or report someone who is bullying.
- Do not retaliate or reply to bullies.
- Save the evidence of offending messages, pictures or online conversations.
- Report online bullying: Such bullying may be reported to a trusted adult, the provider of the service, the school or the police, if the cyberbullying is serious.

LEARNING POINT
CONSIDERING ADVICE ABOUT CYBERBULLYING

Fuller cyberbullying guidance is available at: www.digizen.org/downloads/cyberbullyingOverview.pdf (accessed 28.10.2021). You might wish to access this now and consider the usefulness of the guidance given here to your own context.

Establishing positive school and college environments

As we noted at the beginning of this chapter, educational institutions have the power to be proactive in creating environments that acknowledge and provide for the needs of learners who experience social, emotional and mental health issues and, thus, reduce the possibility of behavioural issues associated with these issues in the first place.

A number of reports have acknowledged the importance of consistently applied policy and practice, and the link between the quality of teaching and learners' behaviour. The Steer Report (Department for Education and Skills, 2005), 'Section 2: Principles and practice: What works in schools', identified practical examples of good practice that can be adopted by all schools to promote good behaviour and, hence, improved learning. The report notes that socially-acceptable behaviour will not necessarily just occur. It needs to be taught by staff who know how to model what they expect through their own behaviour and who have access to training and support for themselves in behaviour and classroom management.

Links between challenging behaviour and failure in schools and colleges

Across the UK, teachers are responsible for promoting good behaviour in schools and colleges, have high expectations of their learners, and maintain good relationships with them. Failure that begins in the early stages of education and continues can be experienced as frustrating and the cause of anxiety for learners. "E're Miss, why do you bother with us thick kids when you can teach them clever kids Latin?' was a question posed to the current author by a demoralised teenager who had failed in school since he started at the age of 5. We cannot generalise from one question asked by one young man. However, his question may reflect some of what one might expect about the potential long-term consequences of not addressing children's difficulties in learning early on. They certainly reflect the comments recorded in Riddick's (1996) study of the personal experiences through education of 22 learners, aged from 8 to 14 years and identified as 'dyslexic', and their families. In this study, for example, children recalled similar feelings of disaffection and of dread of 'visible public indicators' (Riddick, 1996, p. 124) of their difficulties, such as always being the last to finish work.

Responsive classrooms

A previous report into behaviour in schools, the Elton Report (Department of Education and Science, 1989), remains pertinent to today's schools and colleges despite the fact that it was written more than three decades ago. It stresses two important principles in terms of classroom activities:

> The classroom is the most important place in the education system. What happens there every school day decides how well the purposes of the system are being achieved. (Chapter 3, Paragraph 1)

> In order to learn well, children need a calm and purposeful classroom atmosphere. [...] Teachers must be able to keep order. If they cannot, all the children in their charge will suffer. (Chapter 3, Paragraph 2)

Web activity WA7.3
Reflecting on advice and guidance from the Elton Report

On the website we have uploaded a summary of some of important points raised by Elton, and an accompanying reflective activity. You might choose to access this material now.

Classroom management to encourage positive behaviour

Understanding and addressing behavioural issues related to groups of, and individual, learners is, as in other areas of educational need, complex. As we discussed in Chapter 1, there are a number of different theories of learning that are commonly used to underpin classroom management techniques as well as programmes designed to address individual needs arising from anti-social behaviour. Two that we refer to here relate to collaborative problem-solving, with a focus on learner voice, and behaviourism.

Problem-solving and learner voice

Some educators consider that, in classrooms, all children can benefit from support to understand and manage their feelings, work co-operatively in groups, motivate themselves and develop resilience in the face of setbacks. Difficulties in these areas are likely to have a negative influence on learning and achievement.

'Circle Time'

An initiative associated with resolving disputes often used at primary school level in schools in the UK is 'Circle Time' (Mosley, 1996), where learners sit in a circle and listen to what their peers have to say. The circle is a symbol of 'unity, healing and power' in many traditional communities and can be found in the customs of groups as diverse 'as the North American Indians and Anglo Saxon monks' (Tew, 1998, p. 20). 'Circle Time' follows strict protocols of involving both teachers and learners in discussion. In schools, the rules must be followed strictly. No one may put anyone down. No one can refer negatively to anyone else, thus creating 'safety' for all participants. When someone speaks, everyone must listen. Everyone has a chance to speak and everyone's opinions are taken seriously. Members of the class can suggest ways of solving problems, following which individuals can accept the help or refuse it. If a rule is broken, a visual warning is given. If this continues, the miscreant is asked to take time away from the circle (Wearmouth et al., 2005, p. 184).

A variant of Circle Time is 'Circle of Friends', a small-group activity shown by Frederickson, Warren and Turner (2005) as having the potential to result in increased social acceptance of children experiencing difficulties by their peers and increased global self-esteem of the focus child. The values that underpin the Circle of Friends approach are 'full inclusion for all; the belief that there is not social justice until each belongs and has an equal place in our schools and communities' (Newton & Wilson, 1999, p. 5). The Circle of Friends approach works by developing a support network of volunteer peers around individuals in the school community who are experiencing social difficulties. Volunteers from the peer group meet weekly with learners individually, ensuring that relationships are built around him/her. The group problem-solves with the target pupil in order to address any social difficulties that he/she may be experiencing in school. Clearly, these meetings need to be managed very carefully to ensure that they are a positive and supportive experience for the individual child. At the very first meeting (and this occurs without the target child), the rules of the circle are decided. The issue of confidentiality must be emphasised, as well as the times set. There is evidence to indicate that this strategy can be successful in increasing the social acceptance of young people with autism in mainstream classes, with a reduced tendency to blame the child for specific behavioural traits and an increased understanding of autism (Whitaker et al., 2003).

Importance of consistency in the learning environment

Strategies in teaching socially-appropriate behaviour in classrooms are often behaviourist principles (Skinner, 1938; Baer, Wolf & Risely, 1968). As we saw in Chapter 2, behaviourist approaches are based on an assumption that all (mis)behaviour is learned. From this assumption it is logical to assume that learning and (mis)behaviour can be altered by changing the environment, if this is carried out in a systematic, consistent, predictable way. Examples of antecedent conditions (or setting events) that are intended to denote behaviour that is seen as (un)acceptable are classroom and school/college rules that can provide punishing consequences for behaviour that is not appropriate.

LEARNING POINT
REFLECTING ON HOW BEHAVIOURIST PRINCIPLES MIGHT UNDERPIN INDIVIDUAL BEHAVIOUR PLANS

We would like you to think about a particular learner's anti-social behaviour in classrooms. What would you have to take into account if you wished to draw up a behaviour plan for him/her during an early stage in the assess → plan → do → review cycle (Department for Education/Department of Health, 2015) that is based on behaviourist principles?

You might like to reflect on whether and how you might incorporate the suggestions of Rogers (2013) and/or Sproson (2004) below into the plan.

A learner's background is no excuse for poor behaviour (Rogers, 2013). Socially-acceptable behaviour is learned, and can therefore be taught as part of regular classroom activities. 'Positive reinforcers' – teacher praise, rewards of various sorts and positive communications with families – are key factors in encouraging learners to choose preferred behaviour. Learners who disrupt lessons should take ownership of this and be reminded what the rules are: 'Jayson … you're calling out … Remember our class rules for asking questions, thanks' (Rogers, 2013, p. 238). Younger learners can be given non-verbal cues to what appropriate behaviour 'looks like'.

Adult behaviour – modelling and reinforcing ways of behaving in particular situations – is very important. Learners can imitate negative as well as positive behaviour. Abusive and sarcastic language should not be used. Not to be drawn into a power struggle that may be rewarding to some learners is crucial because it may well reinforce their current inacceptable behaviour.

There are a number of techniques that can enable teachers to avoid such power struggles, for example in classrooms, and prevent further anti-social behaviour:

- Build in a brief 'take-up' period for pupils to respond. Make the request, walk away to imply compliance, and acknowledge compliance when it happens (Rogers, 2013, p. 240). This may address the pleasure that some learners may take in not doing what they are asked immediately, if they have an audience.
- Model ways of resolving conflict which meet the needs of both parties and provide win-win outcomes wherever possible, end or reduce conflict, or at least reduce it and avoid leaving either party 'wounded' (Sproson, 2004, p. 319).
- Adopt the 'broken record' approach, that is, repeat a request a number of times, calmly, without being drawn an argument.
- Give what Rogers (2013, p. 242) calls 'directed choices' – alternative activities that divert learners from unwanted behaviour.

Where, on evaluating progress, it is clear that a young person's behaviour has not improved following the first iteration of a behaviour plan, it might be appropriate to review the plan and take further measures in the next iteration, again using behaviourist principles.

Conclusion

As we noted above, there is considerable evidence that young people's overall level of well-being influences their behaviour and engagement in educational institutions and their ability to make good academic progress. Ensuring that teachers and others are aware of, and feel that they have the ability and skills to address, factors that can influence learners' mental health and well-being, both those related to the institutional context and those associated with individual learners, is therefore of prime importance. This includes access to specialist advice from external services such as CAMHS and educational psychology.

After reading this chapter, what do you feel are the most important issues to take into account when considering the needs of learners who experience social, emotional and mental health and associated behavioural issues?

In Chapter 8 we turn to sensory and physical difficulties and needs.

Further reading

Talking therapies

Axline, V. M. (1964) *Dibs in Search of Self: Personality Development in Play Therapy*. London: Penguin.

Franklin, C., Trepper, T. S., McCollum, E. E., & Gingerich, W. J. (2011) *Solution-focused Brief Therapy: A Handbook of Evidence-Based Practice*. Oxford: Oxford University Press.

National Health Service (2018) *Mindfulness*. Available at: www.nhs.uk/conditions/stress-anxiety-depression/mindfulness/

National Health Service (2019) *Cognitive Behavioural Therapy (CBT)*. Available at: www.nhs.uk/conditions/cognitive-behavioural-therapy-cbt/

Parry, S. (2019) *The Handbook of Brief Therapies*. London: Sage.

Roffey, S. (2020) *Circle Solutions for Student Wellbeing* (3rd edn). London: Sage.

Welsh Government Social Research Evaluation Team (2011) *Evaluation of the Welsh School-based Counselling Strategy: Final Report*. Cardiff: Welsh Government. Available at: https://strathprints.strath.ac.uk/34096/1/2011_Wales_SBC.pdf

Attachment theory

Bretherton, I. (1985) Attachment theory: Retrospect and prospect. *Monographs of the Society for Research in Child Development*, 50(1/2), 3–35. Available at: www.researchgate.net/profile/Inge_Bretherton/publication/245549122_Attachment_Theory_Retrospect_and_Prospect/links/59e773d50f7e9bed362bf4ea/Attachment-Theory-Retrospect-and-Prospect.pdf

Bullying

Bullying UK (n/d) Cyber bullying. Available at: www.bullying.co.uk/cyberbullying/

National Bullying Helpline (2020) Bullying: Practical help and advice for children and adults dealing with bullying at school or work. Available at: www.nationalbullyinghelpline.co.uk/

Newton, C., & Wilson, D. (2003) *Creating Circles of Friends: A Peer Support and Inclusion Workbook.* Nottingham: Inclusive Solutions.

8

SENSORY AND/OR PHYSICAL DIFFICULTIES

Major questions addressed in this chapter are:

- What kinds of sensory and physical difficulties are commonly experienced in settings, schools and colleges across the UK?
- How might sensory and physical difficulties create barriers to learning and progress?
- How might barriers to learning experienced by young people with these difficulties be addressed in settings, schools and colleges?

Key terms

Sensory difficulties, hearing impairment, visual impairment, multi-sensory impairment, physical difficulties

Introduction

In general terms, the incidence of sensory and physical difficulties experienced by learners in settings, schools and colleges is low in comparison with overall numbers of those with special or additional learning and/or support needs. For example, as the Department for Education (2019) notes in *Statistical First Release (SFR): Special Educational Needs in England*, its document compiled from the school census across England in January, 2019, of the total number of those with sensory needs, 1.1% related to vision, 1.8% to hearing, and 0.3% to multi-sensory impairments, and 2.9% of the total experienced physical disabilities. Addressing needs relating to sensory and/or physical difficulties is a legislative requirement included in both disability law across the UK and also law that pertains to special or additional learning and/or support needs in the various countries. Both within-person factors, that is the sensory or physical disability, and contextual factors relating to the environment in educational institutions and family circumstances interact to influence learning and achievement. As Sahlén et al. (2019, p. 129) comment in relation to young people with hearing impairments:

> A range of with-child factors, for example executive functions,[1] hearing acuity, age at onset of hearing loss, and age at intervention, interact with environmental and contextual factors, which together drive spoken language development in DHH [deaf and hard-of-hearing] children.

Individual learners have their own personal strengths and needs, interests, family backgrounds, and so on, that, together with their own and their family's views, should be taken into account when designing an intervention plan.

In this chapter we begin with a focus on sensory impairments. Subsequently, there is discussion of a range of physical impairments and approaches to addressing needs of physically-impaired learners.

Sensory difficulties

For learners with a sensory impairment, the greatest challenge, most commonly, is communication (Spencer & Marschark, 2010). For a deaf child, for example, 'a large body of international research has shown that many [...] children have difficulties with different aspects of language' (Sahlén et al., 2019, p. 128). Early on, a child with normal sight and hearing will usually explore its surroundings and interact with others naturally. A child with a sensory impairment may need encouragement to do this. Visual impairment may well delay early development and learning as a result of reduced environmental and spatial awareness, and constraints on social interaction arising from difficulty in recognising facial expression. Slow progress in building relationships with peers may well affect self-confidence. Early intervention and support for learning and development is therefore clearly very important.

---

[1]So-called 'executive functions' comprise the mental processes that enable us to plan, focus attention, remember instructions and juggle multiple tasks successfully (Harvard University, https://developingchild.harvard.edu/science/key-concepts/executive-function/, accessed 25.03.2020).

Hearing difficulties

In this section we first outline the structure and functions of ears to enable clear discussion of the site of impairments to hearing, and move on to discuss common causes of hearing difficulties, likely barriers to learning that are experienced, and interventions and classroom approaches designed to include those learners.

The ear, structure and functions

The ear has, broadly, two functions: hearing and balance.

Hearing system

The hearing system consists of three main parts: the outer, middle and inner ear. All must function efficiently to enable us to hear sound clearly. Impaired hearing occurs when one or more parts do not work properly:

- The outer ear, or 'pinna',[2] is shaped to receive sound waves that pass down the ear canal to the eardrum.
- Sound waves cause vibrations on the eardrum. Three tiny bones, the hammer, anvil and stirrup,[3] increase the strength of the vibrations which pass across the middle ear into an organ called the cochlea[4] in the inner ear.
- The cochlea is filled with fluid and thousands of tiny hair-like sound-sensitive cells. The vibrations cause the fluid and sound-sensitive cells to move. This movement creates a small electrical charge that passes as a signal along the auditory nerve to the brain where it is interpreted as sound.

Balance

In the inner ear are three semi-circular tubes or 'canals' that are filled with liquid and movement-sensitive hair cells that enable us to balance. When we move, the fluid moves and creates electrical signals that are passed to the brain.

Causes of impaired hearing

There are many reasons why a child may have a hearing loss or become deaf. As the World Health Organization (2020) notes, the causes of hearing loss and deafness can be congenital, that is existing at birth or soon afterwards, or acquired.

Both hereditary and non-hereditary genetic factors may be involved, or complications during pregnancy and childbirth. These include maternal rubella, syphilis or certain other infections during pregnancy, low birth weight and/or lack of oxygen at birth, inappropriate maternal drug use,

---

[2]'Pinna' is a Latin word that means 'wing' because of the shape of the outer ear.

[3]All three bones have names that reflect their shapes.

[4]The Latin word 'cochlea' literally means 'snail', again because of the shape.

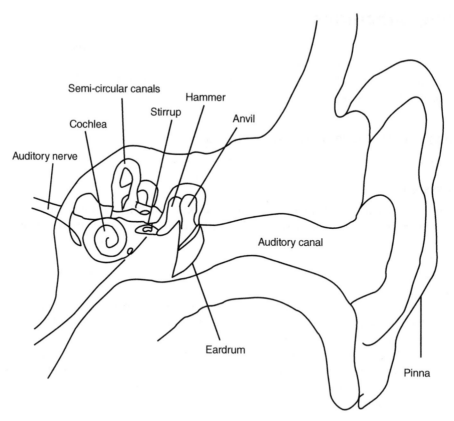

Figure 8.1   Human ear

and severe jaundice shortly after birth that can damage the baby's hearing nerve. Sensorineural deafness is permanent and occurs when there is a fault in the inner ear or auditory (hearing) nerve. Few children are totally deaf, however.

The most common acquired cause of hearing loss among children is chronic otitis media with effusion ('glue-ear'). 'Glue ear' (National Deaf Children's Society (NDCS), 2010a) is a build-up of fluid in the middle ear which prevents sound from passing efficiently through the outer and middle ear to the cochlea and auditory nerve. It affects about one in five children at any time. For most children, the glue ear clears up by itself. A few children need surgery to insert 'grommets' into the eardrums. These are tiny plastic tubes that allow air to circulate in the middle ear and help to prevent the build-up of fluid. Other factors that may cause a loss of hearing are certain infectious diseases, including meningitis, measles and mumps, chronic ear infections, damage injury to the head or ear, wax or foreign bodies blocking the ear canal, and, later on, excessive noise and exposure to loud sounds for prolonged periods of time, for example from use of personal audio devices at high volumes.

Effects on learners of impaired hearing

The degree of hearing loss is measured in decibels (dB). (The decibel is the unit used to measure the intensity of a sound. On the decibel scale, the smallest audible sound, near total silence is 0 dB. The decibel scale is logarithmic. In other words, a sound 10 times more powerful than 0 dB is 10 dB, and 100 times more powerful is 20 dB). Hearing loss can be categorised as:

- Mild: 21–40dB
- Moderate: 41–70dB
- Severe: 71–95dB
- Profound: in excess of 95dB.

As noted above, the most important risk factor for hearing-impaired learners concerns communication and language. Hence a major problem with late identification of deafness is the effect on language development (Goldberg & Richberg, 2004; Moeller et al., 2007). A delay in identification can mean a delay in establishing effective communication with the child, which, in turn, can have a long-term impact on his/her social and educational development. Such delay means that deaf children:

> spend part of their early lives with either severely degraded or no auditory input. If they live in a non-signing family [...] this means that there will be less language input for them than for hearing children. This causes a delay in language development that is difficult, sometimes impossible, to eliminate. (van Berkel-van Hoof, 2019, pp. 155–156)

Therefore, the consequences on development of undetected hearing impairment may be long-lasting (Yoshinaga-Itano, 2003).

> In the early years, a child's brain is still developing and putting the right building blocks in place for future development. If the child's brain is not exposed to lots of communication and language, this can have a knock-on effect on other areas of development later in life, such as memory skills, ability to organise thoughts, solve problems and social development. (NDCS, 2015b, p. 7)

Children with a conductive hearing loss have a higher tendency to behaviour problems, poor motivation and attention, shyness and withdrawal (Spencer & Marschark, 2010). The most vulnerable are those whose conductive deafness started in early infancy and persisted undiagnosed for long periods:

> [...] congenital hearing loss can delay language acquisition and impede communication abilities, which can in turn affect the child's abilities to participate socially and access information. Research has shown that DHH children are at a higher risk of being bullied, mocked, and socially isolated by peers in school (Fellinger et al., 2009). Research has also shown that DHH children experience social and communication barriers in their own families (Hintermair, 2006) because many hearing parents find it hard to communicate effectively with them. (Dammeyer, 2018, p. 483)

Support for the acquisition of communication and language

One of the most important considerations in supporting young children to acquire communication and language skills is that, from birth, all of them, including those with a hearing impairment, need a rich communication and language environment, where there is a lot of interaction between children and adults. It is important for family members and practitioners to think carefully about the clarity of their spoken language (Wilkins & Ertmer, 2002). Using natural speech patterns is more effective in communicating with deaf children than exaggerating lip movements or shouting.

It is obvious that higher-quality language input from families early on is likely to relate to greater language acquisition (Dirks, 2019). However, in addition to linguistic input from families, the language development of deaf children is also 'related to the level of parental sensitivity, the ability to correctly interpret a child's signals and respond appropriately' (Dirks, 2019, p. 418). Cejas and Quittner (2019, p. 123) conclude that, if deaf children are to make the most progress academically, socially and in terms of future life chances, auditory and language training is not enough on its own:

> [...] this surgical procedure [i.e. cochlear implants] should be accompanied by parenting interventions that reduce stress, increase sensitive parenting, and foster a strong parent–child relationship. Early interventions at the family systems level need to be developed and evaluated for this population.

It is important to acknowledge, at home and in settings, schools and colleges, that deaf children may well need more time to communicate than hearing children. This includes extra time to take part in a conversation, for example. When children are very young, gestures, facial expressions and body language constitute a significant part of communication and help to provide visual access to language, which is especially important for children with a hearing impairment. The National Deaf Children's Society offers the following advice to families in this regard:

> It's important to make sure that you face your child as much as possible and maintain eye contact to get their attention. This will allow your baby to see your face clearly as they begin to watch faces and lips during communication. You should also try to make sure that your face is in the light. For example, try and avoid having your back to a window. This will help your child to see your face and gestures. (NDCS, 2015a, p. 10)

Methods of communication

There are several different methods of communicating that are available to deaf children, their families and carers, and teachers and others. Major 'types' of approach are Auditory-Oral (or 'Oral/Aural'), Sign-Bilingual, or Total Communication. Before discussing these approaches it is important to acknowledge, as the (NDCS, 2015b, p. 45) comments, that, in general terms, the evidence for the effectiveness of any one method being better than others for deaf children as a whole is not clear. It seems that there is some evidence for all these approaches being successful for some young people.

Auditory-Oral methods

The aim of an Auditory-Oral approach is to encourage deaf children to use whatever residual hearing they have to develop good speaking and listening skills (Beattie, 2006). Cochlear implants, hearing aids and radio aids are used to maximise the child's 'residual' hearing (Spencer & Marschark, 2010. 'Hearing aids and cochlear implants should be offered as early as possible so that babies and young children have the opportunity to access sound and develop hearing pathways' (NDCS, 2015b, p. 8).

Cochlear implants

Cochlear implants are devices that replace the function of the normal cochlea by converting auditory signals into electrical impulses and directing these into the auditory nerve. Across the world, the numbers of people with such implants is increasing year on year. The degree to which hearing improves after implantation seems to be variable and unpredictable, implying an important focus on specific training (Glick & Sharma, 2017). Heimler, Pavani and Amedi (2019) highlight the advantages of using systemic multi-sensory approaches, for example pairing visual linguistic inputs such as sign language with newly-acquired sound inputs. In terms of mental health issues among deaf children, there is evidence to suggest that the use of cochlear implants reduces, but does not eliminate, the risk (Dammeyer, 2019).

Hearing aids

Web activity WA8.1
Development of hearing aids

On the website we have uploaded a brief history of the development of hearing aids. If you are interested in this, you might access the materials at this point.

Most hearing aids work by making sounds louder, and there are different types of hearing aid used by children that do this. The most common are behind-the-ear models (NDCS, 2020). These have a microphone that picks up sounds, a processor that amplifies the parts of the signal, that is the sound frequencies, needed and a receiver that sends the amplified sounds into the ear through the earmould which is fitted into the ear and custom-made for the individual.

There are also 'bone conduction hearing aids' that work by changing the sound from an acoustic signal into a mechanical signal, a vibration. The receiver is a small vibrating pad fixed behind the ear, usually on the 'mastoid' bone, the large bone behind the ear. This pad allows sound to be conducted through the skull bone rather than through the outer and middle ear.

Bone conduction hearing aids may be suitable for learners who have conductive deafness that could be caused by malformation of the outer ear or of the canal, chronic ear infections or long-standing glue ear. When the vibrations are transmitted through the bones of the skull to the cochlea they are converted into sound as in normal hearing, thereby bypassing the outer and middle ear.

Sign Bilingualism

The term 'bilingualism' implies competence in two languages. So-called 'Sign Bilingualism' in the UK means using British Sign Language (BSL) (or Irish Sign Language in Ireland) together with the spoken language of the home (Moores, 2008). There is an assumption that a visual language is essential for deaf children to benefit from education, have full access to the world around them, and to connect with Deaf culture, the Deaf community and the hearing world (Burman, Nunes & Evans, 2006). BSL cannot be used simultaneously with spoken language because it has linguistic rules that are different from English. It uses body language, including head position, facial expressions and gesture, as well as hand movements. Fingerspelling is used to represent words such as names, which have no signs.

Total Communication

Total Communication means, as its name suggests, communicating through whatever combination of modes works best: sign, speech, fingerspelling, body language (gesture, facial expression, and so on), lip-reading and Cued Speech. Signed/Sign Supported English (SSE) – English language supplemented with the use of signs – uses BSL signs and fingerspelling (Moores, 2001) in the word order of English. Signed English also uses BSL signs with specially developed 'markers' made with the hands, and fingerspelling, to represent the word order and grammar of the English language. This last feature makes it useful to support the teaching of reading and writing. Fingerspelling – spelling with the fingers – means that each separate letter has to be indicated with the fingers and palm of the hand (Padden & Gunsals, 2003). Lip-reading – reading words from the lip patterns of a speaker (Spencer & Marschark, 2010) – is never enough on its own. Many speech sounds are invisible on lips. Lip patterns vary from one person to another. Lack of clarity around the mouth caused, for example, by beards or moustaches, or eating while talking, can make it difficult to lip-read. Cued Speech uses natural speech with 'cues': eight hand shapes in four different positions to represent the sounds of the English language (Hage & Leybaert, 2006). Some letter sounds – 'p', 'm' and 'b' – look the same on the lips. Some sounds, for example 'd', 'k' and 'g', cannot be 'read' on the lips. Hand shapes are 'cued' near to the mouth to make clear the sounds of English which look the same when lip-read, or sounds that are not visible, to reinforce the association between the sounds and letters of spoken English.

Ongoing debates and differences of opinion

In some places there is a serious difference of opinion between those who believe that deaf children can be taught to speak using Auditory-Oral approaches, that is, assisted by hearing aids, cochlear implants, radio aids, and so on, and be integrated into mainstream society, and those who believe they should be taught through sign language. Some argue that mental health problems related to, for example, feelings of isolation and, sometimes, bullying, are best prevented by supporting hearing and spoken language skills, while others argue that sign language support and a bicultural approach are better. Specific support for social-emotional development has been shown to be beneficial for some young people, but the learning of coping strategies to support children to participate in social interactions often requires a level of competence in verbal conversations. Teaching specific strategies, such as turn-taking, which may be carried out through having a personalised approach that fits the individual deaf person, have been shown to be helpful in maintaining the flow of conversation (Tye-Murray, 2003).

Some, for example Vissers and Hermans (2019), argue for an approach that takes account of the many factors that affect a child's biological, psychological and social development. What suits the child best may depend on the degree of hearing loss, the extent of the delay in language acquisition and, of course, what the child him/herself and the family feel about his/her situation. Which approach is the most effective for any individual child, family and setting 'is the one which works for them, both fitting in with the family's culture and values and, most importantly, allowing the child to develop good self-esteem, a positive self-image, successful relationships, and to achieve her [sic] potential in all aspects of her life' (NDCS, 2015a, p. 50).

Including learners with hearing impairments

Key to successful inclusion is the ethos of the classroom, setting, school or college in which young hearing-impaired children are placed. There is a strong argument that 'reviewing and adapting teaching styles, presentation methods, listening conditions and differentiation/adaptation of the curriculum to address the needs of deaf pupils will also improve the learning conditions for many other pupils in the school' (Royal National Institute for Deaf People (RNID), 2004, p. 8).

Adaptations to learning environments

For educational purposes, young children with hearing impairments will probably require adaptations to their environment in order to access the curriculum.

Radio aids

Deaf children often use assistive listening devices to help them to hear what a speaker is saying, particularly in noisy listening conditions. In educational institutions, personal FM systems, 'radio aids', 'can help reduce effects of background noise in, for example, a school classroom, and help a child to concentrate on one person's voice, often their teacher' (NDCS, 2008, p. 31). These aids have a transmitter, microphone and receiver. In a class, the teacher wears the transmitter, and the sounds are transmitted by radio waves to the deaf learner's receiver. This receiver picks up the radio waves and converts them back into sound. The learner's hearing aids or implants amplify the sound so it can be heard by the learner. Either teachers of the deaf or audiologists will usually assess whether a radio aid would be useful and appropriate for a young child. Criteria used for making this decision may well include the child's age, hearing, listening and language levels, ability to use a hearing aid independently, emotional development, family views, the environmental acoustics and the appropriateness of using hearing aids within the context.

Soundfield systems

Soundfield systems, which some local authorities provide for use at home and for use in class-rooms, are designed for similar reasons as radio aids. Here, a microphone worn by a speaker is linked to an amplifier by either an infra-red or FM radio transmitter. The speaker can walk around a room fitted with loudspeakers, with no need for wires. The soundfield system amplifies speakers' voices to a clear level of sound above background noises (NDCS, 2008). Most hearing-impaired learners who use hearing aids or cochlear implants will still continue to need radio aids in rooms with a soundfield system.

Sound waves reverberate and, as a result, increase the degree of background noise in rooms that have numbers of hard surfaces (Moeller et al., 2007). Soundfield systems and adequate consideration of the acoustics in rooms at home or teaching spaces in Early Years settings and schools can improve the listening environment for all learners. For example, a good listening environment at home might mean keeping background noise low by turning off the television or noisy electrical appliances during conversations, and using soft furnishings – carpets, rugs, and so on – to absorb sound and reduce echo.

In classrooms, hearing-impaired learners may need the additional support through visual and written forms of language, the possibility of lip-reading and multi-sensory clues as well as hearing aids (Harris & Moreno, 2006). Teachers should therefore highlight key terms and concepts, and in order to facilitate lip-reading and the use of hearing aids where the maximum range is often two metres, should place themselves in an appropriate position in relation to learners.

Case study: Using Total Communication at home and in educational contexts

It is often useful if siblings and the rest of the family, peers and teachers in Early Years settings, schools and colleges learn to use Total Communication with learners who experience hearing impairments of a severe nature. 'Billy' was very fortunate in this regard. He had been born with a profound hearing impairment which had been identified a few days after his birth and he had been given cochlea implants. Professionals experienced in advising families about how to help their children supported his parents at an early stage to learn some of the elements of Total Communication, including Cued Speech, to supplement what he could hear through the implants. He went to a nursery school where the staff were offered professional development related to hearing impairments and made a real effort to encourage his language develop-ment. Later, in his primary school, where there was a soundfield system, a specialist teacher came in on a regular basis to monitor his progress and support the classroom teacher to ensure the system was working effectively and that Billy could access what he needed in order to take part in classroom activities with his peers. She also offered to teach the pupils in the whole school how to understand and use Signed English at an appropriate level.

Practical considerations in classrooms

A number of educators have argued that teachers in classrooms at any level should be aware of the needs of deaf learners in very practical terms.

Web activity WA8.2
Responsiveness of classroom context

On the website we have uploaded a list of practical considerations for the classroom, together with an activity. You might choose to access this now.

Encouraging participation through mindful use of 'translanguaging'

Swanwick (2019) focuses on the role of language as an integral part of the process of learning for all young people in classrooms, including for those with hearing impairments. Clearly, encouraging the participation and scaffolding of the learning of all young people in classrooms, enabling social participation and responding to the variety of communication needs of deaf learners through classroom dialogue can be challenging. Swanwick (2019, p. 90), for example, notes that:

> Deaf learners often struggle to develop essential learning skills such as the ability to organize their learning, solve problems, make predictions, see generalizations, and make connections between concepts […]

She advocates a focus on 'translanguaging', 'that is, teachers' mindful use of sign, spoken, and written languages that promotes inclusivity and engagement and is supportive of language and curriculum learning' and draws on the language repertoire of deaf students in individual classrooms (Swanwick, 2019, p. 94). This may involve switching between spoken, sign and written language, fingerspelling, and so on, to check comprehension and introduce new concepts and vocabulary. There are provisos in this approach, of course. Translanguaging will enhance learning and language development of hearing-impaired learners if:

1. it is embedded within an inclusive and additive language context
2. the diverse language repertoires of individuals are recognized and nurtured, and
3. practitioners have the bilingual skills and agility to lead and respond to translanguaging practices that enhance language development and learning. (Swanwick, 2019, p. 98)

Visual difficulties

The Royal National Institute for Blind People (RNIB) (2018) reports that there are more than 25,000 blind and partially-sighted learners aged 16 and under in the UK. Up to half have other disabilities (Morris & Smith, 2008), including 30% who have severe or profound and multiple learning difficulties. Many people who are classed as blind have some 'functional' vision, and it is important to teach the child how to make best use of this (Davis, 2003). Where a distinction is necessary for any reason, the term 'blind' is used to refer to pupils who rely on tactile methods in their learning, for example Braille or Tactile diagrams (see below for discussion of both methods), and the term 'low vision' is used with reference to children and young people who are taught through methods which rely on sight (Mason, 1997).

Some children are at higher risk of vision impairment, including those who are very premature and very low birth weight babies, children from the most economically deprived backgrounds (Cumberland, Pathai & Rahi, 2010), and children with learning difficulties (Woodhouse et al., 2014). A young person's experience of vision impairment in educational contexts varies, depending on a number of factors. They include, for example, access to assistive products such as glasses or white canes, and the extent to which the setting, school or college buildings are accessible and appropriate transport is available.

Below we first outline the structure and functions of eyes to enable clear discussion of the site of impairments to vision, and move on to discuss common causes of visual difficulties, likely barriers to learning that are experienced, and interventions and classroom approaches designed to include those learners.

Structure of the eye

Light enters the eye through the cornea, passes through the lens and is refracted back to the retina (see Figure 8.2). The retina contains light-sensitive cells that generate an electrical signal that travels through the optic nerve to the visual cortex of the brain where it is processed into an image. Different parts of the cortex are responsible for different elements of vision: movement, shape, colour, and so on. In normal vision, these elements are integrated into a coherent whole. Malformation of the eye and/or malfunctioning of the optic nerve or parts of the visual cortex can create visual problems.

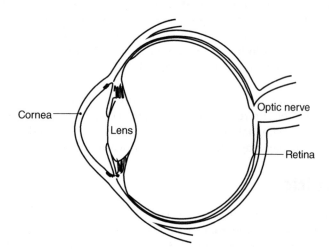

Figure 8.2   Human eye

Causes of vision impairment

Vision impairment might result from a variety of genetic or hereditary factors, for example congenital disorders of the optic nerve and/or retina, damage to the eye before, during or after birth, or damage to the visual cortex or other parts of the brain associated with information processing.

Practical effects of vision impairment

Many blind people actually have some sight, for example peripheral or tunnel vision, or may find it easier to see in certain light conditions. Partially-sighted learners make up the majority of vision-impaired learners. Some of the difficulties partially-sighted learners may experience include low acuity in near or distance vision, or both, loss in central vision – the area of the visual field that discriminates fine detail – loss in peripheral vision, irregular patches of poor vision, low sensitivity to contrast, light sensitivity, difficulties in eye movement, and colour loss. While vision impairment varies widely in its effects, the most important consideration is the practical implications for an individual learner in a setting, school or college:

- Vision impairments can affect academic progress, particularly in literacy acquisition and concept development. These learners are unlikely to have access to the same incidental learning through vision that is available to sighted learners – for example, noticing actions, events, and so on, without anyone specifically pointing them out. Blind or partially-sighted learners may be very tired by the degree of concentration required to complete tasks and the extra time needed to complete tasks. Their access to new information and learning may be limited by this (Davis, 2003). Many will be unable to learn to read and write without specialist tuition to do so.
- In terms of acquiring social skills, many may find it hard to recognise body language, for example facial expressions and gestures, and may need support in developing social skills. Sometimes young people with visual impairments encounter negative attitudes and stereotyping and may lack confidence and self-esteem as a result. They may be less accepted by their peer group and have fewer friends.
- Mobility and awareness of the environment may well be affected, especially for those learners with more severe vision impairments.
- For some, the growing realisation of the restrictions that their vision impairment may impose upon them, usually in comparison to their sighted peers, may be a trigger for a series of negative emotions, and leave them vulnerable to psychological stress, frustration and even depression. They may experience greater feelings of failure. They may also be more dependent on their parents in many areas, which may adversely affect the development of a sense of independence, one of the most important factors in relation to their self-esteem and adjustment.

According to the RNIB (2018), with appropriate support and understanding the impact of these factors can be minimised or removed altogether.

Addressing difficulties

Sensory stimulation is very important for brain development from birth. 'As the child with VI [visual impairment] has little incidental motivation to use his vision, there may be a tendency for him [sic] to withdraw into passivity or self-stimulation within his own body, e.g. eye-poking, hand-flapping' (Blairmires et al., 2016, p. 57). Family members, carers, teachers and others should therefore use touch or noise to communicate, for example, pleasure and approval. Young children will benefit from personal, undivided attention, tuning in to what is important to the child at the time, exploring objects together and giving a running commentary on what is going on, introducing low-vision aids and the use of information and communication technologies (ICT) where appropriate.

It is essential to ensure that babies and young children with visual impairment who cannot make sense of the world visually do so by other means. The RNIB has published very useful material relating to ways to support young children to develop tactile skills. They emphasise the importance of offering as wide a range of tactile experiences as possible right from the beginning:

> Before they start to explore with their hands, infants gain a wide variety of information through their mouths, so it is essential that blind babies have opportunities to suck and mouth foods of different consistencies as well as objects that are pleasing – and safe! The child will need to be encouraged to hold, reach out, grasp, squeeze, twist, press, poke, explore texture, weight and hardness. They will need to move from using the whole palm to finger pads in order to determine shape pattern. These are the prerequisites of braille, should this become their preferred medium. (RNIB, 2015, §1.3)

'Treasure Baskets', originally developed by Elinor Goldschmied (Hughes, 2015), are particularly relevant for babies and young children with visual impairments because they offer direct hands-on sensory experiences. A Treasure Basket is a shallow hardwearing basket containing a collection of everyday items that are safe to handle and made of natural materials that are chosen to stimulate one of the five senses of touch, taste, smell, sound and whatever residual sight the child may have. The contents therefore vary in weight, size, texture, colour, taste, temperature and sound. Children are encouraged to explore the contents of the basket using their senses to discover what an object is and what it does when it is handled.

In schools, the majority of blind and partially-sighted children are educated in inclusive (mainstream) education. However, there is evidence that blind and partially-sighted children are increasingly being deprived of specialist support, and learning materials and examinations are not consistently made available in alternative formats. It is crucial, therefore, that teachers and others in settings, schools and colleges are aware of the individual needs of young people with visual impairments, and, as with other forms of need, implement what is contained in an individual learning or support plan, take the views of those learners and their families very seriously, and have access to external forms of specialist advice where appropriate.

Safety and access in the learning environment

In considering the appropriateness of the learning environment in settings, schools and colleges, two prime considerations are safety and access. In settings, schools and colleges where there are learners with visual impairments, classrooms should be well lit with signposting that includes Braille, symbols and/or large print. Passageways should be clear of hazards. Contrasting coloured walls and floors, and edges of steps highlighted with paint or coloured strips, can be very important also.

Web activity WA8.3
Skills needed to travel within an environment

On the website we have uploaded materials related to the skills needed to travel within an environment, and an activity associated with this. You should access this now.

Special consideration of the classroom environment, for example lighting and where to site quiet or loud areas, Braille and/or tactile/large print signs, bulky equipment such as CCTV, a Brailler and computers, may well be necessary (Mason, 2001).

All settings, schools and colleges have an anticipatory duty to plan for disabled learners. An accessible physical environment can do a great deal to reduce barriers to participation and learning for learners with vision impairment. There is a balance to be struck between providing an environment that is safe and accessible for learners with visual impairments and preparing them to take an independent role in a society that is not always designed to meet their needs.

Web activity WA8.4
Carrying out an environmental audit

On the website you will find an activity related to an audit of the environment. You should access this now.

Access to the curriculum

In terms of learning materials, tactile materials with a variety of textures and smells can be used to differentiate and modify pictures, books, models, toys, games and mathematics equipment, depending on the age and stage of the learner, and the learning environment.

Learners may need teaching of reading and writing through specialist codes such Moon, a tactile code based on the shapes of letters in the alphabet, developed by William Moon in 1847, or Braille (see below). They may also need specialist teaching of mobility, tactile and keyboard skills, as well as social and life skills generally. For such specialist or additional teaching, it is important to discuss with the mainstream teacher – and also, in many circumstances, with the learner and his/her family – whether and when to withdraw the learner from the mainstream classroom. It is crucial that s/he does not become socially isolated and the mainstream teacher maintains full responsibility for his/her learning and progress.

Braille

Around 3% of blind and partially-sighted learners aged 5–16 use Braille as their main format for reading and writing (Morris & Smith, 2008). Braille was invented by Louis Braille, a blind French schoolboy, over 200 years ago. This code consists of six dots arranged in two columns of three.

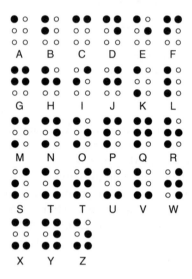

Figure 8.3   Braille alphabet

Braille is a code used by people who are blind or visually impaired to read and write. It is a tactile system through which letters and words are represented using raised dots in various combinations to represent letters of the alphabet, punctuation, numbers and whole words. These braille dots are positioned like the figure six on a die, in a grid of two parallel vertical lines of three dots each. From the six dots that make up the basic grid, 64 different configurations can be created. It is not a separate language.

There are two grades of braille: uncontracted (previously Grade 1) and contracted (previously Grade 2). Uncontracted braille includes a letter-for-letter and number-for-number translation from print. When every letter of every word is expressed in braille, it is referred to as uncontracted braille. Books or other reading materials can be transcribed in uncontracted braille. Contracted braille has special signs for common words and combinations of letters. There are 180 different letter contractions and 75 short-form words used in English in contracted braille. For beginning readers, some reading schemes have been adapted to include uncontracted or contracted braille on interleaved clear plastic sheets, so that the pictures and print story can be seen underneath. This enables shared reading between sighted and blind readers at home and in settings and schools to share books. These short cuts reduce the volume of paper needed for reproducing books in braille and make reading faster. Particular subject areas, for example music, mathematics, science and foreign languages, have their own specialist codes. Unified English Braille was developed by the International Council on English Braille (ICEB) to bring together several existing braille codes, including codes for mathematics, sciences and literary material. This was adopted in the United Kingdom in October 2011.

Web activity WA8.5
Understanding the production of braille

Just as printed materials can be produced with paper, pencil, typewriter or printer, braille can also be written in several ways. We have uploaded a description of how this might be done on the website. If you are interested you might access this material now.

Daily literacy instruction for young braille readers is essential (Koenig & Holbrook, 2000). Braille instruction must be systematic, regular, adequate to the child's needs, and provided by knowledgeable and appropriately trained personnel to give the child who is blind the best opportunity to become a proficient reader (Koenig & Holbrook, 2000; Barclay, Herlich & Sacks, 2010).

Blind learners may have individual braille tuition alongside normal classes. However, it is good inclusive practice to make sure braille users take part in literacy activities alongside the sighted learners in their class. Some schools also help braille users to feel included by introducing basic braille to all learners in a class, holding braille awareness activities or braille clubs.

Web activity WA8.6
Access to education for vision-impaired learners

It is important to find out the most appropriate way to present materials for individual learners. On the website we have uploaded some suggested principles for managing the preparation of resources and an activity associated with this material. You might access this now.

A number of published learning resources are already available in modified formats. You may wish to investigate the following website to check the range of what is there: www.clearvisionproject.org/ (accessed 28.10.2021). The books all have added braille (or Moon), print and pictures, making them suitable for vision-impaired and sighted children and adults to share.

The RNIB book-lending service offers free access to thousands of 'talking books': www.rnib.org.uk/reading-services (accessed 28.10.2021).

LEARNING POINT
MAKING LESSONS MORE INCLUSIVE WITH A MULTI-SENSORY APPROACH

Lessons can be made more accessible to learners who have vision impairment by adopting a multi-sensory approach, for example using audio or tactile resources alongside or instead of visual resources. Alongside braille resources, learners with little or no sight but good tactile skills may also use tactile resources – pictures, diagrams, charts and graphs – to gain access to curriculum information. Tactile pictures/diagrams can be useful when a picture/diagram is not easy to describe in words and the shape or pattern is vital to understanding a concept. Increasingly, pictures and diagrams on websites have a text description that can be read by a screen reader.

Some vision-impaired learners may find it more efficient to process information through listening than through seeing. Many older learners rely heavily on recording devices to take notes or to listen to audiobooks.

If you are a teacher or learning/classroom assistant, look at one of your lesson plans. How accessible is it for a learner with a vision impairment? What amendments might make it more accessible?

Think about any concepts or information that you have assumed all learners will understand, but may be new to a learner with a visual impairment. Think also about the amount of reading and writing learners are required to do and the facilities available to all learners to achieve this.

Supporting students with a vision impairment in further education

During post-16 education, colleges and sixth forms have to make 'reasonable adjustments' so that any learners with a disability or impairment are not disadvantaged. There are all sorts of support and equipment that a college might offer and the college will look at what works best for an individual. Some examples of support may include a support teacher or worker, or a sighted guide, materials in alternative formats such as braille or large print, assistive computer technology, such as closed-circuit television, computers with speech synthesisers and magnification, and so on. They may also be able to offer assistance during assessments or exams, so that all learners are assessed fairly. The type of support available varies between colleges and it is important that young people are encouraged to contact and visit any further education establishments as early as possible to discuss their requirements and confirm the college will meet their needs. Although there is no longer a legal requirement for colleges to produce a Disability Equality Scheme, some colleges may still have a DES or a Single Equality Scheme which you may wish to review. It is also important to consider the Public Sector Equality Duty and what action the college is taking on equality, especially in relation to the delivery of services for students.

Disclosing a disability and other needs

Letters and forms for completion, which are sent to all prospective and future students or are available online, should provide an opportunity to encourage disclosure of a disability, any support needs or additional requirements. On the initial letter, there should also be the opportunity for the student to indicate their preferred medium (e.g. large print, disk, BSL) for future communications. Any information received should be noted and acted upon (such as always using the preferred medium for future communications or arranging for an interpreter to be present at interview). Enrolment and other forms should be designed to facilitate their completion by all students. Completion by electronic means, if possible in advance, should be considered. There should be the opportunity to declare a disability by means of carefully worded questions on the forms, together with an explanation as to the advantages of declaration and how the information will be used.

Apprenticeships

Colleges are expected to make reasonable adjustments and provide support with the training-related aspects of an apprenticeship, paid for through Lead Scotland. Support costs for apprentices in the workplace should normally be covered by the Access to Work scheme (www.gov.uk/access-to-work, accessed 28.10.2021).

Accessing available funding

In England, the Education and Skills Funding Agency (www.gov.uk/government/organisations/education-and-skills-funding-agency, accessed 28.10.2021) offers advice about funding related to further education.

Lead Scotland is a voluntary organisation set up to support disabled young people, adults and carers across Scotland to access learning opportunities (www.lead.org.uk/, accessed 28.10.2021).

Careers Wales (https://careerswales.gov.wales/courses-and-training/funding-your-studies/funding-students-learning-difficulties-disabilites, accessed 28.10.2021) offers advice about funding for students with disabilities of various kinds post-school.

In Northern Ireland, NI Direct offers information on a wide range of government services, including education, training, employment and welfare benefits (www.nidirect.gov.uk/, accessed 28.10.2021).

Multi-sensory impairment

Multi-sensory impairment means difficulty in both vision and hearing. The incidence of deaf-blindness is very low. 'Estimates of 1 in a 1,000 are probably over counting, and 1 in 4,000 may be an underestimate' (National Assembly for Wales (NAW), 2019, p. 4). Very few babies are born totally blind and deaf.

Children may be born with multi-sensory impairment, or may acquire it later from illness or injury. For example, premature birth and/or severe infections during early childhood may cause deaf-blindness. In previous years, Rubella (German measles) during pregnancy was a major cause of deaf-blindness. Vaccination against Rubella means that it is now uncommon. In the UK, for example, children are offered a triple vaccine against measles, mumps and Rubella, at 1 and 3 years of age (www.nhs.uk/conditions/vaccinations/mmr-vaccine/, accessed 28.10.2021).

Learners with multi-sensory impairment have a limited, and potentially confused, experience of the world around them as a result of the much reduced and possibly distorted auditory and visual information that they receive (Aitken, 2000). Combinations of different degrees of vision and hearing impairment can have quite different effects that lead to quite different outcomes, for example, for a young person who is severely sight-impaired but has a moderate hearing loss, to a child who is severely hearing-impaired but has a moderate vision loss. Taylor (2007, p. 205) notes the difficulties experienced by many of these young people in communicating:

> These include: a reduced and confused experience of the world, becoming passive and isolated, and the tendency to be echolalic or repeating the last word said to them, all of which limit their ability to make choices. Aitken and Millar (2002) also highlight the effects of hearing impairment on individuals' communication, including isolation from information and from other people.

Some children become skilled at using touch, others in using the sense of smell as a means of learning about the world and in communication. Others may feel differences in air pressure to sense movement around them.

The effects of deaf-blindness on development may be summarised as problems with communication, mobility and orientation, and/or access to information. Meeting the learning needs of deaf-blind learners therefore needs to include programmes designed to enable them to:

- learn to communicate, and then learn through communication;
- learn to mobilise, and to use that movement to learn;
- learn to access information, and then use this information to learn.

Uses of information and communication technology

Assistive technology is not an end in itself. The goal of assistive technology is to give children and young people with disabilities access to literacy and communication in the school, home and community. Information and communication technology (ICT) has enormous potential to support the learning in learners with vision impairment across the age and ability range. As well as providing an important alternative means of access on an individual basis (for example, through the use of a laptop or braille device for reading and recording in lessons), assistive technology can also provide learners with access to the many mainstream ICT-based resources that increasingly form part of all children's teaching and learning.

The RNIB website has some very useful guidance on, and examples of, ICT in action to support the needs of learners with visual impairments (https://www.rnib.org.uk/advice/technology-useful-products, accessed 24.05.2022).

Difficulties in motor movement

Motor skills are muscle movements and are critically important in all aspects of learning. Gross and fine motor skills work together to provide co-ordination. Gross motor skills are required for movement of large body parts, for example arms and legs, for walking, running, crawling, and so on. Fine motor skills are the collective skills that are needed for smaller movements in the wrists, hands, fingers, feet and toes: writing, picking up objects between the thumb and finger, using scissors and other tools. Balance is crucial to every action. Static balance is essential to maintain stillness. For example, a child needs control of the head, shoulders and hips before s/he can stand securely. Dynamic balance is important to motor movement. This kind of control and balance is required for so-called 'bilateral co-ordination': co-ordination and control of both sides of the body simultaneously so that a child can run, jump, climb, skip, and so on. Hand–eye co-ordination enables a child to perform many day-to-day activities, for example to see, stretch out and pick up a toy. Foot–eye co-ordination is essential to kick a ball. Children also need bodily and spatial awareness, so that s/he knows where his/her bodily parts are in relation to each other, and where they function in space.

Coulter et al. (2015) provide a very useful overview of children's usual progression in gross motor skills. The developmental sequence is hierarchical, developing from the head down to the feet, and from the midline of the body to the fingers. Fine motor skills also typically develop in a predictable pattern in the early years of childhood (Exner, 2005). A 2- to 3-month-old baby first bats at a toy, then, by 6 months of age, is grasping, releasing and transferring objects between his/her hands (Coulter et al., 2015). Then comes the use of fingers to explore things, pick up small objects using a pincer grasp, self-feed and dress. By 5 years of age the majority of children can copy squares, triangles, spontaneously write a few letters, draw a recognisable house and person, and thread a large needle. As time goes by, children learn to use 'school tools': scissors, markers, crayons, pencils and glue.

Difficulties in motor co-ordination may result in problems in both gross and fine motor skills at a young age (Macintyre, 2014): clumsiness; losing balance; difficulty in climbing; jumping up with both feet, pedalling tricycles, and throwing and catching balls; uncertainty in hand dominance; inability to use scissors and grip pencils properly; difficulty undressing generally; and inability to use toilet facilities unaided.

Serious physical impairments as well as sensory impairments may be identified at the Newborn and Infant Physical Examination (NIPE), which is carried out within three days of the child's birth. We discuss this assessment in Chapter 9. In addition to the hearing and vision tests outlined above, the baby is examined to ensure there are no problems with the hips, heart and (for boys) genitals (www.nhs.uk/conditions/pregnancy-and-baby/newborn-physical-exam/, accessed 28.10.2021). Once difficulties have been identified, either at the newborn stage or later on, a referral to health professionals is likely and, if so, a plan will be put in place with advice from the relevant health professionals, if appropriate.

Below we outline a number of physical difficulties that may be experienced by learners: muscular dystrophy, dyspraxia, cerebral palsy, congenital heart defects, cystic fibrosis and Tourette syndrome, together with some general principles for addressing needs in educational institutions.

Muscular dystrophy

Around 8,000 to 10,000 people in the UK have a type of muscular dystrophy (Pohlschmidt & Meadowcroft, 2010). Muscular dystrophy (MD) is an inherited disorder caused by incorrect or missing genetic information that prevents the body from making the proteins needed to maintain healthy muscles effectively, potentially including the heart. Muscles in the body gradually weaken and eventually stop working so that, over time, walking, sitting upright, breathing easily and moving limbs becomes impossible. There is no cure, but medical scientists are working on ways to improve muscle and joint function and slow muscle deterioration.

There are different types of muscular dystrophy; some start in infancy, others may not appear until early adulthood. The most common and most severe form is Duchenne muscular dystrophy (MD), which affects around one boy in 35,000, but not usually girls. Girls can carry the gene that causes Duchenne, but usually do not have physical symptoms. Each son of a carrier has a 50% chance of being affected and each daughter a 50% chance. In Duchenne MD, a problem in the genes results in a defect in dystrophin, which is an important protein in muscle fibres. Most boys need to use a wheelchair by the age of 12. The respiratory and heart muscles also may weaken in the teen years.

Dyspraxia

Dyspraxia – δυσ (dys) bad or difficult; πραξία (praxis) action – can be defined as 'a common disorder affecting fine and/or gross motor coordination in children and adults' that may also affect speech (Dyspraxia Foundation, 2020, https://dyspraxiafoundation.org.uk/about-dyspraxia/, accessed 03.04.2020). Young children with dyspraxia experience difficulty in activities requiring co-ordination, balance and control. An early sign is that a baby is 'floppy', with poor muscle tone. Often dyspraxic children miss out the crawling stage and the skills in motor movement that develop with it. Many day-to-day activities that require gross and fine motor co-ordination – using a knife and fork, tying shoe laces, writing neatly, and so on – are difficult. All dyspraxic individuals are different, and require careful observation to identify the effects of dyspraxia and develop an individualised plan to meet personal needs.

Cerebral palsy

Cerebral palsy is one of the most common congenital childhood disorders and is usually caused by brain damage that happens before or during a child's birth, or during the early years. Cerebral palsy affects muscle tone, movement and motor skills. Learners with cerebral palsy often experience difficulties in feeling, perception, cognition, communication, epilepsy, and also secondary musculoskeletal problems (Rosenbaum et al., 2007). Individual young people are affected differently, depending on which part of the brain is involved. Learners with cerebral palsy may need to miss class time for visits to the doctor or to take medication in school or college, so may well need support to catch up with classroom activities and assignments.

Congenital heart defects

Congenital heart defects are abnormalities in the structure of the heart, ranging from mild to severe, that develop in foetuses early in pregnancy. For example, there may be holes in the walls between the heart's chambers, abnormal heart valves, or abnormalities in the blood vessels entering or leaving the heart. Some cause serious symptoms at birth, requiring intensive hospital care. Others may not be diagnosed until the teen years or later. Learners of any age with congenital heart defects may have special needs that require consideration. For example, they may tire easily, or need to avoid activities that require a lot of exertion or going outdoors on hot days, or need extra time to move around the setting, school or college, and may miss class time to visit professionals, and so on.

Cystic fibrosis

Cystic fibrosis is a genetic disorder affecting the lungs and digestive system. The cystic fibrosis gene disrupts the balance of salt and water that is needed to maintain a normal thin coating of fluid and mucus inside the lungs, pancreas and other organs. The result is that the mucus becomes thick, sticky and hard to move, and the germs it traps remain in the lungs, which can become infected. Thick mucus in the pancreas blocks enzymes from reaching the intestines to digest nutrients properly.

Tourette syndrome

Tourette syndrome is a genetic condition that causes sudden, uncontrollable, repetitive muscle movements, such as eye blinking, grimacing, head jerking or shoulder shrugging, and vocal 'tics', such as throat clearing, sniffing, humming, 'echolalia', that is repeating other people's words, or 'coprolalia', which is involuntary swearing. During stressful situations, tics can become more severe, more frequent or longer. Tourette syndrome is a neurological condition, not a psychological one, and doctors can prescribe medicines to help control symptoms that interfere with school work or daily life.

Addressing physical difficulties

Learners with physical impairments are, above all, individuals with their own strengths, needs and interests. It is really important for staff in settings, schools and colleges to ensure that they are aware of individual learners' physical needs, familiarise themselves with advice from health and other professionals, and pay close attention to what is written on education or learning plans. Regular supervision from a clinic is very important to manage particular physical conditions as effectively as possible. Some young people, for example those with muscular dystrophy, may well need:

> [...] specialised equipment to aid their mobility, to support their posture and to protect and restore their body shape, muscle tone and quality of life. It is vital that children with physical needs have access to appropriate forms of therapy, for example physiotherapy and hydrotherapy, and that their carers receive training to enable them to manage their physical needs confidently on a day-to- day basis. (Mencap, undated, p. 5)

A learner's mobility, then, can be limited through disease, injuries or genetic issues, muscular dystrophy, cerebral palsy, and so on. Mobility may be limited in the upper or lower body, or both. Depending on the needs of individual learners and their age and stage of learning, those with limited mobility may use splints, casts, leg braces, canes, crutches, walkers or wheelchairs; may need extra time, as well as help, moving around classrooms, between classes and throughout school; may need special seats, desks or tables, and extra space for wheelchairs or other equipment; and may need a learning support assistant or other students to take notes for them, or have class lectures, discussions and activities recorded via video or audio. Some may need help moving around in class or reaching things, assistive devices for writing and speaking, occupational therapy, physiotherapy and speech therapy during the school day. Teachers should have realistic expectations for learners with physically debilitating conditions. Care routines may be exhausting and health care appointments can take up big chunks of time. If, for example, a student with a congenital heart defect misses class time for doctor visits or hospitalisations, s/he should be allowed extra time for assignments and provision to make-up work, if appropriate.

Conclusion

For a child with a sensory impairment, the greatest challenge is communication. A young child with a visual difficulty may need help and encouragement to explore his/her physical environment and interact with others. Normal progress in language and cognitive development may be problematic for a child with a hearing impairment, so intensive support may be needed for a young child. Early assessment of learning needs and appropriate intervention are therefore clearly very important. Whatever means of communication are developed with young children, it should enable them to acquire cognitive and other skills.

Gross and fine motor movements have critically important contributions to make to all aspects of a young child's learning. The classroom environment may need to be altered in some way, and teaching approaches revised. Other changes may be needed. The accommodations that are needed will depend on the specific difficulties that are experienced, the classroom context and the curriculum. The classroom should be free of obstacles and easy to navigate. Learners should know that they can ask for help without embarrassment when needed and to plan their routines and tasks ahead of time.

Why do you think it is so important to take individual strengths, needs, interests, experiences and family backgrounds into account when devising intervention plans for learners who experience sensory and/or physical difficulties and needs? Is there any difference in this regard for learners with any other area of difficulty, in your view?

Further reading

Vision and hearing impairments

Broadley, F. (2021) *Supporting Life Skills for Young Children with Vision Impairments and Other Disabilities*. London: Routledge.

Morgan-Jones, R. (2020) *Hearing Differently: The Impact of Hearing Impairment on Family Life*. London: Whurr.

Ravenscroft, J. (2020) *The Routledge Handbook of Visual Impairment*. London: Routledge.

The following websites contain a wealth of information:
National Deaf Children's Society: www.ndcs.org.uk/
British Deaf Association: https://bda.org.uk/

National Blind Children's Society: www.nbcs.org.uk
Royal Society for Blind Children: www.rsbc.org.uk/

Physical difficulties

Ekins, A., Robinson, S., Durrant, I., & Summers, K. (2017) *Educating Children with Life-limiting Conditions: A Practical Handbook for Teachers and School-based Staff.* London: Routledge.
Soan, S., & Hutton, E. (2020) *Universal Approaches to Supporting Children's Physical and Cognitive Development.* London: Routledge.
Vickerman, P., & Maher, A. (2018) *Teaching Physical Education to Children with Special Educational Needs and Disabilities.* London: Routledge.

The following websites contain a wealth of information:
Scope: www.scope.org.uk/
Muscular dystrophy: www.musculardystrophyuk.org/
Dyspraxia Foundation: https://dyspraxiafoundation.org.uk/
Cerebral palsy: www.cerebralpalsy.org.uk/
Cystic Fibrosis Trust: www.cysticfibrosis.org.uk/
Tourettes Action: www.tourettes-action.org.uk/

9

ASSESSMENT AND PLANNING

Major questions addressed in this chapter are:

- What is the place of assessment in addressing learning, behavioural and sensory needs?
- What constitute appropriate ways for assessing the kind of difficulties that are either experienced or are a matter of concern for the learners, family or teachers, and the curriculum area?
- How can we ensure that assessment of needs is appropriate to the individuality of the learners?
- What principles underpin different kinds of assessment?
- What is the legally-required content of plans that are designed to meet needs?

Key terms

Formative assessment, criterion-referencing, norm-referenced (standardised) testing, standard deviation, reading age, assessment of hearing, assessment of vision, family views, assessment of AD/HD, assessment of autism, assessment of dyslexia, statutory assessment

Introduction

Before discussing the issue of assessment in this chapter, it is necessary to return to the rationale for assessment in the first place. As we discussed in Chapter 1, legislation related to special, additional or support needs in educational contexts across the UK is strongly associated with the principle of equity: putting in place the additional, extra or special resources that are required to enable all learners to access the curriculum and make progress. A child or young person is assessed as having special or additional learning or support needs if s/he experiences a difficulty in learning or behaviour, or an emotional issue or a disability, which requires special or additional educational or support provision to be provided of a kind that is not normally available in schools and colleges. Such a requirement must be seen within the learning context of the individual young person. Where the curriculum and teaching are adapted to be accessible to individual students, it is obvious that fewer learners will experience difficulties of the kind that require special or additional provision to be made to address them. As the *Code of Practice* in England (Department for Education/Department of Health, 2015, §1.14) notes: 'High quality teaching that is differentiated and personalised will meet the individual needs of the majority of children and young people.' From this argument there are two corollaries:

- we should know how well adapted classrooms are to meet all learners' needs and whether the curriculum, teaching approaches, resources, and so on themselves are responsible for creating barriers to the learning of individuals;
- where we are sure that the barriers are not within the learning context, we have to be able to have a reliable, effective way to identify the extent of individual learners' needs.

The chapter will therefore open with a discussion of the importance of the learning environment in influencing progress in learning and behaviour. It will continue by discussing assessment in the very early years of life that ensures that babies and toddlers have access to support for their physical and/or sensory needs from the beginning. The chapter will go on to consider assessment and planning in classrooms as exemplified by the assess–plan–do–review cycle outlined in the *Code of Practice* (DfE/DoH, 2015) in England.

The chapter will continue with the following topics:

- principles of different kinds of assessment, roles and functions:
  - o observation in settings, to illustrate issues related to assessment in the early years;
  - o formative assessment in classrooms (Assessment for Learning) – the power of teacher feedback to young people;
  - o criterion-referenced assessment, together with examples;
  - o summative and standardised assessment, together with examples;
- the significance of understanding the barriers to learning from the young people's and families' perspectives;
- frameworks for planning, from individual education/behaviour plans/provision maps, with examples of plans/maps and reflective activities to consider experiences of difficulties at different ages and stages, to the development of formal statutory plans with resourcing protected by law, for example as in England.

Assessment of the learning environment

Whichever view we may take of the learning process, behaviourist, constructivist, social constructivist, and so on (see Chapter 2 for discussion of theories of learning), it is perfectly clear that the environment in which children and young people learn will have a strong influence on learning, progress and behaviour. Whether special or additional provision is required must be seen within the learning context of the individual child.

It is obvious that in classrooms where the work is tailored to the needs of individual learners, fewer will experience difficulties of the kind that require special, additional or support provision to be made in order to address them. When assessing whether or not a learner has such needs, it is important to know whether, in the learning environment, lesson activities, tasks and resources take account of the full range of learning needs and any requirements on individual learning and/or education plans of whichever kind are used in the setting, school or college.

One way to assess the degree to which the learning environment predisposes to positive learning and behaviour is to carry out an audit of teaching in the classroom. The authors of the *Primary National Strategy* (Department for Children, Schools and Families, 2005) developed a very useful inclusive teaching checklist to evaluate the extent to which pedagogy in classrooms is inclusive of all learners. It has been archived and is now available at: https://webarchive. nationalarchives.gov.uk/ukgwa/20110207024342/http://nationalstrategies.standards.dcsf.gov. uk/node/317753 (accessed 28.10.2021).

Web activity WA9.1
Auditing the learning environment

You might to choose to assess the degree to which the learning environment is conductive to positive learning and behaviour by using the list uploaded on the website as an auditing tool.

Assessment during the early years

These days, assessment of the difficulties and needs that may be experienced by individuals begins very early in life. Within three days of a child's birth, serious physical as well as sensory impairments may be identified at the Newborn and Infant Physical Examination (NIPE; see www. nhs.uk/conditions/pregnancy-and-baby/baby-reviews/). In relation to physical impairments, the baby is examined to ensure there are no problems with the hips, heart and (for boys) genitals. In addition, hearing and vision tests are carried out (www.nhs.uk/conditions/pregnancy-and-baby/ newborn-physical-exam/, accessed 28.10.2021). About two or three in 10,000 babies are born with problems with their eyes.

Once a child's difficulties have been identified, either at the newborn stage or later on in the early years, there is likely to be a referral to health professionals, including physiotherapists, occupational therapists and speech and language therapists, and a plan put into place to address the difficulties. Plans should clearly take account of the outcomes of the assessment of difficulties, specify ways to address these and include clear targets, in which the child and family should be involved. Advice from the health professionals may well be incorporated into the plans.

Identification through noticing

Observation through the informal process of 'noticing' is a very important aspect of identifying any particular cause for concern in children's learning in the early years. Purposeful observation of a child provides a useful opportunity to assess and monitor a child's development in fundamentally important areas, for example personal, social and emotional, physical, and communication and language. Such observations can provide information about how a child behaves, but not usually the reason for this.

Assessment in schools and colleges

It seems sensible that, as exemplified by the requirement in the Children and Families Act 2014 in England, assessment of need should start with a whole-school/whole-college approach to screening learners' current levels of attainment on entry, and subsequently progress should be monitored and recorded systematically so that individual difficulties can be identified quickly. We might follow the advice of the *Code of Practice* (DfE/DoH, 2015) in England that recommends a repetitive cycle of assessment of need followed by planning to meet the needs that have been identified, implementing the plan and reviewing the success of the plan. Such a cycle can lead to adjustments to teaching that can result in good progress and improved outcomes. It is useful at this point to have a look at the principles of formative assessment that are clearly compatible with ensuring that teacher assessment is used in an effective way to support learning.

Formative assessment: 'Assessment for Learning'

Assessment can be an effective way to promote learning but it depends on the kind that is used. Ongoing continuous formative assessment can provide teachers and others with opportunities to notice what is happening during learning activities, recognise the level and direction of the learning of individuals and see how they can help to take that learning further. As the Assessment Reform Group (1999, p. 2) comment, 'There is no evidence that increasing the amount of testing will enhance learning' on its own. Results from externally-imposed summative tests, especially where there are very high stakes attached to these results, can have very negative effects on students (Wearmouth, 2009).

Shifting the emphasis of the purpose of day-to-day assessment in classrooms to learning has resulted in many places in a focus on 'Assessment for Learning' (AfL), that is, ongoing, day-to-day formative assessment to collect information on what children do or do not understand and the adaptation of teaching in response to this. In a seminal piece of work, Black and Wiliam (1998) demonstrated clearly that student achievement, particularly that of lower achievers, can be raised through formative assessment in the classroom. They concluded that improving learning through assessment depends on five 'deceptively simple' factors: providing effective feedback, actively involving learners in their own learning, modifying teaching in response to the results of assessment, recognising the influence of assessment on learners' motivation and self-esteem, and enabling learners to assess themselves and understand that they need to do to improve (Assessment Reform Group, 1999, p. 5). We can see from these conclusions how closely they reflect the requirement to elicit learners' views of their learning: assessment must involve learners so that they have information about how well they are doing to guide subsequent learning in a constructive way that shows them what they need to do, and can do, to make progress.

Criterion-referencing

Sometimes we also need to know whether a learner has reached a particular threshold or level in his/her learning. So-called 'criterion-referencing' means comparing a learner's achievements with clearly stated criteria that specify key features of learning, achievement and quality at different stages of learners' development (Dunn, Parry & Morgan, 2002). Specifying clear criteria for an assessment clarifies what is required of learners but also assists teachers or others in deciding what they need to teach next. The descriptors of levels of performance and the overall criteria should be clear enough to serve as indicators of what learners have to do to succeed (Wearmouth, 2009). Teachers can compare a sample of the learner's work with the criteria in order to identify specific strengths and weaknesses, identify individual teaching and learning needs and prioritise new learning goals.

However, where learners continue to make inadequate progress, there should be further investigation of the learner's difficulties, drawing on:

- teachers' assessments/experience of the learner;
- the individual's development in comparison with peers;
- the views and experience of parents/families/carers, the learner's own views and, if relevant, advice from external support services.

For higher levels of need, schools should have arrangements in place to draw on more specialised assessments from external agencies and professionals.

It is clear from this that educational institutions will need a range of individualised assessment 'tools' to support closer identification of need, for example:

- standardised tests;
- criterion-referenced assessment checklists;
- profiling tools, for example for behaviour;
- observation schedules and prompt sheets;
- questionnaires for parents;
- questionnaires for pupils;
- screening assessments, for example for dyslexia.

Formal, norm-referenced (standardised) assessment

Making a decision about the seriousness or significance of barriers to learning raises questions about how to assess for difference between those who do, or do not, experience these barriers at a level that warrants additional or special attention. For some areas of need it is possible to design a testing tool that enables measurement of current attainment and comparison of the score with the average of that of the national cohort of peers. Comparison of an individual's score with that of peers is what we call 'norm-referencing'. To appreciate this kind of testing it is important to be aware of the very important issues of validity and reliability, without which we can have no confidence in the assessment. Further, we need to understand the test standardisation process, as well as a number of important concepts related to standardised tests and test procedures: 'measure of spread' of scores, validity and reliability, interpretations of percentile ranks, confidence bands and reading ages, and the advantages and disadvantages of this kind of assessment.

LEARNING POINT
VALIDITY AND RELIABILITY

The terms 'validity' and 'reliability' both relate to the trustworthiness of tests. Broadly, the 'validity' of a test is the degree to which that assesses what it is intended to test. 'Reliability', on the other hand, generally means whether we would obtain the same result on the same test with the same cohort of individuals if we did the test procedure again.

Read the following and note down your responses to the questions:

We might ask whether a test tests what we expect it to test with populations other than the samples used in the standardisation process. Are the norms and content of a test of reading or cognitive ability developed and standardised in Britain valid for young people from a completely different culture and new to the UK? What do you think about this issue?

Another issue relates to the age of a text. To what extent would you say that the norms of a spelling test standardised in the UK 25 years ago are still valid? What might some of the problems be?

Why do you think the concept of reliability is so important for standardised test procedures?

Process of standardisation

A standardised test is a test that is administered and scored in a consistent – standard – manner. Standardised tests are designed so that the questions, administration of the test, scoring and interpretation are consistent – in other words, they are carried out in the same way for everyone. Standardised tests are developed in a very structured way to ensure that they have validity and reliability. They involve a number of stages, for example:

- the framework to sample the skills and/or knowledge to be assessed is designed;
- a large number of questions are written and trialled with learners in schools/colleges;
- questions that prove not to be useful during the trials are rejected;
- tests for a standardisation trial are developed;
- the standardisation trial with a statistically significant and nationally representative sample of pupils is carried out;
- the norm-referenced measures are developed to enable comparison of learners' scores to those of peers nationally.

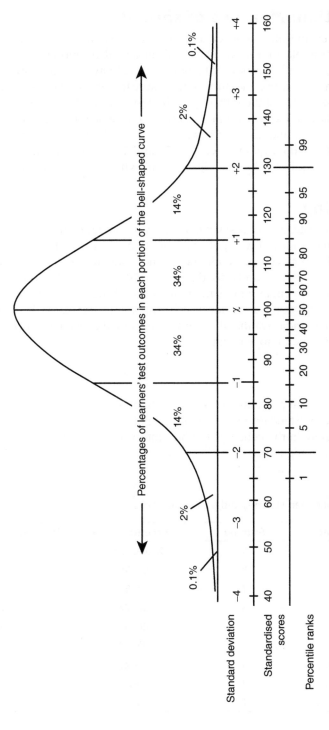

Figure 9.1 The relationship between standard deviation, standardised scores and percentile ranks under a normal distribution curve

Standard deviation: Measure of spread

Typically, the norm-referencing measures convert the mean (average) raw scores of the whole nationally-representative sample to a score of 100. Typically, also, during the development of these measures, for example for educational attainment and ability tests, the raw scores are calculated around the mean so that the 'measure of their spread', or so-called 'standard deviation' of scores, is set to 15. Irrespective of the difficulty of the test, about 68% of students in a national sample will have a standardised score within 15 points, or one standard deviation of the average (i.e. between 85 and 115), and about 95% will have a standardised score within 30 points, or two standard deviations of the average (between 70 and 130). These examples come from a frequency distribution, known as the 'normal distribution', which is shown in Figure 9.1.

Percentile ranking

In percentile rankings, the outcomes of assessment are given in a range from 0 to 100, with 0 the lowest, 100 the highest and a mean (average) score of 50. A glance at Figure 9.1 indicates that there is a fixed relationship between percentile ranks and standardised scores. The same mean raw score would be converted to a standardised score of 100 in a normal distribution, and to 50 as a percentile. A learner's percentile rank is the percentage of individuals in the sample of the same age who gained a score at the same level or below that of the learner's score. So performance at the 75th percentile indicates that the learner performed as well as, or better than, 75% of the sample when age is taken into account.

Stanines

Stanine scores are derived from percentile ranks. Percentile ranks are divided into nine categories called stanines (short for 'standard nine') and the digits '1' to '9' are used as category labels. The mean lies approximately in the centre of the fifth interval. Table 9.1 shows the relationship between stanines and percentile ranks.

Table 9.1   Relationship between stanines and percentile ranks

Description of achievement	Stanine	Percentile rank	Percentage of learners
Very high	9	96 and above	4
High	8	89–96	7
Above average	7	77–89	12
Average	6	60–77	17
Average	5	40–60	20
Average	4	23–40	17
Below average	3	11–23	12
Low	2	4–11	7
Very low	1	0–4	4

Confidence band

A so-called 'confidence band' is the range of scores within which we can be confident that the accurate assessment of attainment is likely to fall. (Tests of the sort discussed here measure attainment, that is, the level achieved by a learner in a given area, for example spelling, mathematics, and so on, at any particular time, not 'ability'.) It is impossible to obtain a perfect measurement of an individual's attainment, that is the hypothetically 'true score'. Errors can be introduced through factors such as the learner's state of mind during the text, tiredness, and so on, regardless of how carefully assessment tests are devised and administered.

'Reading age'

'Reading age' is a common term in educational contexts to indicate the age at which the raw score from a reading test is the average. For the sample of learners tested in each age group, the average raw score is worked out and then any irregularities are smoothed out in the graph that results.

Reading 'ages', however, are not fixed and exact measures of reading attainment. Reading is a learned behaviour that is closely linked to development and age, access to good literacy teaching prior to the assessment, and a measurement of reading age represents a snapshot of a progression in literacy development at a particular point in time. Thus, a child's reading age that is lower than that of peers does not necessarily suggest general low ability. It may be that the learner has had little consistent schooling, for example.

Increases in performance with age are smaller for older age groups. This raises issues for using this measurement with older students, because accuracy and rate of reading would show no improvement beyond a certain point.

LEARNING POINT
ISSUES ASSOCIATED WITH NORM-REFERENCING

Note down your responses to the following:

What do you think are the main advantages to using norm-referenced assessments?

Using such assessments would enable you to compare a learner's outcomes with those of others nationally. You could also use assessments of this sort to see if a learner experiences comparable difficulties across a range of areas in the curriculum. What would you need to assess in this regard?

Are there any disadvantages to norm-referenced assessment in your view?

- How might a young person feel if s/he were always assessed as being right at the bottom in terms of percentile ranking?
- What could you do to support him/her to maintain self-respect and personal motivation in this situation?

What effect might there be on teacher expectations of a young person if his/her test scores always fall in the bottom 'tail' of a normal distribution?

- Does this matter? If so, why?

Assessment of sight

As a general rule, assessment of a child's vision begins very early in UK countries. Eye tests are offered routinely to newborn babies and children to identify any problems early on in their development. Within 72 hours after birth, parents are offered a physical examination of their baby by a health professional, for example a doctor, midwife, nurse or health visitor. At the Newborn and Infant Physical Examination, the professional looks into the baby's eyes with an ophthalmoscope to check their appearance and movement. The appearance and movement of the baby's eyes are checked for cataracts, a clouding of the transparent lens in the eye, and other conditions. The examination cannot identify how well the baby can see. Further checks may be carried out when the child is between 6 and 8 weeks old, between that point and compulsory school age, and on entry to school.

The vision of each eye is recorded separately, as well as both eyes together. It can be difficult to accurately assess vision in very young children, so it can be very helpful to have an idea of 'normal' milestones for the development of a child's vision. A young child can usually:

- at birth, focus on objects 8–10 inches away, but not be able to use both eyes together;
- at 3 months: visually follow moving objects and look around with eyes beginning to work together. 'By twelve weeks the child should be able to move his [sic] eyes in a range of 180 degrees to a moving finger held 20 to 25 cms away from his face' (Dixit, 2006, p. 112);
- at 6 months, turn his/her head to see objects and pick up toys that s/he has dropped;
- at 12 months, point and gesture, judge longer distances, show an interest in pictures, place shapes in frames and follow a rapidly moving toy held in front of him/her without moving his/her head;
- at 18 months, recognise familiar objects, be interested in exploring and scribble with crayons or pens;
- by 2½ to 3, be able to point to a flying bird, moving car or train, and so on.

In the early years, looking at a young child's eyes can offer a lot of information about how s/he sees the world:

- the child may not look at a speaker when s/he speaks;
- the eyes may look unusual, squint or seem sensitive to light;
- the child may rub the eyes, or have an excessive amount of tears;
- s/he may tilt the head to look at something;
- s/he may be excessively clumsy, bump into things and/or have poor balance;
- when looking at something, the eyes should be still and not drift.

Referral to an ophthalmologist or orthoptist if there is a concern about a young child's vision will be able to give some indication of the degree of possible visual impairment.

For young children, a test of vision may be carried out using objects, pictures or symbols. When the child can recognise or match letters, his/her vision is tested using charts with rows of letters and numbers of decreasing sizes. These charts are called Snellen or LogMAR charts.

The most well-known chart used to test sharpness of sight is the Snellen eye chart, originally devised by a Dutch ophthalmologist, Dr Hermann Snellen, in 1862. The Snellen chart displays rows of letters or letters and numbers, the biggest at the top, becoming smaller as the child reads down the chart. Other versions are available to test the sight of children who cannot read the alphabet.

More recently, the LogMAR chart has been introduced to test eyesight. This is described by the Royal College of Ophthalmologists (2015) as 'more accurate than other acuity charts' and is therefore now quite commonly used in eye clinics. A comparison between Snellen and LogMAR charts is available at www.rcophth.ac.uk/wp-content/uploads/2015/11/LogMAR-vs-Snellen.pdf (accessed 28.10.2021).

Measures of visual acuity, such as Snellen and LogMAR, relate to the recognition of letters or symbols with high contrast, but tell us nothing about the quality of vision, for example seeing larger objects and objects with poor contrast, or whether vision is more or less efficient when using both eyes together (Strouse Watt, 2003).

The International Statistical Classification of Diseases, ICD-11 (World Health Organization, 2019, available at https://icd.who.int/browse11/l-m/en#/http://id.who.int/icd/entity/1103667651) classifies vision impairment into two groups: distance and near presenting vision impairment. It is important to recognise here that the point of reference is what a person with normal vision can read at a distance of 6 metres, so 6/6 means having the ability to see fine detail from a distance of 6 metres as well as people with normal vision.

Distance vision impairment:

* Mild – visual acuity worse than 6/12. The learner can read at 6 metres or less what a normally-sighted person can read at 12 metres.
* Moderate – visual acuity worse than 6/18. The learner can read at 6 metres or less what a normally-sighted person can read at 18 metres.
* Severe – visual acuity worse than 6/60. The learner can read at 6 metres or less what a normally-sighted person can read at 60 metres.
* Blindness – visual acuity worse than 3/60. The learner can read at 3 metres or less what a normally-sighted person can read at 60 metres.

Near vision impairment:

* Near visual acuity worse than N6 or N8 at 40 cm with existing correction. Near vision is measured using a small handheld chart that has paragraphs of text that is smallest at the top and largest at the bottom. These are of a standard size and 'normal' near vision is known as N6, with 'N' referring to near and the '6' referring to the size of the letters; N5 is better than N8, for example.

Children with the same eye condition may have very different strengths and needs from each other, with different interests, background experiences, and so on, as well as differing degrees of useful vision (Miller & Ockleford, 2005). A whole range of information is therefore needed to ensure that support for a young child is appropriate, including the views of the learner and the parents/family, medical and school records as well as the clinical assessment of vision.

Assessment of hearing

There is a variety of tests that can be used to find out how much hearing a child has. The tests used will depend on the child's age and stage of development. 'One to two babies in every 1,000 are born with a hearing loss in one or both ears' (Blairmires et al., 2016). It is possible to test the hearing of all children from birth onwards. Babies 'begin to develop language and communication from their earliest months', so early screening means that 'much can be done to positively support and encourage that development [...] when early identification of deafness is combined with effective early intervention, with parents and professionals working together, language outcomes for deaf children can be similar to those for hearing children' (NDCS, 2015a, p. 6). Since 2006, babies have been screened to test their hearing within a few days of their birth.

Two screening tests are carried out soon after birth. The first one tests for Oto-Acoustic Emissions. It involves putting an earpiece in the baby's ear with a microphone and speaker that emits a clicking sound. A properly functioning cochlea will produce a response that the earpiece picks up. The second tests Auditory Brainstem Response, that is, that sound received by the cochlea is transmitted as a signal through the auditory nerve to the brain. Headphones are placed on the baby's head, and sensors on the ears. If, following the screening tests, the decision is taken that hearing aids will be needed, the audiologists will inform a range of services, including, possibly, Education and Speech Therapy, so that ongoing advice and support can be given to the family. Pre-school teachers of the deaf may offer the family advice about options relating to modes of communication. This may include the offer of tuition in signed communication, the management of hearing aids or cochlear implants, where used at home and in Early Years settings. They may also provide support to the family, including liaison with other professionals that may include social services, speech and language therapists, Children's Centres and audiology clinics.

For children of school age, hearing is usually measured with behavioural tests using pure tones. The sounds come through headphones and each time a child hears a sound they respond by moving an object, pressing a button or saying 'yes'.

Quantification of hearing loss

A decibel (dB) is a measure of sound pressure level. Normal voice measures 60 dB at a distance of one metre, a raised voice 70 dB at one metre, and shouting 80 dB at one metre. The severity of a hearing impairment is measured in decibels of hearing loss and is ranked according to the additional intensity above a nominal threshold that a sound must be before being detected by an individual.

Four categories of hearing impairment are generally used: mild, moderate, severe and profound. As noted by the National Deaf Children's Society (2020):

- with 'mild deafness: 21–40 dB' a learner could hear a baby crying but not necessarily whispered conversation;
- with 'moderate deafness: 41–70 dB', a learner could hear a dog barking but may have difficulty following speech without a hearing aid;
- with 'severe deafness: 71–95 dB', a learner would hear drums playing but even with the use of a hearing aid would usually need to lip-read or use sign language;

- with 'profound deafness: >95 dB', a learner might hear a large lorry but not drums playing. Even 'with cochlear implants or hearing aids the child may require additional communication support (for example through sign language or cued speech) to access speech, especially within background noise or within a group conversation' (NDCS, 2015b, p. 65).

Deaf children with the same level of deafness may experience sounds differently. About 20% of primary age children suffer from conductive hearing loss caused by middle-ear problems; this reduces to 2% by secondary age.

Observation

Observation is a method that can be useful in assessment of learning and behaviour. Of course, observing children in the environment of the classroom or school is something that is a part of teachers' everyday practice. As Sharp (2009, p. 83) notes:

> Observation is used in education if the purpose is to capture something of the dynamics and complexities of particular activities and events as they unfold right before your very eyes.

It should be systematic and carefully planned so that it enables an effective means of recording and provides a reliable evidence base for interpreting the degree to which learning and/or behaviour are problematic. Direct observation can be particularly useful to find out whether people do what they say they do, or behave in the way they claim to behave.

Observation is not an easy option – it requires careful organisation and practice. Nonetheless, it can reveal characteristics of groups or individuals which would have been impossible to discover by other means (Bell, 2010).

There are a number of different formats that may be adopted. The first step is to make decisions about exactly *what* the focus will be: people, activities or events, or a combination of these; the behaviour of an individual, a group or a whole class; or specific situations such as lessons or playground activities. Choice of time frames is important, for example a sample of what goes on during short predetermined time periods, or a whole day spent shadowing one individual. Another choice to be made is who will carry out the observation. For a member of staff working in his/her own institution, it might be difficult to maintain a detached, non-participant stance, and the observer may find him/herself drawn into what is going on despite their best intentions. On the other hand, making notes while engaged in the hurly-burly of classroom activity brings its own problems. Whichever choice is made, it is also important to the effect the observer might have on the activity or behaviour s/he is observing.

In summary, in all observation studies, the observer should be constantly aware of the need to be clear about the choices that have been made and the reasons underlying the decisions. S/he will be selecting the events that are noted and making interpretations of what is seen. This will inevitably involve some personal judgements, and there is the danger that the observer might not be impartial or could be influenced by his/her own assumptions or preferences.

Time and interval sampling

In order to collect evidence of a young person's learning and behaviour that might be viewed as typical of him/her, it is possible to use time and interval sampling. 'Observation schedules' can be designed to include particular events or behaviours. Time sampling means observing for a set number of seconds. Within a predetermined interval, such as every 20 or 30 seconds, the teacher records the number of times a behaviour has been observed during that time period. The assumption here is that, if a recording is made regularly and systematically, it will represent what the student's learning or behaviour patterns are like, generally.

Time and interval sampling can be carried out across different lessons and in different contexts. Decisions about the practical aspects of it will, to a large extent, be dictated by the kinds of concerns raised in relation to the learning and behaviour of individual students, the discussion that has already taken place in relation to what is already known about the learner, and the context for the observations.

Using checklists

Pre-set lists of behaviours can be used as checklists against which the frequency and seriousness of incidents of behaviour can be assessed in different contexts. A checklist might have a range of scores next to each behaviour, so that a score can be given against each one as a baseline. Teachers' scores of the behaviour of the same learner might be compared to analyse whether the behaviour is different or the same in different contexts. Alternatively, the same learner's behaviours can be scored at a later date to see whether the teacher's perception is that the behaviour has improved or deteriorated. It has to be said, however, that the reliability of any kind of checklist is open to personal interpretation or the influence of the learning environment, and so on.

Web activity WA9.2
Appropriate use of behaviour checklists

We have uploaded an example of a behaviour checklist with an invitation to adapt this to suit your circumstances. You might choose to access this now.

Assessment of communication difficulties

For some learners, difficulties in receptive and expressive language, both spoken and written, sensory impairment, and making relationships might make meaningful discussion problematic. Communication with some young people with profound and multiple learning disabilities can mean careful observation and interpretation of reflexes, actions, sounds and facial expression by those who know them the best (Porter et al., 2001). Inflexible thought processes, lack of personal insight and dislike of change may inhibit some autistic children from participating in meaningful discussion (Preece, 2002). A variety of useful tools have been developed to elicit the views of learners who have difficulty in expressing themselves verbally but understand what is happening around them, for example cue cards (Lewis, 2002, p. 114) that can act 'as prompts for ideas about […] people, talk, setting (indoor/outdoor variants), feelings and consequences about the particular event under discussion […], and "Talking Mats"' (Cameron & Murphy, 2002) that support learners to express their views by moving symbols about on mats. 'Talking Mats' is described as

> a social enterprise whose vision is to improve the lives of people with communication difficulties by increasing their capacity to communicate effectively about things that matter to them. Our […] communication tool is based on extensive research and was designed by Speech and Language Therapists. (www.talkingmats.com/, accessed 28.10.2021)

Material on the website (www.talkingmats.com/projects/) describes how the technique has been used in a range of contexts and situations.

Assessment of autism

The American DSM criteria are very influential and form the basis, for example, of the Autism Diagnostic Observation Schedule (ADOS) that is used in some local authorities in the UK as a diagnostic tool. However, the DSM is an American publication. Many assessments of autism spectrum disorders in the UK are based on *The International Statistical Classification of Diseases* (ICD), published by the World Health Organization. In the most recent version, the ICD-11 (WHO, 2019, 6A02), autism is described as 'persistent deficits in the ability to initiate and to sustain reciprocal social interaction and social communication' and also as a 'range of restricted, repetitive, and inflexible patterns of behaviour and interests'. So-called 'deficits' are described as 'sufficiently severe to cause impairment' in everyday living, including in educational, family and work contexts, and are usually a 'pervasive feature' of the individual's behaviour that is 'observable in all settings'.

LEARNING POINT
CONSIDERATION OF FORMAL ASSESSMENT TOOLS

Assessment of children using the profiles outlined above can be critiqued on a number of grounds. Two, for example, relate to subjectivity and lack of specificity in interpretation, and to the potential demoralising effects of behaviour associated with autism described as a 'disorder' or a 'deficit'.

Please consider the views of the authors below and reflect on the following questions:

- From what you have read in the outline of the assessment instruments, how clearly might you be able to relate the elements to children you teach and/or whom you know well?
- How useful to you in informing you how to support an autistic child is the term 'disorder' in describing autistic behaviour?

(Continued)

Grandin and Panek (2013, pp. 4–5), for example, comment on subjectivity in assessment:

> […] autism can't be diagnosed in the laboratory […] Instead, as with many psychiatric syndromes […] autism is identified by observing and evaluating behaviors. Those observations and evaluations are subjective, and the behaviors vary from person to person. The diagnosis can be confusing, and it can be vague. It has changed over the years, and it continues to change.

Linked to the issues of vagueness and subjectivity, it can be difficult, as Sheehy (2004) notes, to separate out the effects of autism from those of profound difficulties in learning, given that 80% of children with autism score below 70 on norm-referenced intelligence tests (Peeters & Gilberg, 1999). Increasingly, severe general learning difficulties are correlated with an increasing occurrence of autism (Jordan, 1999).

Smith (2019, p. 192), writing from her own experience, comments on some of the negative consequences of formal identification of autism as a disorder:

> many families may well not recognise their children in professionals' descriptions of them as 'disordered', and in formal lists of 'symptoms' and characteristics of autistic behaviour. Use of descriptors such as these may well be experienced as highly negative and damaging to a child and to a family's sense of self-worth, and not at all helpful in considering how most sensitively and effectively to address the developmental needs of an autistic child. Out of such terminology and lists may emerge a stereotype of autism that masks the individuality and humanity of the child so labelled, creates a sense of 'otherness' and distances the child from peers and families from professionals.

What do you think?

It is useful to be aware of formal profiles that may be used to identify a young person as autistic, but for a practitioner or family member a less formal way may be more helpful. The National Institute for Health and Care Excellence (NICE) (2017) has provided three 'Signs and symptoms' tables for use with pre-school, primary and secondary-aged children in Appendix 3 of its publication *Autism in under 19s: Recognition, Referral and Diagnosis*. These are available at www.nice.org.uk/guidance/cg128/resources (accessed 20.03.2021). These tables 'are not intended to be used alone, but to help professionals recognise a pattern of impairments in reciprocal social and communication skills, together with unusual restricted and repetitive behaviours' (Appendix-C). NICE has also produced a set of scenarios, *Autism: Recognition, Referral and Diagnosis of Children and Young People on the Autism Spectrum*, to assist professionals 'to improve and assess users' knowledge of the recognition, referral and diagnosis of autism in children and young people' (NICE, 2011, p. 4). It is available at www.nice.org.uk/guidance/cg128/resources/clinical-case-scenarios-183180493 (accessed 28.10.2021). In it NICE gives advice in relation to each of the young people whose experiences are described here. We cannot stress too much, however, that the material provided here is not intended as a substitute for identification of autism and advice and guidance about individual learners' needs from fully-qualified professionals where the issue has reached a very serious level of concern.

Assessment of attention deficit/hyperactivity disorder

Attention deficit/hyperactivity disorder (ADHD) is characterised by hyperactivity, impulsivity and inattention, which are judged excessive for the age or level of overall development of the individual. Indicators should be apparent in early life (NICE, 2018).

LEARNING POINT
IDENTIFYING SIGNS OF AD/HD

NICE (2019) offers very useful information for teachers and others on identifying AD/HD. See www.nice.org.uk/guidance/ng87/chapter/Recommendations#recognition-identification-and-referral (accessed 28.10.2021). You might choose to access this now.

How useful do you find this material in your own context?

Recognising dyslexia

It is really important for families, teachers, learners themselves and others to be able to recognise barriers to learners that may indicate the possibility of dyslexia.

Case study: Initial screening for dyslexia

In Chapter 6 we discussed dyslexia and specific difficulties in learning. 'Jason' arrived at his secondary school depressed, frustrated and very angry. He was very articulate in conversation with his friends and, after a while, with the special educational needs co-ordinator (SENCo), but unable to translate his cognitive ability into achievement in reading and written tasks. He was blind in one eye, and in a previous school had been assessed as experiencing difficulties in learning as a result of his sight impairment. However, in his new school, in discussion with Jason and his parents, the SENCo decided to carry out an informal assessment as a first step to assess whether he experienced any barriers to his learning that are indicative of dyslexia.

In discussion with other members of staff, she accessed his written work across a range of curriculum areas, which confirmed that there was an obvious gap between his written work and his oral skill. His ability to express his thoughts aloud was much better than his writing, which had many crossings out, with letters out of order and often confused in orientation: b/d, p/g, m/w. When he tried to copy from the board, he was slow, and often wrong. His reading accuracy, expression, rhythm and tone were poor, and his comprehension of text was much better than reading it aloud accurately. Beyond literacy learning, he experienced other

(Continued)

difficulties: planning his work, left/right directionality, rapid discrimination of sounds, fine and gross motor co-ordination, and excessive tiredness because of the barriers to learning he faced.

The next step for the SENCo was to put immediate plans in place to support his literacy acquisition and share with other staff members the outcome of the informal assessment so that they could differentiate appropriately for him in the classroom, and to involve Jason and his family in the plans that were being made.

There is a positive ending to this narrative. Some time later, when the school could demonstrate that it had made appropriate arrangements for Jason using its own resources but that he still needed special provision to meet his needs, dyslexia was formally identified by the Educational Psychologist and the local authority funded special provision for him, including access to a specialist support teacher. When he left the school, it was to go to university to study for a degree.

Have a look at the list of indicators above. How useful might you find this as an initial screen for possible dyslexia?

The NHS (2018) has published a useful discussion of ways to identify possible dyslexic difficulties on its website. This is available at: https://www.nhs.uk/conditions/dyslexia/diagnosis/

You might choose to access this material now.

Access arrangements and reasonable adjustments

Under the terms of the 2010 Equality Act, in order to support their young people with disabilities to access the curriculum, including examinations, schools and colleges are required to make 'reasonable adjustments'. In this particular case, difficulties in learning, including dyslexia, may constitute such a disability for which reasonable adjustment should be made. All schools and colleges now have to have specialist assessors to assess difficulties and disabilities in order to make the case for access arrangements. Such assessors may be qualified members of their own staff, or external professionals who carry out the assessments (Joint Council for Qualifications (JCQ), 2021). There is also a legal duty placed on awarding bodies not to discriminate against disabled candidates during examinations.

In order to evaluate whether a young person has a significant level of difficulty in learning or a substantial impairment, it is common to use a battery of tests to assess young people's literacy levels, numeracy skills and cognitive ability, using assessments of reading, spelling, mathematical, verbal and non-verbal skills. Formal assessment made of the barriers to learning experienced by disabled students or those with special educational needs should be valid and reliable so that adjustments made for individuals can be seen as a fair way to enable access to examinations. This means that assessors must understand the rationale underpinning norm-referenced tests, be thoroughly familiar with test procedures, and able to interpret the outcomes.

Adjustments will not be approved as 'reasonable' if they are overly costly to the awarding body, require unreasonable timeframes or undermine the 'security and integrity' of the examination. It would not be reasonable to adjust assessment objectives within a particular qualification. The JCQ (2021, chapter 5) lists useful examples of reasonable adjustments for disabled candidates. Some of the most common are 25% or more additional time, use of a computer reader or reader, candidates reading the paper aloud to themselves, or use of a reading pen, use of a scribe or speech recognition technology, use of word processors, and other adjustments that may be considered 'reasonable' in particular circumstances and for particular disabled students.

It must be stated very clearly, however, that evidence of the disability is not sufficient to make the case for reasonable adjustments for disabled students. Also required is evidence of the normal/usual way of working within the candidate's educational institution.

Planning to meet identified needs

Where, despite effective differentiated teaching and inclusive approaches in the classroom, learners continue to make inadequate progress, current legislation across the UK refers to individual plans for recording the nature of a student's difficulties and how they are going to be addressed. Across the UK also, as discussed below, it is expected that both families and learners will be actively involved in creating and assessing the effectiveness of the individual plan.

LEARNING POINT
EFFECTIVENESS OF PLANNING TO MEET INDIVIDUAL NEEDS

Guidance given in *The Code of Practice* (Department for Education/Department of Health (DfE/DoH), 2015) was written for the English context, but broadly reflects what might be considered good practice generally. Now look at the description below. Consider the extent to which you might use this guidance as a template against which you might evaluate your own practice in planning provision for individuals. Might you need to make amendments to this guidance to suit your own national context? If so, what are these?

The *Code* suggests that individual plans should be 'crisply written' and record 'only that which is additional to or different from the differentiated curriculum plan that is in place as part of normal provision'. It should contain:

- information about the short-term targets, which should be three or four in number;
- 'the teaching strategies and the provision to be put in place';
- 'when the plan is to be reviewed';
- 'the outcome of the action taken'.

Effective planning, as outlined in the *Code*, is that which:

- focuses on the child or young person as an individual, not the SEN label;
- uses clear ordinary language and images, not professional jargon, so is easy for children, young people and their parents to understand;
- highlight the young person's strengths;
- enables the young person, and his/her family to say what they have done, what they are interested in and what outcomes they are seeking in the future;
- tailors support to the needs of the individual;
- organises assessments to minimise demands on families;
- brings together professionals to agree overall approach.

(Continued)

The class teacher, SENCo, any teaching assistants, the student, parents/carers, and outside agencies, if appropriate, should all be involved in the planning process. It is imperative, for example, that:

- teachers work closely with TAs or specialist staff to plan and assess the impact of targeted interventions;
- planning and review time is explicitly planned for and regularly takes place;
- there is joint planning time with support staff, which might necessitate
  - paying support staff to join planning/department meetings
  - quick and concise communication tools to convey outcomes of targeted provision
  - targeted provision work carried out in pupil's class/subject books so teachers can see what work has been carried out and to what standard and pick up emerging issues.

The effectiveness/impact of support should be reviewed in line with the agreed date so that:

- impact on progress and pupil's/parents' views feed back into the analysis of the young person's needs;
- the SENCo and teacher revise support in light of progress;
- involvement of external specialists is considered where the young person *continues* to make little progress. This involvement should be shared with parents and recorded.

Statutory advice in the *Code* advises that the teacher and SENCo should negotiate with parents and the student and agree:

- interventions and support, together with expected impact on progress;
- a date for review.

The plan should then be recorded on the school's information system.

Taking account of learners' views

The right to be heard constitutes a human right. The UK signed up to the United Nations' *Convention on the Rights of the Child* (UNCRC) (UNICEF, 1989, https://downloads.unicef.org.uk/wp-content/uploads/2010/05/UNCRC_united_nations_convention_on_the_rights_of_the_child.pdf) in 1990. This is a legally-binding international document that sets out a number of rights of every child: civil, political, economic, social and cultural, irrespective of race, religion or ability. Legislation across the UK requires young people's views to be taken into account when needs are assessed and learning or behaviour plans are developed. However, the importance of listening to what young people have to say has significance beyond solely the law. It is crucial also in terms of the way we understand the learning process.

LEARNING POINT
LINKING LEARNERS' SELF-ADVOCACY TO
UNDERSTANDINGS OF THE LEARNING PROCESS

In Chapter 2 we discussed a number of ways of understanding human learning. You might like to look back at the sections on 'Constructivist approaches' and consider how this applies to listening to learners' views of themselves and their learning in practice.

Young people are active agents in constructing their own understandings, so, if we are to support them, we need to try to understand how they feel about barriers to their learning, behaviour, motor skills, or in any other area in which they experience difficulties, and what they know will assist them most effectively. How learners make sense of their own situation, the impression that is conveyed of others' views of them, how they understand their worlds, their experiences, tasks in classrooms, and so on, is fundamentally important. It may well be problematic for teachers to support learning through the zone of proximal development if they do not pay attention to what young people say, how they react to things and what they do. Eliciting students' views requires professionals to have very finely-tuned listening skills and demonstrate non-judgemental responses in order to create a space in which young people feel safe to talk about themselves, their difficulties, and so on. 'Children will make decisions about people they can talk to and trust, and those they cannot' (Gersch, 1995, p. 48).

Web activity WA9.3
Using 'Talking Stones' to elicit learners' views

On the website we have uploaded a description of the use of a projective interview technique, 'Talking Stones', as a strategy to help learners talk about problematic relationships and situations as they see them (Wearmouth, 2004b). This is a technique not to be used lightly. As with any other personal conversations with learners, there are issues of safety and confidentiality to be considered. We would advise you to take close account of the safeguarding procedures in your own place of work. Once a student has begun to disclose personal information, it may be difficult for an inexperienced teacher-interviewer to bring about closure in a way that leaves the student in a frame of mind sufficiently comfortable to return to regular classroom activities. Sometimes also, as with other conversations of a personal kind, when abuse or other information is disclosed, it may need to be referred to the safeguarding officer in the setting, school or college. What do you think?

Engaging with parents and/or carers

Parents' and/or carers' entitlements to be consulted when decisions are taken about their children are enshrined in law across the UK. A number of guides for parents and carers have been published to enable families to understand their rights, for example *The Parents' Guide to Additional Support for Learning* (Enquire, 2014), which is funded by the Scottish government, and the *Special Educational Needs and Disability (SEND) – A Guide for Parents and Carers* (DfE, 2014d), published in England.

Although parents and families have a legal entitlement to be involved actively, levels of confidence in this process may be very different between families. Not all are comfortable in formal educational contexts, especially if their own educational experiences were problematic.

Web activity WA9.4
Factors affecting home–school partnerships

On the website we have uploaded principles agreed by groups of special educational needs co-ordinators as important to take into consideration when working in partnership with families, together with a related activity. You should access this material now.

Statutory assessment of needs

If, despite the process of assessment and planning, a learner fails to make 'adequate progress', then additional special action should be taken. Those who experience extreme longer term or more extreme difficulties may be the subject of statutory assessment.

England: Education, Health and Care Plans

In England, where a learner's degree of educational need is such that it requires a higher level of resourcing than is available from a school or college's special resources, an Education, Health and Care (EHC) Plan might be needed. Local authorities (LAs) have the legal duty to carry out an EHC needs assessment, issue the plan and ensure that the special educational provision that has been specified is made available. An LA has a clear duty to assess a child or young person's education, health and care needs where s/he may have special educational needs and may need special educational provision to be made at a level or of a kind which requires an EHC Plan. An EHC needs assessment can only be requested to assess educational needs, *not* solely health and/or care needs, irrespective of severity.

The test which local authorities must apply in coming to a decision about an EHC Plan is set out in the Children and Families Act 2014 (§37 (1)). Based on the evidence gathered:

(1)   Where, in the light of an EHC needs assessment, it is necessary for special educational provision to be made for a child or young person in accordance with an EHC plan –

(a)   the local authority ***must*** secure that an EHC plan is prepared for the child or young person, and

(b)   once an EHC plan has been prepared, it must maintain the plan.

There are specific requirements for the contents of an EHC Plan. An EHC Plan specifies:

- the child's or young person's special educational needs;
- the outcomes sought for him or her;
- the special educational provision required by him or her;
- any health care provision reasonably required owing to the learning difficulties and disabilities which result in him or her having special educational needs;
- social care provision which is being made for the child/young person under the Chronically Sick and Disabled Persons Act 1970 and any social care provision reasonably required by the learning difficulties and disabilities which result in the child or young person having special educational needs, to the extent that the provision is not already specified in the plan.

If an EHC Plan does not contain all of the sections which are needed, it will not be legally compliant.

Scotland: Co-ordinated Support Plans

In Scotland, statutory provision for learners with additional support needs associated with complex or multiple factors which require a high degree of support from education authorities and other agencies is organised through a 'co-ordinated support plan' (Scottish Government, 2017). The criteria required for a plan are, first, that:

- an education authority is responsible for the school education of the child or young person;
- the child or young person has additional support needs arising from –
  - o one or more complex factors,[1] or
  - o multiple factors.

Then there is a requirement that:

- those needs are likely to continue for more than a year, and
- those needs require significant additional support to be provided –
  - o by the education authority in the exercise of any of their other functions as well as in the exercise of their functions relating to education, or
  - o by one or more appropriate agencies (within the meaning of section 23(2)) as well as by the education authority themselves.

The views of the parents/family, the young person, representatives of relevant agencies and any others who provide support must be sought. There are statutory requirements related to its

---

[1]Factors are interpreted as 'complex' if they have, or are likely to have, 'a significant adverse effect on the school education of the child or young person' (Scottish Government, 2017, p. 77, § 13). Examples given in the *Supporting Children's Learning Code of Practice* of the source of such factors are the learning environment, family circumstances, disability of health, and social and emotional factors.

contents (Additional Support for Learning (Co-ordinated Support Plan) (Scotland) Amendment Regulations 2005) (SSI 2005/518):

- the education authority's conclusions about:
  - o the factor(s) from which the additional support needs arise;
  - o the intended educational objectives;
  - o the additional support required to achieve the objectives.
- details of who should provide this support;
- the name of the school the young person is to attend;
- the details of the person who will co-ordinate the additional support;
- the details of a contact person within the local authority who can offer advice and further information.

There should be a particular focus on positives in a young person's life, and a timetable for a review of the plan.

Parents/families and young people can refer particular matters, for example statutory parts of the plan and prescribed decisions, to the Additional Support Needs Tribunals for Scotland.

Wales: Individual Development Plans

In Wales, the new 'additional learning needs (ALN)' system has introduced a new statutory Individual Development Plan (IDP) to replace existing support plans. All learners with ALN will be entitled to an IDP, irrespective of the complexity of their difficulty in learning or disability. There is a right of appeal to the Education Tribunal for Wales.

Northern Ireland: Statement

In Northern Ireland, formal assessment may result in the issuing of a statutory Statement of Special Educational Needs which is usually drawn up for one of two reasons: access to special resources and expertise, a special curriculum, or an environment with higher than normal staff support that is guaranteed; or to address parental or professionals' wishes that the young person should be educated in a special school, or other form of special provision. A Statement is required to describe the special educational needs, the provision that is needed, the objectives of the provision, the necessary resources, how progress will be monitored, the name of the school, and any identified 'non-educational' needs and provision. The special provision is mandatory, and the school named must admit the learner. Families have a statutory right to be involved in the statementing process, and have a number of legal rights in decision-making. Evidence and advice must be collated from a range of professionals that include the learner's head teacher, a doctor and an educational psychologist.

Conclusion

The principle of equity underpins legislation across the UK: putting in the additional, extra or special resources that are required to enable all learners to access the curriculum and make progress means that clear, systematic, fair assessment of difficulties in the first place is paramount. Both assessment and planning need to take account of the views and experiences of the learners and their families, the interests and strengths of those learners as well as the barriers to learning that have been identified, and also the contexts in which interventions will be put into place. When used thoughtfully and from a well-informed position, assessment, planning and provision can transform the future life chances of individual learners.

As you reflect on what we have discussed in this chapter, what do you consider is the place of assessment in addressing learning and behavioural needs?

How, in your view, can settings, schools and colleges ensure that assessment of needs is appropriate to the individuality of the learners?

In Chapter 10 we address the issue of difficulties in literacy acquisition.

Further reading

Assessment of classroom environments

Fraser, B. J. (1998) Classroom environment instruments: Development, validity and applications. *Learning Environments Research*, 1, 7–34.

Gadsby, C., & Evans, J. (2019) *Dynamically Different Classrooms: Create Spaces that Spark Learning.* Carmarthen: Independent Thinking Press.

Gettinger, M., Schienebeck, C. J., Seigel, S., & Vollmer, L. (2011) Assessment of classroom environments. In M. A. Bray & T. J. Kehle (eds), *The Oxford Handbook of School Psychology* (pp. 260–283). New York: Oxford University Press.

McMillan, J. H. (2013) *Sage Handbook of Research on Classroom Assessment.* London: Sage.

Formative and summative assessment

Black, P., & Wiliam, D. (1998) Assessment and classroom learning. *Assessment in Education: Principles, Policy & Practice*, 5(1), 7–74.

Black, P., & Wiliam, D. (2018) Classroom assessment and pedagogy. *Assessment in Education: Principles, Policy & Practice*, 25(6), 551–575.

National Foundation for Educational Research (NFER) (n/d) *An Introduction to Formative and Summative Assessment.* London: NFER. Available at: www.nfer.ac.uk/for-schools/free-resources-advice/assessment-hub/introduction-to-assessment/an-introduction-to-formative-and-summative-assessment/

Eliciting families' and learners' views

Department for Education (DfE) (2017) *Engaging Parents and Families.* London: DfE. Available at: https://assets.publishing.service.gov.uk/government/uploads/system/uploads/attachment_data/file/634733/Practice_example-Engaging_parents_and_families.pdf

Goodall, J., & Vorhaus, J. (2010) *Review of Best Practice in Parental Engagement.* London: Institute of Education. Available at: https://assets.publishing.service.gov.uk/government/uploads/system/uploads/attachment_data/file/182508/DFE-RR156.pdf

Sartory, E. A. (2014) Eliciting and foregrounding the voices of young people at risk of school exclusion: How does this change schools' perceptions of pupil disaffection? Unpublished doctoral thesis, University of Exeter. Available at: https://core.ac.uk/download/pdf/43093815.pdf

Dyslexia assessment

National Health Service (2018) *Diagnosis: Dyslexia*. Available at: https://www.nhs.uk/conditions/dyslexia/diagnosis/

Phillips, S., & Kelly, K. (2018) *Assessment of Learners with Dyslexic-type Difficulties*. London: Sage.

Reid, G., & Guise, J. (2017) *The Dyslexia Assessment*. London: Bloomsbury.

10

DIFFICULTIES IN LITERACY ACQUISITION

Major questions addressed in this chapter are:

* What is known about how learners acquire literacy?
* How do different theories of literacy acquisition help teachers and others to conceptualise what they can do to support literacy acquisition for these young people who experience difficulties at different ages and stages, and at home?
* In which ways can families and community members support the literacy acquisition of those who experience difficulties?

Key terms

Decoding, phonics, motivation, cultural issues, paired and shared reading, comprehension, spelling, planning writing

Introduction

To participate fully in society, it is important to be literate. Literacy is part of our 'cultural toolkit' (Bruner, 1996). Human action is mediated by tools and signs – 'semiotics'. This includes language, writing, and all sorts of conventional signs (Vygotsky, 1981).

> These semiotic means are both the tools that facilitate the co-construction of knowledge and the means that are internalised to aid future independent problem-solving activity. (Palincsar, 1998, p. 353)

In settings, schools and colleges, being able to handle written text competently and confidently is a key part of meeting the day-to-day expectations of classroom life. As the OECD (2016, p. 5) notes:

> The ability to locate, access, understand and reflect on all kinds of information is essential if individuals are to be able to participate fully in our knowledge-based society. Achievement in reading literacy is not only a foundation for achievement in other subject areas within the educational system, but also a prerequisite for successful participation in most areas of adult life.

Most conceptualisations of what comprises 'reading skills' are as a composite primarily of two cognitive skills: technical (decoding and syntactic) and comprehension (Clark & Teravainen, 2017). Many of us who have taught children to read might argue that the process of reading is more complex than a simple reduction to the acquisition of these sets of skills, however.

LEARNING POINT
REFLECTING ON PERSONAL EXPERIENCES
OF LEARNING TO READ

Take a few minutes to reflect on the following questions:

- What memories do you have of learning to read yourself?
- What kinds of texts were you given in the early days?
- What helped you to learn to read?
- Did anything stand in the way? If so, what was it?
- How much did you enjoy reading?
- How important is enjoyment in reading important for learners, do you think?

These days many recognise the importance of other factors also. For example, the OECD (2016, p. 7) interprets reading more widely than a composite of technical skills:

> Changes in our concept of reading since 2000 have led to an expanded definition of reading literacy, which recognises motivational and behavioural characteristics of reading alongside cognitive characteristics.

Expanding on this point, Clark and Teravainen (2017) explain that, in addition to the two cognitive skills, 'reading' should also be seen to include affective processes (enjoyment, motivation, positive attitude, confidence and personal identity as a reader) and behaviours (frequency and breadth of reading, and ability to self-monitor). Learners who enjoy reading and are motivated to read, read more often and have higher reading scores (Clark & Teravainen, 2017). We might also assume that enjoyment, motivation and frequency of practice apply to writing achievement also.

In the text below, we first discuss the technical (decoding) and comprehension skills involved in reading and ways to approach the teaching of learners who experience difficulties that takes account of the individuality and diversity of learners. We then turn to issues of enjoyment, confidence and engagement in learning to read. Subsequently, we consider writing, as product or process, and ways to support technical skills as well as confidence. Finally, we offer examples of classrooms where learners' positive identities as readers and writers have been encouraged.

Understanding literacy acquisition

There is no programme that is uniquely positioned to support literacy acquisition (Bond & Dykstra, 1967; Adams, 1994). There are different understandings of the process of reading and writing that influence understandings of what constitutes 'best practice' for all learners as well as which programmes will support those who experience literacy difficulties most effectively. In addition, interventions need to take account of individual differences in any one aspect of the process of reading, interpreting and writing text, or all of these.

Models of the reading process

As we noted above, conventionally reading has been seen as composed primarily of two cognitive skills: technical (decoding and syntactic) and comprehension (a search for meaning).

Reading as decoding

The view of reading primarily as decoding is sometimes called 'bottom-up'. This means starting with the details, that is the letters, and working upwards to form an understanding of the whole text. From this perspective, reading comprises the process of decoding the abstract and complicated alphabetic code, identifying symbols with sounds, combining the sounds into words and phrases, and reconstructing the author's meaning (Adams, 1994). First the letters of the alphabet and the principles of sound–symbol identification must be learnt, and then this should be applied to decode words and then to text in order to read.

Teaching about the association between sounds and letter symbols in written language is often referred to as a phonics approach. The idea that letters represent the sounds of spoken language is an abstract concept that some children find it difficult to grasp.

A phoneme is the smallest unit of sound in a word. Phonemic awareness refers to spoken language. It is the ability to identify and think about individual sounds in spoken words, for example identifying and repeating the first and last sounds in words, blending individual sounds into words, /t/a/p/ tap, segmenting a word into its phonemes (separate sounds).

From a bottom-up view, beginning with the detail of the letter sounds and combining them into whole words and texts, it seems clear that children who cannot hear or manipulate the phonemes in spoken words are likely to experience difficulty learning how to relate these phonemes to letters when they see them in written words. Learners identified as poor readers are often weaker in phonemic awareness than competent readers (Stanovich, 2000).

Phonological knowledge usually includes larger segments of speech, for example words, syllables, onset (the beginning of a word) and rime (the cluster of letters that comes after the initial sound of a one-syllable word). Many learners with difficulty in literacy acquisition also have difficulties in phonological processing (Stanovich, 2000). It is important that learners develop this knowledge early on through, for example, repeated exposure to rhymes, songs, shared books, poems, and so on that can encourage interest and enjoyment in language and literature.

The implication of a bottom-up approach is to emphasise frequent practice with the learning of phonics, common letter blends and digraphs, spelling of whole words and word families, and attention to every letter in left-to-right order in words (Adams, 1994).

Teaching phonics

There are two main approaches to phonics teaching, synthetic and analytic phonics, and it is important for teachers and others to understand the difference between them. In synthetic phonics, the pronunciation of the word is worked out through sounding and blending. In analytic phonics, children analyse letters sounds after the whole word has been recognised.

Synthetic phonics

In synthetic phonics, letter–sound correspondences are taught in isolation and then learners blend individual letters together to form whole words. At the start of schooling, children are taught a small group of letter sounds, for example 'a', 'i', 'n', 'p', 's' and 't', which make up more three-letter words than any other six letters, and then shown how these can be blended to pronounce words. Other groups of letters are then taught and the children blend them in order to pronounce new words.

Multi-sensory teaching approaches

Particularly where learners experience difficulty in acquiring phonic knowledge, one way to reinforce links between sounds and symbols is to take a multi-sensory approach to teaching. Multi-sensory approaches utilise two or more modalities simultaneously: auditory, visual, kinesthetic and tactile. When teaching letter sounds, the teacher might integrate hearing, sight and motor movement by encouraging learners to make the sound out loud while writing the letter(s) at the same time. The intention is that the memory of the motor movement will integrate with the sound and look of the letters, that is their auditory and visual representation.

Many commercially-produced reading programmes now incorporate multi-sensory teaching. Just to take one example, 'Toe by Toe' (Cowling & Cowling, 1993) is designed to develop decoding skills and phonological processing using a multi-sensory approach.

As Ehri (2002) comments, a significant amount of research indicates that explicit teaching of the alphabetical code can result in improved reading accuracy. However, whether the gains are generalised to word recognition, writing vocabulary, text reading and reading comprehension is less certain. Many advocate instead teaching phonics in the context of reading and writing whole words; in other words, using an analytic phonics approach.

Analytic phonics

Analytic phonics involves the analysis of consonants, vowels, blends, diagraphs and diphthongs within whole words. Teaching involves pointing out English spelling patterns in real words. Typically, children are taught one letter sound per week and shown pictures and words beginning with that sound. Then they are introduced to letter sounds in the middle of words, and so on. Some educators consider that specific exercises are unnecessary because learners acquire this information incidentally as they are exposed to text-rich environments and real texts.

Many of us would agree that teaching beginning readers phonics is very important. However, there is a strong argument for suggesting sensitivity to the individuality of the learner and his/her prior experiences here. When learners experience difficulty in reading acquisition, it is really important to find a way to maintain their engagement, interest and belief in themselves as able to achieve. Depending on their age, interests and prior experiences in the classroom, exposure to phonics, phonics and more phonics to the exclusion of other techniques may be experienced by students as boring and demoralising (Wearmouth, 2004a). For older students, for example, there were occasions when the current author, as a teacher, turned to a 'whole-book' approach (see below) with the choice of reading materials designed to match the learners' interests for the sake of re-igniting their interest in literacy learning, left aside phonics for a while and returned to teaching phonics at a later date.

Reading for meaning

The second approach, that is sometimes called 'top-down', sees reading as the active *construction* of meaning. Top-down processing means working from a general understanding of a passage and then working down to more detailed information to check things out, often known as the 'psycholinguistic guessing game' (Goodman, 1996). From this perspective, there is an assumption that the reader has expectations of what a text might be about that s/he then tests as s/he reads, and confirms or rejects the expectations as s/he proceeds.

LEARNING POINT
REFLECTING ON PSYCHOLINGUISTIC
UNDERSTANDINGS OF THE PROCESS OF READING

It is really important to be aware of, and to recognise, different understandings of the reading process so that we can provide learners with a balanced approach and highlight one or other of these at different points to engage learners' interests and meet their needs in reading acquisition. Read the description of a psycholinguistic approach below. How far, from your own experience of teaching learners to read, do you concur with Goodman's view?

(Continued)

Goodman (1996, pp. 110–111) describes psycholinguistics as follows: '[…] as we read, our minds are actively busy making sense of print, just as they are always actively trying to make sense of the world. Our minds have a repertoire of strategies for sense-making. In reading, we can call these psycholinguistic because there's continuous interaction between thought and language.'

He goes on to say that everything readers do is part of their attempt to make sense and construct meaning out of print. It is not necessary to pay attention to every single part of every word to read a text. Do you agree with this? 'Readers become highly efficient in using just enough of the available information to accomplish their purpose of making sense' (Goodman, 1996, p. 91).

Given this assumption, that readers do not need to scrutinise every detail of every word to be able to read, Goodman is highly critical of phonics instruction for children who experience difficulties in literacy acquisition. He says: '[…] much misunderstanding still exists about reading and written language in general. I believe that this confusion exists largely because people have started in the wrong place, with letters, letter–sound relationships and words. We must begin instead by looking at reading in the real world, at how readers and writers try to make sense with each other' (Goodman, 1996, pp. 2–3).

There is a view of current approaches to teaching reading in the UK that there is too much emphasis on phonics. What do you think about this? Can we find a way to teach phonics that will interest and engage learners?

The psycholinguistic understanding has been associated with the whole-book approach to teaching children to read through reading. There are many examples of reading programmes of this sort. In the UK context, for example, Waterland, an infant teacher, disillusioned with what she called 'feeding the cuckoo method', developed the 'Apprenticeship Approach' (Waterland, 1985) that operated from an assumption that reading may be learned by young children working like apprentices learning to read from real books alongside competent readers. This approach emphasised meaning and enjoyment. Later it was refined as Paired Reading (Topping, 1995) (see below).

'Interactive' approach

A further teaching approach is the 'interactive' model which assumes that readers use bottom-up and top-down information simultaneously. For example, identification of sounds with symbols interacts with the reader's anticipation of what the word is likely to be from the context of the text, and the outcome is the construction of meaning – in other words, reading. This interactive approach assumes 'a complex, multifaceted activity' which requires 'broad-based instruction':

Children need to learn processing skills, using context and knowledge of syntax to focus on the general meaning of the whole, and also decoding skills focusing on individual letters and words. They need specific teaching of both 'top-down' and 'bottom-up' skills; a certain amount of phonic instruction; careful monitoring in order to give early help to those who make a slow start; interesting meaningful texts; teachers who are enthusiastic about literacy throughout the whole primary range; encouragement from home; and lots of practice. (Wragg et al., 1998, pp. 32–33)

Some readers may rely heavily on visual and auditory cues, others on meaning and context. Readers' difficulties in one area can be compensated by strengths in another. Stanovich (2000) calls this the 'Interactive Compensatory' model. Readers who cannot easily recognise words at a glance, for example, may be able to use context to aid recognition.

Addressing difficulties in reading

There is a very wide range of teaching programmes used to support the reading acquisition of those students who experience difficulties. Careful planning is required to address learning needs within a broad, balanced view of literacy and a global understanding of them as individuals as well as within the context of the school and classroom curriculum within which the plan is to be realised.

Motivation

At the beginning of this chapter, we argued that motivation, positive attitude, confidence and personal identity as a reader are crucial factors in learning to read. 'Self-efficacy' – a sense of 'I can do' – theorists (e.g. Bandura, 1982; Schunk, 1989) stress that, if a learner is to succeed, it is important for her/him to believe that s/he has the ability to perform well. Encouraging pupils to set 'proximal' goals, that is achievable goals within a short time span, for example by indicating the number of tasks to be completed in one lesson, generally leads to higher self-efficacy and greater achievement than setting 'distal' goals, that is end goals, for example, by indicating how many sessions it takes to complete an entire learning programme (Bandura & Schunk, 1981). It has to be stressed, however, that many learners with difficulties in the literacy area will not be able to read, write or spell better simply through trying harder. These students therefore also need strategies to help them improve their literacy level (Palincsar & Brown, 1984).

It is really important that learners know that they have knowledge on which they can draw to understand what they are reading – especially when learners experience difficulties. Learners might be encouraged to ask themselves what they already know, what they want to know, and what they have learnt?

In advance of beginning to read a text, teachers might identify and discuss the vocabulary that may be unfamiliar and/or overview the content of the text.

The comments teachers make about students' learning and performance have also been shown to affect pupil motivation. For example, feedback that sets out specific information about what the learner did well and what could be done differently, and how this could be achieved, as well as comments about how the pupil's current level of achievement compared with past achievement, have been shown to enhance pupils' self-perceptions of success, and to lead to improved levels of achievement when compared to grades or comments that compare pupils with peers.

Respectful acknowledgement of cultural differences

In order to engage the interest of learners who experience difficulties in literacy acquisition, it can be really important to draw on high-quality reading materials, written and illustrated by writers from learners' home communities in a variety of genres. Learners who experience difficulties should have access to a wide range of rich literacy texts and activities. Learners need the chance to talk about what they are reading, and what teachers and peers understand from reading the same text (Glynn, Wearmouth & Berryman, 2006).

When they are very young, children learn to speak and think within their own cultural contexts. Early on, their frames of reference for doing these things come from these contexts. From babyhood, people they know talk to them and talk to each other. There is an important question about how learners can take the step 'from speaking to understanding writing on a page or screen, to realise that knowledge of life and language can help them make sense of words and texts' (Gregory, 1996, p. 95). Orally told stories, rhymes, songs, prayer and routines for meeting and greeting people all have an important role in literacy acquisition and are shared within many cultures long before children begin any form of formal education. In order to support children's motivation and belief in themselves as able to achieve, teachers need to create a means to mediate students' own cultural contexts and the school cultural context (Wearmouth, Berryman & Whittle, 2011; Bishop, Berryman & Wearmouth, 2014). Learners will only engage with a text if they can understand what they are reading. To do this they need prior knowledge and experience. Vygotsky (1962) contends that all mental processes have social origins. The sense of words is rooted in experience with others. From what they hear and see, and how others respond to them, babies actively begin to construct language and to communicate their own ideas with those around them.

In recent years, it has become increasingly obvious that, to enable students in schools from an increasingly diverse range of cultural backgrounds to acquire literacy to a standard that will support them to achieve academically, it is important to adopt teaching approaches that acknowledge, and are responsive to, them as culturally situated. It is obvious, therefore, that when the home cultures of students in any one school vary widely, the tools and frames of reference they appropriate for literacy learning outside the school may well also vary to a significant degree. The degree to which teachers-as-mediators of literacy are sensitive and responsive to students' existing culturally-based literacy-related frames of reference can be highly significant to literacy learning and cognitive achievement (Wearmouth, 2017). To take an extreme example, branded into the memory of the author of this book is her anger and sense of futility when her secondary students in West Cameroon, West Africa, who were taking an English Literature examination paper set by an English university examination board, were faced with an 'unseen' poem that began:

> For days these curious cardboard buds have lain
>
> In brightly coloured boxes. Soon the night
>
> Will come. We pray there'll be no sullen rain
>
> To make these magic orchids flame less bright.

> (https://fromtroublesofthisworld.wordpress.com/tag/for-days-
> these-curious-cardboard-buds-have-lain/, accessed 30.10.2021)

The students were not even given the title of the poem (Scannell's 'Gunpowder Plot') as a cue into what the poem was about. Clearly, the examiners in England had little understanding that the poem might be completely divorced from the prior frames of reference of students brought up in a Cameroonian context. School success is less likely for those whose home cultures provide them with a different set of mediational tools and different concepts of what constitute appropriate texts (Heath, 1983; Moll & Greenberg, 1990; Applebee, 1993) unless teachers create the means to bridge between the home and school (Wearmouth et al., 2011). In order that all students from increasingly diverse cultural backgrounds make progress in their literacy learning, it is essential that schools 'teach to and through the strengths' (Gay, 2010, p. 31) of their students by '[...] using the cultural knowledge, prior experiences, frames of reference, and performance styles of ethnically diverse students to make learning encounters more relevant to and effective for them'.

Support for learners for whom English is an additional language

Students' ability to use spoken language affects the development of all other communication skills. It is especially important to recognise this when students are learning at school in a second language. This situation is faced by many recent immigrants to English-speaking classrooms in different countries. The Education Department of Western Australia (1997) highlights the importance of recognising and responding to the following when teaching children for whom English is a second language:

- the diversity and richness of experience and expertise that children bring to school
- cultural values and practices that may be different from those of the teacher
- that children need to have the freedom to use their own languages and to code-switch when necessary
- that the context and purpose of each activity needs to make sense to the learner
- that learning needs to be supported through talk and collaborative peer interaction
- that the child may need a range of 'scaffolds' to support learning and that the degree of support needed will vary over time, context and decree of content complexity
- that children will need time and support so that they do not feel pressured
- that supportive attitudes of peers may need to be actively fostered
- that it may be difficult to assess children's real achievements and that the active involvement of parents will make a deal of difference, as will on-going monitoring. (Education Department of Western Australia, 1997, pp. 4–5)

Writing from a UK perspective, and from a wealth of experience of supporting children for whom English is an additional language, Gregory (1996, p. 95) poses the question: 'What enables learners to take the step from speaking to understanding writing on a page or screen, to realise that knowledge of life and language can help them make sense of words and texts?' Gregory advocates addressing the issue of building from the known into new literacy acquisition by explicit scaffolding of children's learning through:

- recognising children's existing linguistic skills and cultural knowledge and building these into both teaching content and teaching strategies;

- limiting the size of the reading task by introducing explicitly common new lexis and language 'chunks';
- modelling chunks of language orally and in an idealised way through puppets and/or songs and socio-dramatic play;
- devising home–school reading programmes which recognise the role of both parent and child as mediator of different languages and cultures and which families feel comfortable with. (Gregory, 1996, p. 112)

Encouraging engagement, interest and progress in reading acquisition through collaborative learning

Collaborative learning, peer to peer, can be very powerful in encouraging learners' confidence in themselves as able to learn and achieve in terms of literacy acquisition.

Paired and shared reading

Co-operative learning strategies offer learners opportunities to build relationships and a sense of belonging, as well as provide fun and enjoyable learning experiences (Brown & Thomson, 2000, p. 54) as they model, discuss, share and evaluate their learning as they plan work together, revise, edit each others' work and discuss the content of texts and the process of reading. However, co-operative learning does not just happen. Peer tutoring has been shown to be particularly effective in the teaching of reading, provided the tutor is properly prepared and supported and the pupil is willing to accept such help. Westwood (1997) summarises four essentials of peer tutoring as:

- clear directions as to what they are to do and how they are to do it;
- a specific teaching task to undertake and appropriate instructional materials;
- a demonstration of effective tutoring behaviours; and
- an opportunity to role play or practise tutoring, with feedback and correction.

Peer tutors, too, can be struggling readers themselves, providing their reading competence is at a level higher than that of their tutee. There is ample evidence over a long period (Glynn et al., 2006) that peers can learn to implement responsive and interactive reading and writing tutoring procedures, and that their own reading and writing skills may be enhanced as a result of engaging in interactions with tutee students around shared literacy tasks. More skilled and knowledgeable learning partners, such as peers who challenge and explore, can serve as both guides and collaborators in literacy learning activities in classrooms and draw on cultural resources and experiences to construct new knowledge to make sense of their world. Collaborative reading and writing activities can provide children with the opportunity to scaffold peers' learning through observing, guiding or offering assistance, while the less skilled learner is motivated to initiate language interactions and respond to peer questions and challenges. In their seminal study of comprehension-fostering and comprehension-monitoring activities, Palincsar and Brown (1984) showed how reciprocal oral language exchanges between a learner and more experienced other could have demonstrable effects on levels of reading comprehension. The researchers selected four concrete activities in which to train learners and tutors, which embodied the elements: 'self-directed summarizing (review), questioning, clarifying and predicting' (p. 121).

These activities were embedded in the dialogue between more competent other and learner that took place during the reading of text. The success of their initial research project has been replicated many times with pairs of tutors and learners and within small groups.

Web activity WA10.1
Using reciprocal reading to develop comprehension skills

If you are interested in reading more about the seminal work of Palincsar and Brown, you might choose to access the material we have uploaded on the website.

Paired reading

A very well-known, 'tried and tested' programme based on the principle of learning to read through reading that also has all the potential advantages of encouraging interest and engagement in reading is 'Paired reading' (Topping, Duran & van Keer, 2015). This can be used in school with classroom assistants, more competent peers or volunteers from the local community as the tutors. Alternatively, it can be organised for use with families.

LEARNING POINT
POTENTIAL OF 'PAIRED READING' TO SUPPORT ENGAGEMENT AND INTEREST IN READING

Have a look at the principles that Topping (1996; Topping et al., 2015) set out for families interested in how to use 'Paired reading' techniques. As you do so, consider whether and how you might adapt this for use with struggling readers in schools or college:

- What kind(s) or reading materials will you suggest?
- What ongoing guidance might families or others need to maintain the programme?
- What kind of success criteria would you suggest for this programme – that is, if the programme is successful, what would it look like?

In summary, the learner should choose high-interest reading material irrespective of its readability level (provided it is within that of the helper) from any source. Why do you think this might be important?

Families, peers in schools/colleges, learning support assistants, and so on, should commit themselves to an initial trial period in which they agree to do at least five minutes of Paired reading on five days each week for eight weeks or so. How important is this regularity, do you think?

(Continued)

If this is used with family members, friends and neighbours, can all be encouraged to help, but must all use the same technique?

The learner should be asked to feed back on the quality of the tutoring s/he receives.

The learner should be encouraged to talk about a book s/he has chosen to encourage the motivation to read. How do you think talk can contribute to a learner's comprehension skills?

The learner might wish to begin to read an easy text on his/her own. If s/he makes a mistake, there is a very simple way to correct this. After pausing for 4–5 seconds to allow self-correction, the reading partner should just model the correct way to read the word, the learner should repeat it correctly and the pair should carry on.

Reading partners should support learners through difficult text by reading together – both members of the pair should read all the words out loud together, the tutor modulating speed to match that of the learner while giving a good model of competent reading.

On an easier section of text, the learner may wish to read without support. The learner should signal for the partner to stop reading together, by a knock or a touch. The partner should go quiet, while continuing to monitor any mistakes, praise and pause for discussion of meaning. While reading alone, the learner may make a mistake which s/he cannot self-correct within 4–5 seconds. Then the partner should model the correct word, as above, and both should read together again.

The pair should continue switching from reading together to reading alone to give the learner as much help as is needed according to the difficulty of the text, how tired the s/he is, and so on.

During Paired reading sessions, it is important to praise learners for their achievements where praise is pertinent.

(Adapted from Topping, 1996, p. 46)

There is another technique, McNaughton, Glynn and Robinson's (1987) *Pause, Prompt, Praise*, that is also based on collaborative learning and views proficiency in reading as resulting from the ability to use every relevant piece of information around and within a text to understand it. Following Clay (1979, 1991), the authors of *Pause, Prompt and Praise* emphasise the importance of supplying reading material at a level appropriate to the learner so the learner meets some unfamiliar words but can read enough of the text to make sense of it. Tutors are taught to pause to allow for self-correction, consider the type of errors, and then prompt to offer word meaning or sound–symbol identification and praise to reinforce the use of independent skills.

Word recognition

'The 100 most frequently used words account for more than 55% of the words children read and write, and the 300 most frequently used words account for 72%' (Eldridge, 1995, p. 165). Many have irregular letter–sound associations, for example 'they', 'what', 'are'. Given the frequency of these words, a lot of energy will have to be expended and comprehension will be hindered (Stanovich, 2000) if word recognition is not automatic. Learning letter sequences is challenging for learners who are dyslexic and/or who have poor visual perception and retention. Most may learn through systematic, sequential teaching through shared and guided and personal reading opportunities which may involve the rereading of familiar texts, daily writing practice, access to word charts of commonly used words, word games, use of dictionaries, and so on. However, others may need specially focused multi-sensory teaching (see above).

'Three-Level Guides'

An example of a collaborative activity designed to support learners to read a text closely and develop their comprehension skills by providing a clear purpose and direction for reading is 'The Three-Level Guide'. The guide is a series of statements, some true and some false, written by the teacher about a text. Learners are asked to agree or disagree with these statements and justify their opinions. The activity is intended to support learners to think about a text, statements that are important and can be verified directly from the text, those statements that require them to make inferences from prior knowledge, and how they can apply information from texts. These three levels are:

- reading the lines for literal understanding;
- reading between the lines to make inferences;
- reading beyond the lines to apply understanding.

The learners should first try to decide for themselves whether:

- a statement reflects what is actually stated in the text;
- the statement might be true, or not, depending on inference;
- the statement is something with which the author might concur.

They then discuss and justify their choice with a partner or a small group. As a collaborative activity, learners learn from each other as they discuss the statements.

Web activity WA10.2
Developing appropriate 'Three-Level Guides'

We have uploaded an activity related to the development of a 'Three-Level Guide' on the website. You might choose to access it now.

Effective use of recordings to support reading acquisition

Some researchers have noted how repeated reading, 'reading mileage' (Davey & Parkhill, 2012), can support reading speed and fluency. Reading fluency, confidence and positive responses to text can be enhanced through opportunities to read along with a recording of the text (LeFevre,

Moore & Wilkinson, 2003). Repeated exposure to text, aurally and visually, can reinforce word recognition, thus freeing up cognitive 'energy' for comprehension.

In recent years, there has been rapid growth in the sales of audiobooks. Just to take one example, 'Pickatale' is a mobile audiobook and storybook app for children aged 0–12 years.

> An audiobook option allows children to follow the text while a narrator reads, with words highlighted in time with the audio. This function is designed to help younger children or less confident readers start to recognise different words and pronunciations. Older children or more confident readers can choose to read the book unaided; but if they get stuck, interactive settings allow them to click on words or images for audible help. (www.thebookseller.com/news/interactive-storybook-app-pickatale-comes-uk-1102091#, accessed 30.10.2021)

A number of benefits for the use of audiobooks have been identified. Best (2020, p. 2), from a review of the literature, concludes that there is strong evidence that engagement with audiobooks can have a strong positive influence on reading skills and enjoyment, 'especially given that some children can understand audiobooks that are two grade levels beyond their measured reading comprehension levels (Nawotka, 2019)'. The National Literacy Trust's report on children, young people and digital reading (Best, 2020) indicates that disengaged boy readers are more than twice as likely to say that they read fiction on screen compared with their more engaged peers (25.4% vs 9.8%) (Clark & Picton, 2019).

The publisher Scholastic (Scholastic Parents Staff, 2019) has also described positive outcomes from reading with audiobooks:

- exposure to new vocabulary can increase word-recognition ability;
- access to higher-level texts can improve comprehension and give struggling readers access to content more appropriate for their age and interests;
- audiobooks can be a private experience, with the title unknown to others. If a learner wants to 'read' a lower-ability or lower-aged book, they can do so without scrutiny from their peers. Novelty – listening on a device – might be considered more 'fun' than reading a paper book, particularly when a production features a dramatic reading or famous voice.

Case study: Learning to read through reading with audio recordings

Read the following account of the way in which a young man, 'Julian', learnt to read through reading texts that really engaged him while listening to audio recordings, and how this enabled him to enjoy discussing the plots and characters of novels that he shared with his friends.

'Julian' arrived at his secondary comprehensive school, aged 11, as a highly articulate, but very dyslexic, non-reader. His younger brother had caught up with him a long time before in terms of his reading and Julian was completely lacking in self-confidence as a result. Also, the friends who had arrived with him at his new school were all placed in top sets, but he was in the bottom, because he could not read, and this made things worse for him.

The special educational needs co-ordinator talked with Julian about his situation and found him to be disaffected and depressed. He was quite reticent about himself to start with, but when he finally talked, he told her that previous teachers in his primary school had adopted a phonics approach to teaching reading, but to no avail. What he really wanted to do, he said, was to be able to read what his friends were reading so that he could join in their discussions. The SENCo, who was new to her post at the time, decided that, given his age and status as a non-reader, there was nothing to lose by setting phonics instruction on one side for the time being and trying to teach him to read by engaging with his interests instead. She talked with his parents and with him, and made an agreement with him that she would systematically record 30 minutes' worth of *Hitchhiker's Guide to the Galaxy* five days a week, and he would take the recording home every day and listen to the recording twice while following the text with his eyes. This procedure was followed by recordings of *The Hobbit*.

After seven months, Julian's father phoned the school to tell the SENCo that his son had read *The Daily Mirror* newspaper that week at the breakfast table for the first time ever. Julian was promoted to the upper sets in his year group, he seemed much happier, and for six months he avoided any contact with the SENCo. She assumed this was because she reminded him of all the pain he felt when he could not read. Without warning, however, he appeared in her room and volunteered to help others who could not read to read.

Several years later, and with a lot of support for his spelling and writing that he was now prepared to accept, he was accepted at university.

This is a factual account with the young man's name anonymised. Is there anything about it that surprises you? How might you adopt this approach for non-readers that you know?

Attentive listening to children's reading

Choice of reading material to engage non-readers is important. So, too, is listening to struggling readers read. The listener should be responsive to the learner's understanding of, and interest in, the text and any difficulties that s/he experiences. When the current author first began to teach in the area of special educational needs, she noticed how listening to young people read seemed at best a perfunctory activity. She strongly agreed with Wragg et al. (1998, pp. 264–265), who highlighted research findings which stressed factors that are important in listening to learners' reading in classrooms.

Web activity WA10.3
Effective listening to children's reading

On the website we have summarised Wragg et al.'s (1998, pp. 264–265) findings together with an activity. You might choose to access this material now.

Views of the writing process

Readers and writers use their knowledge in complementary ways. Readers construct meaning by interacting with words, grammatical structures and other language patterns in texts. Writers start with meaning that they represent in texts through grammatical structures and other language patterns (Ministry of Education, New Zealand, 2005 p. 123). Writing might be seen as the composite of two technical skills: production of the surface features and the mechanics of text, grammar and spelling (Smith & Elley, 1997), or skill in processes such as brainstorming, drafting, revising, editing and publishing content and meaning (Graves, 1983). However, similar to reading, affective aspects must also be taken into account, especially when learners experience difficulty: motivation to learn, interest, engagement and personal identity as a writer.

Surface features and the mechanics of text

The issue of spelling in the English language is problematic. English developed from a number of different languages, and has an alphabetic writing system in which there is no direct consistency between the symbols and the sounds of the language. As Barton (1995, p. 97) comments, '[…] the symbols (the letters) may best be described as providing a clue to the sounds'. Some words do have consistent sound–symbol correspondence, but, even so, different pronunciations of English around the UK and across the world, particularly with vowel sounds, means that there may be a difficulty in understanding each other's speech.

English also incorporates meaning of words derived from other languages in its spelling system, typically Latin. For example, 'portare', to carry, gives us portable, import, export, transport, and so on. There are also homophones that sound the same in speech but are differentiated in writing by their spellings, for example 'red' and 'read'. Each has to be learned separately: '[…] we are never sure of the spelling of a new word we hear until we have seen it written down; we are often unsure of how to pronounce a word we come across in reading until we hear it spoken (Barton, 1995, p. 100).

Teaching spelling

Spelling in the English language is complex, in part because many English words are derived from a number of different languages: Latin, French, German, and so on. Given the complexity, it is hardly surprising that teaching spelling can be approached from a range of ways, for example from a partist approach to individual letter–sound identification and combinations of letters into words, or a holistic, whole-word approach.

- Words to be learned might be grouped in terms of similar letter–sound patterns within them. These may be hierarchically organised, phonically regular combinations of letters and sounds that the learner is expected to know. There is a disadvantage here, however. Learners may spend a great deal of time learning long lists of words, but may show little or no generalisation of these patterns into similar words that they may need when they write.
- Choice of words to be spelt can be made on the basis of what the learner needs and wishes to spell for the purpose of his/her writing, or from lists of words in common use. In order to avoid difficulties later on, children need to be familiar with vowels and syllables

at an early stage and to be taught techniques for learning the spelling of words they want or need to use.

• Some teachers may correct all spelling errors. Others may correct only words or sentence structure with which they feel students should already be familiar. Some may encourage students to proof read their own, or peers', work before handing it in.

LEARNING POINT
CHOOSING A STRATEGY FOR TEACHING SPELLING

One way to strengthen new spellings is to take a multi-sensory approach to teaching which emphasises the spelling of the whole word, focusing on all modalities – auditory, visual, kinesthetic and tactile:

> Multi-sensory teaching is teaching done using all the learning pathways in the brain (visual, auditory and kinaesthetic–tactile) in order to enhance memory and learning. It is crucial that, whatever pathways are being addressed in a particular exercise, they are directly focused upon by both teacher and child. For example, they look at, feel, move and say the names of the wooden letters they are using to compose a word. When 'writing' a word in the air, the left hand holds the right elbow and the eyes follow the pointing finger. A tray with salt or sand on it or the reverse side of a piece of hardboard can be used to 'write on' with a finger. The rough surface maximises the sensory input and in both cases the letters and the final word are said out loud. (Johnson, 2002, p. 275)

Read the text below and consider whether you might employ the multi-sensory strategy to support the spelling acquisition of learners who experience difficulties.

   How might you put this into practice?

   How would you select the words to be spelt?

Reason and Boote (1994) describe one multi-sensory approach which, while lengthy at first, can, in their view, be slimmed down as students gain confidence and competence in spelling. Words should be chosen to reflect students' current writing needs and interests:

• Look at the word, read it, and pronounce it in syllables or other small bits (re-mem-ber; sh-out).
• Try to listen to yourself doing this.
• Still looking at it, spell it out in letter-names.
• Continue to look, and trace out the letters on the table with your finger as you spell it out again.
• Look at the word for any 'tricky bits'; for example, gh in right. (Different pupils find different parts of a word 'tricky'.)
• Try to get a picture of the word in your mind: take a photograph of it in your head!
• Copy the word, peeping at the end of each syllable or letter-string.
• Highlight the tricky bits in colour (or by some other means).

(Continued)

- Visualise the word again.
- Now cover it up and try to write it, spelling it out in letter-names.
- Does it look right?
- Check with the original.
- Are there some tricky bits you didn't spot (i.e. the parts that went wrong)?
- Repeat as much of the procedure as necessary to learn the words thoroughly.

(Reason & Boote, 1994, p. 138)

Peer tutoring spelling

A different spelling approach, 'Cued spelling' (Topping, 2001), with its breakdown into specific steps, lends itself to being implemented in either peer-tutoring or co-operative learning contexts in schools and colleges, and the potential advantages that paired learning can bring with it if handled constructively. Each pair can be encouraged to keep a spelling diary, each page including space to write the master version of up to 10 words on all days of the week, with boxes to record daily Speed Review and weekly Mastery Review scores and spaces for daily comments from the partner and weekly comments from the teacher.

Web activity WA10.4
Reflecting on the usefulness of 'Cued spelling'

We have uploaded a summary of the steps in 'Cued spelling' (Topping, 2001) on the website with an activity accompanying it. You might choose to access this now.

Focusing on the planning process

Focusing on the process means taking a holistic approach: seeing the piece of writing in its entirety and planning the hierarchy of steps to reach the end point. Hayes and Flower (1986) conceptualise writing as incorporating a hierarchical series of goals that writers achieve through engaging in the cognitive processes of planning, translating and revising. Planning involves generating information to be included in the script, selecting and organising what is relevant, and deciding on criteria for judging successful completion of the script. Translation involves converting the plan into the script. Revising includes editing for grammatical errors as well as structural coherence. These processes overlap and competent writers revisit each of them many times before the writing task is complete. Competent writers can also switch their attention between these processes according to their perception of what is required for successful task completion (Bereiter & Scardamalia, 1986).

Seeing the process of writing like this can be very useful because it enables teachers to focus on the individual processes of writing production. The use of strategies intended to highlight planning processes is an area that has been researched thoroughly in relation to students with difficulties in literacy development.

Writing frames

An example of the planning process is the use of writing frames to generate and organise ideas (Englert & Raphael, 1988; Graves, Montague & Wong, 1990). 'Writing frames' are a way of providing learner writers with a support or 'scaffold', that offers, for example, some headings, subheadings and connectives for linking paragraphs when writing an explanatory information text; the layout, greeting, opening sentence and closure when practising a letter; and sentence openings for making contrasting points when presenting an argument. The theory behind this is that, by expressing these thoughts in a visible way, we can subsequently rethink, revise and redraft, and reflect upon our own thinking (Wray, 2002).

'Mind-mapping'

'Mind-mapping' (Buzan, 2000) is a visual representation of thought processes. As such, it can be a useful way to begin planning a structure for producing extended text. Learners first think about and then produce a 'mind map' of the topics to be included in their writing text before beginning to develop the plan. Once learners have produced their mind map, they can then look at it and rearrange the content in a coherent order to suit what they wish to write about and produce the structure for their text. This can be a way of reducing what we might call the 'cognitive load' involved in the writing process by separating out content from the structuring process, and then focusing on the technical aspects of producing the text.

'Paired writing'

'Paired writing' is a further example of a collaborative approach to support literacy acquisition. Topping (1995, 2001) suggests that this technique should be used for three sessions of 20 minutes per week for six weeks.

Web activity WA10.5
Reflecting on ways to use 'Paired writing'

On the website we have uploaded a description of 'Paired writing', and an activity to go with it. You might access this material now.

Using narrative to plan writing

Over the years, the value of peer collaboration has been researched in relation to overall improvement of literacy both for students with and without difficulties in literacy acquisition. Literate language includes 'story grammar'. As Westby (1991, p. 352) comments, narrative is a core part of many aspects of our lives: 'We dream, remember, anticipate, hope, despair, love, hate, believe, doubt, plan, construct, gossip and learn in narrative'. Narratives contain essential elements such as problem-solving, persuasion, comparisons, and so on (Montgomery & Kahn, 2003). For this reason, writing in a narrative genre can be seen as an early step towards later expository text. Broadly, this is more formal factual text that provides clearly structured information about a topic.

Case study: Using scaffolded story writing

Julia was an English teacher who was very interested in supporting those of her learners who found writing difficult to improve to a level where they could be proud of their achievements. In looking for an interactive group activity to support these learners, she came across a strategy called 'scaffolded story writing' (Montgomery & Kahn, 2003) that appeared at first sight to be useful to her. Following the advice of these authors, she first introduced the idea of what an author does in writing a text, and then discussed with her pupils five elements of an effective narrative: interesting character(s), context, a problem, possible solutions, and a credible ending (Apel & Masterton, 1998). She then set up a series of questions related to 'comprehension, organisation, sequence of ideas, and metacognition' (Montgomery & Kahn, 2003, p. 145) and encouraged her pupils to discuss possible approaches with each other to support their thinking about the stories they wanted to write.

Over the course of a term Julia found that her pupils really began to enjoy sharing their ideas with each other. Some of them took their stories home to show their families, which had never happened before, and she had some very positive comments from families at the next parents' evening.

If you are interested in trying out this strategy, you will find examples on the internet at http://dyslexiacatalyst.com/teachers/how-to-scaffold-creative-writing/#:~:text=Scaffolding%20(Framework),d)%20decide%20how%20to%20finish (accessed 30.10.2021).

Acknowledgement of cultural considerations in writing tasks

For some learners, in order to support a sense of being included and to maintain engagement in the classroom, it may be very important to acknowledge cultural differences and the culturally-related resources they bring with them to settings, schools and colleges. It is important to acknowledge the 'politically influential "accountability" movement [that] has urged teachers to narrow the curriculum and concentrate on "basics" like phonics and spelling' (Dyson, 1997, p. 171). However, in order to build from the known to the yet-to-be-learnt, teachers have a responsibility to scaffold literacy learning by ensuring access to cultural resources that are meaningful to the learners and supportive of their well-being and self-esteem. In the United States, a central concern to Anne Haas Dyson (1997, 2003) is support for the acquisition of literacy, particularly writing, in ways that are relevant to learners. A particular focus is on the cultural resources that young people bring into schools that can be built upon to support literacy learning. Dyson investigated how young school children in urban American classrooms appropriated superhero figures from popular culture to take on powerful cultural storylines in ways that enabled both literacy and social learning. In this research, she showed how children, irrespective of socio-economic or ethnic background, could build from 'the very social and symbolic stuff of their own childhoods' (Dyson, 2003, p. 328) to engage with school literacy practices. She conducted a close examination of the way in which children often recontextualise materials from the media: popular songs, characters from films, and so on, in various activities at school, in their play and verbal interactions with peers and adults. In one particular classroom in her study, children used songs and reflections on characters from the film *Space Jam* for:

> [d]rawing adventures, making lists of valued knowledge, announcing and reporting the results of sports events, composing and recalling songs, telling and retelling stories.... (Dyson, 2003, p. 349)

As they recontextualised media materials from *Space Jam* in their practices at school, the children were able to experience challenges, social expectations and ideological tensions:

> In the 'scary story' event [in a classroom writers' workshop] the girls [...] struggled quite vividly with symbolic and social tensions as they negotiated what one had to 'say', 'write' or communicate with gesture in a joint performance for the official sharing time practice. (Dyson, 2003, p. 349)

Use of media materials was only possible, however, because the curriculum in the classroom was 'permeable [...] that made space for and productively engaged their social and symbolic – their textual – resources' (Dyson, 2003, p. 349).

Conclusion

We have argued that learning both reading and writing need enjoyment, motivation, positive attitude, confidence and personal identity as a reader and writer. Interventions intended to support learners who experience difficulties should therefore take account of these elements as well as technical aspects of the skills of literacy, frequency of practice, and so on.

As you reflect on the discussion in this chapter, we would like you to consider the following question. What kinds of approaches or strategies in your view are likely to be the most effective in encouraging engagement and interest in literacy learning among learners who experience difficulties?

Further reading

Comprehension

Centre for Literacy in Primary Education (CLPE) (2020) *The Power of a Rich Reading Classroom*. London: Sage.

Clarke, P. J., Truelove, E., Hulme, C., & Snowling, M. J. (2013) *Developing Reading Comprehension*. London: Wiley.

Gill, A., Stephenson, M., & Waugh, D. (2021) *Developing a Love of Reading and Books: Teaching and Nurturing Readers in Primary Schools*. London: Sage.

Read Naturally (2020) *Comprehension*. Available at: www.readnaturally.com/research/5-components-of-reading/comprehension

Reading Rockets (2020) *Comprehension*. Available at: www.readingrockets.org/teaching/reading-basics/comprehension

Woolley, G. (2011) *Reading Comprehension: Assisting Children with Learning Difficulties*. New York: Springer.

Writing

Topping, K., Nixon, J., Sutherland, J., & Yarrow, F. (2000) Paired writing: A framework for effective collaboration. *Reading*, 34(2), 79–89.

Wray, D., & Lewis, M. (n/d) An approach to scaffolding children's non-fiction writing: The use of writing frames. Available at: https://warwick.ac.uk/fac/soc/ces/research/teachingandlearning/publications/framesrai.pdf

Wyse, D., Andrews, R., & Hoffman, J. (2017) *The Routledge International Handbook of English, Language and Literacy Teaching*. London: Routledge.

Spelling

British Dyslexia Association (BDA) (n/d) *How Can I Support My Child?* London: BDA. Available at: www.bdadyslexia.org.uk/advice/children/how-can-i-support-my-child/spelling

Reading Rockets (2020) Spelling and Dyslexia. Available at: www.readingrockets.org/article/spelling-and-dyslexia

Useful literacy websites

National Literacy Trust: https://literacytrust.org.uk/

The Children's Literacy Charity: https://thechildrensliteracycharity.org.uk/

Book Trust: www.booktrust.org.uk/

Reading Matters: http://readingmatters.org.uk/

11

NUMERACY DIFFICULTIES

Major questions addressed in this chapter are:

*   How can teachers and others understand difficulties in numeracy in ways that enable them to support numeracy acquisition for these young people in settings, schools and colleges?
*   What support might parents and families offer their children at home?

Key terms

Effective mathematics teachers, difficulties in mathematics learning, dyscalculia, family support

Introduction

Mathematics learning is an area of the curriculum in which many learners experience difficulties. For some, this may relate to general difficulties in learning. However, as the American DSM-5 (American Psychiatric Association, 2013, pp. 66–67) notes, some learners have difficulties in this area that cannot be explained as being caused 'by intellectual disabilities, uncorrected visual or auditory acuity, other mental or neurological disorders, psychosocial adversity, lack of proficiency in the language of academic instruction, or inadequate educational instruction'. In other words, some learners have a specific difficulty in the learning of mathematics. This may be in the mastering of:

> number sense, number facts, or calculation (e.g., has poor understanding of numbers, their magnitude, and relationships; counts on fingers to add single-digit numbers instead of recalling the math fact as peers do; gets lost in the midst of arithmetic computation and may switch procedures)

and/or it may be in using mathematics to reason:

> e.g., has severe difficulty applying mathematical concepts, facts, or procedures to solve quantitative problems. (APA, 2013, p. 66)

An alternative term used to refer to specific difficulties in learning mathematics is 'dyscalculia'. Whether the difficulties that are experienced are general or specific, the challenge for those with an interest in mathematics education is to be aware of what teachers and others might do to support improvement in learning and progress.

We begin this chapter by asking you to reflect back on your own experience of mathematics learning and the lessons you learnt from this. We continue with a focus on what research tells us about effective mathematics teachers and pedagogy in inclusive mathematics classrooms. We continue by identifying particular areas in mathematics where learners may experience particular difficulties, and offer practical, well-theorised ways to support learning in each.

Lessons from prior experiences

In previous chapters of this book, we have discussed the notion of personal frames of reference that is such an important issue when we consider how and why teachers teach the way they do.

LEARNING POINT
CONSIDERING PERSONAL EXPERIENCES OF MATHEMATICS LEARNING

Think about your own learning of mathematics and what you remember about mathematics lessons at the early stages and then in secondary and, if appropriate, further and/or higher education.

How easy or difficult did you find the learning at the various stages?

How interested were you in mathematics?

- Were there any areas that particularly interested you?
- Were there any that you found boring, or you thought were irrelevant?
- To what extent did your achievement in mathematics coincide with your interest in it?

To what do you attribute your own achievement, or lack of achievement, in mathematics?

To what extent do you think the teacher made a difference to your success or lack of success?

On reflection, what lessons can you take from your own experience to apply to mathematics teaching in order to be really effective?

From her own personal experience as both learner and teacher, the current author would assert that what teachers do in mathematics classrooms is largely dependent on:

- what they know and believe about mathematics (hence, as a non-specialist mathematician, when tasked with teaching mathematics to the lowest sets in secondary schools, she took an HE distance learning course in mathematics to improve her subject knowledge);
- what they understand about the teaching and learning of mathematics;
- what they know about their learners.

How far do you agree with this view?

Attributes of effective teachers of mathematics

A range of research suggests that effective mathematics teachers have what Shulman (1987, p. 7) first termed good 'pedagogical content knowledge':

> the most powerful analogies, illustrations, examples, explanations, and demonstrations — [...] the most useful ways of representing and formulating the subject that make it comprehensible to others. [...] Pedagogical content knowledge also includes an understanding of what makes the learning of specific topics easy or difficult: the conceptions and preconceptions that students of different ages and backgrounds bring with them.

First, there is the question of mathematical subject knowledge itself, and, second, of knowledge, awareness and understanding of the learning process and an approach to teaching mathematics that is dependent on this.

Given that many learners experience difficulty in the area and, as a result, anxiety, we would add teachers' knowledge of, and relationship with, their learners, and also teacher expectations. Anthony and Walshaw (2007) confirm the importance of a classroom atmosphere that learners experience as non-threatening from a synthesis of 600 studies of effective mathematical pedagogy.

Importance of teachers' mathematical subject knowledge

When teachers are fully conversant, and confident, with the relevant mathematical concepts, they are able to identify points at which they can elaborate on students' current understandings and help them to move towards more complex and sophisticated appreciation of mathematical concepts. Those who are unsure about mathematical ideas may use examples and metaphors that prevent, rather than help, students' mathematical understanding (Bliss, Askew & Macrae, 1996; Ruthven, 2002). Sound content knowledge enables recognition both of the conceptual (mis)-understandings learners are using in their methods and where those (mis)understandings might be leading (Kilpatrick, Swafford & Findell, 2001; Shulman & Shulman, 2004; Hill, Rowan & Ball, 2005). As Askew et al. (1997, p. 3) concluded from the Effective Teachers of Numeracy Project in the UK: 'Highly effective teachers of numeracy themselves had knowledge and awareness of conceptual connections between the areas which they taught in the primary mathematics curriculum.' Many studies (Boaler, Wiliam & Brown, 2000; Sullivan, Mousley & Zevenbergen, 2003) reflect the author's own experiences of ways in which low attainers are often presented with a very limited 'diet' of activities in mathematics lessons, where the four rules of number customarily dominate and there is little focus on students constructing their own understandings. Sometimes strategies used by teachers can support learners to complete tasks rather than to help move them towards independence, as Myhill and Warren (2005) concluded from a study of whole-class teaching in three schools. In using 'heavy prompts' that point learners to the 'right' answers, teachers tended to miss opportunities for insight into learners' prior knowledge or understanding. In a study of the views and experiences of nearly 1,000 students, Boaler et al. (2000) found that those in lower streamed classes had fewer instructional opportunities to learn. Teaching strategies were very narrow, resulting in profound and largely negative learning experiences. Teachers often seemed to ignore students' backgrounds and needs and, similar to those in Bartholomew's (2003) study, talked to them in ways that highlighted the difference between these students and those achieving highly in mathematics.

Knowledge of appropriate and effective pedagogy

Each young person who experiences difficulties in mathematics learning is different, and it is really important to engage with each one individually to tease out the root(s) of the problem. Teachers' beliefs, expectations and understandings of all students as active agents in their own learning are as important in the area of mathematics as in any other area of the school curriculum (Anthony & Walshaw, 2007).

There is now considerable evidence that indicates the beneficial effects on learning when learners are encouraged to articulate their mathematical thinking (Lampert, 1990; O'Connor, 1998; Fraivillig, Murphy & Fuson, 1999). It is important for the teacher, as the more expert other in the learning process, to listen to what learners have to say, draw out the specific mathematical ideas that students are using to work out the answers to problems, share other methods and ways of working through mathematical problems (Hiebert et al., 1997), and reframe student talk in mathematically appropriate language. As we have discussed in relation to socio-cultural views of learning, constructive feedback has a powerful influence on learning and achievement (Hattie, 2002) in the way in which it connects a learner's current level of knowledge and understanding and the standard to be reached.

Many learners who experience difficulty in mathematics are not confident enough to either ask questions or contribute to discussion in the classroom. In a previous chapter, we discussed how important it is to create a safe place for learning so that learners are prepared to volunteer their answers, knowing that they will not be humiliated by either the teacher or their peers if they are wrong. Effective teachers neither embarrass learners nor ignore wrong answers. They use mistakes to enhance the teaching. They might, for example, comment on the strategies that learners are using in the mathematics lesson, talk about the mathematical concepts that students are learning and encourage students to monitor their own progress. Encouraging focused – not random – talk in the classroom is important for another reason also. It is crucial that learners do not become overly dependent on teachers and that teachers encourage them to ask questions about why the class should carry out particular activities in mathematics lessons, and what the point is (Noddings, 1995).

In the chapter on literacy learning, we noted how small-group work can provide the context for social and cognitive engagement, and dialogic space for 'interthinking' (Littleton & Mercer, 2013) to share ideas and elaborate understandings on the interpersonal plane. Peers can serve as an important resource for developing mathematical thinking also. However, as Helme and Clarke (2001) noted in their research in secondary classrooms, the teacher has a very important role in establishing social rules governing participation in the classroom so that lower-attaining learners are not inhibited from engaging in mathematical learning tasks.

Use of mathematical language in the classroom

As Walshaw (2004) notes, the kind of language that is used and the way that mathematics is talked about and arguments are made and understood in classrooms are really important in mathematical learning and the way in which mathematical knowledge is constructed by learners. All should learn this mathematical language. Specialist terms should be taught to learners at whichever level is appropriate and deliberately used to scaffold mathematical thinking. Mathematical language is not simply vocabulary and technical usage terms. It also includes the ways that mathematicians use language to explain concepts. There is a strong argument (Zevenbergen, Mousley & Sullivan, 2004) for a very clear, determined approach to teaching mathematics where the teacher:

- helps learners to 'see through' mathematical language used to describe a problem to the problem itself;
- is very clear in explaining the mathematics that is required to work out the problem;
- is sensitive to, and respectful of, class and cultural differences between the learners, and between the learners and the teacher so that learners are not alienated;
- accepts mathematically correct alternative responses to the problem.

Choice of task, tools and activity necessarily influences the development of mathematical thinking. Some students will need concrete materials to aid their mathematical thinking for far longer than others.

Influence of teacher expectations

Learning and behaviour are influenced by the nature of the learners' relationship with the teacher, which itself is influenced by the value and worth they see reflected in the teacher's behaviour towards them. Since the seminal study of Rosenthal and Jacobson (1968), there has been a great deal of work on the importance of positive teacher expectations in promoting learners' achievement.

Case study: Considering the effect of teacher expectations of learners in mathematics lessons

Read the text below and, as you do so, note down:

- how you might have felt as a learner in the classroom of this particular teacher;
- what, in a school or college, might be done to alter the situation;
- what difference it might make to the learning of the pupils to be able to discuss their work with their peers;
- what prior preparation might be useful to ensure that group work in the classroom is positive and effective in supporting learning and achievement in mathematics lessons.

In a study carried out at a London (England) school, Bartholomew (2003) concluded from the messages conveyed to pupils that mathematics teachers appeared to value those in the top stream more highly than others. One teacher, for example, took a friendly approach to a top-stream class, but behaved in an authoritarian way towards his low-stream class, 'insisting that students queue outside the room in absolute silence and eventually counting them in and seating them alphabetically. They had to remain in their seats in silence, were given no opportunities to ask questions, with the result that many students were extremely confused as to what they were meant to be doing' (Bartholomew, 2003, p. 131).

Skills needed for mathematics acquisition

LEARNING POINT
CONSIDERING SKILLS IN MATHEMATICS ACQUISITION

In Chapter 6 on difficulties in cognition and learning, we noted how some learners experience difficulties related to information-processing, memory, sequential reasoning, use of symbols, moving from concrete to abstract thinking, and so on. How far do you think learners need these skills to become competent mathematicians?

Chinn (2012, p. 9) follows the Russian psychologist Krutetskii (1976) in listing the skills of competent mathematicians. These include:

- thinking in the abstract rather than in 'concrete numerical relationships';
- making generalisations and 'abstract[ing] oneself from the irrelevant';

- operating with numerals and other symbols;
- following 'sequential, segmented [step-by-step], logical reasoning';
- reversing mental process;
- being flexible in thought;
- using spatial concepts.

More recent research (Cragg & Gilmore, 2014) suggests that so-called 'executive function skills' – working memory (holding and manipulating information in mind), ignoring information that is irrelevant to the problem at hand and holding back unwanted responses – and flexible thinking (the ability to flexibly switch attention between different tasks) play a critical role in the development of mathematics proficiency.

Areas of difficulty in mathematics learning and effective programmes to address them

A recent systematic review of the literature has concluded that there is currently a lack of high-quality, evidence-based learning programmes for children and adolescents with specific difficulties in mathematics learning from primary grades and up (Haberstroh & Schulte-Körne, 2019). The evidence there is suggests that individualised teaching, multi-sensory teaching methods, building confidence, high teacher expectations as discussed above, and parental support, are likely to help learners with difficulties to improve numeracy (Peninsula Cerebra Research Unit (PenCru), 2018). Current tools and strategies to support children and young people with dyscalculia all have a broadly similar focus: improving specific arithmetical skills, including approximation, counting skills, recognising small quantities, and understanding that things have a precise quantity associated with them, and that adding or taking things away alters quantities (Gifford & Rockliffe, 2012).

In the section below we identify particular areas of mathematics where learners commonly experience barriers and suggest ways to address each in turn: concepts of 'number-ness', number bonds, mathematical terminology, relational signs, problem-solving, place value and 'zero', multiplication, negative numbers, money and time.

Establishing an understanding of 'number-ness'

Some children, especially those who experience difficulty in comprehending language and understanding the way that symbols can represent meaning, are also likely to find it problematic to acquire and use written symbols for numbers. Learners' ability to understand symbolic representation depends on understanding what the symbolic representation refers to. However, many use mathematical symbols without having grasped the concepts that underpin them (Chinn, 2012). As Grauberg (2002) comments, 'Where is the "f" in 5?'. We might well think about Piaget's (1964, 1969) seminal work on the four stages of learning to justify the handling and counting of everyday items to support developing an understanding of number-ness.

In the UK as well as the USA, young children usually learn to count in a sequence of one-digit numbers. Reciting number sequences tells us nothing about a child's grasp of the meaning of individual numbers, what we might call 'number-ness'. 'An ability to recite these numbers is a perfect example of the child giving the parent or the teacher an illusion of learning, of knowing' (Chinn, 2012, p. 81). In some other countries, the preference is for emphasising small quantities without counting what is known as 'cardinal' aspects of number. If we consider what it takes to recognise a small number, for example 3, as a quantity, it involves only one operation, the matching of a symbol, which might be either sound or visual, to an amount. Logically, this would seem to take less cognitive effort than remembering that 3 comes after 2 and before in a number sequence and simultaneously counting up to 3. Matching a symbol to a concrete amount also establishes the meaning of the number and, hence, the beginnings of number-ness, that is 'the powerful abstract qualities of a number – which means the concept of "twoness", "threeness", "n-ness"' (Grauberg, 2002, p. 12). If we provide children with activities involving the same numbers of different types of material, we can support them 'to see what is common to all (the fact that there are, for instance, 'two' of each) and we want him to learn to ignore what is irrelevant (e.g. size, colour, feel)' (p. 12).

It is possible to use other number systems, for example tally charts, first, where one bundle represents 5 and is clearly made up of five. Or, for some children it might be important to use concrete aids to establish number learning, for example Cuisenaire rods and/or an abacus, for much longer than for other children.

Understanding and using number bonds

In mathematics education, a number bond, sometimes called a 'number pair', is simply the pair of numbers that add to a given number, for example some of the pairs of numbers that add to 10 are 4 + 6, 7 + 3, 8 + 2. Number bonds should become so familiar that children can recognise and complete them almost instantly, with automatic recall. Learning number bonds is clearly really important in the beginning stages of mathematics learning. In the current author's experience, however, learners may continue to lack automaticity in this area even in secondary schools.

Multi-sensory approaches to learning number bonds

Learners who have little idea of the meaning of numerals or number terms might be supported to develop their understanding through a multi-sensory approach using concrete materials: dice, dominoes and/or cards. The arrays of dots from 1 to 10 can provide a clear way to visualise, understand and learn number bonds. Card games can be used for practice. Number bonds should be remembered as number 'facts' (e.g. 6 + 4 = 10), and also as a number that should be added to another to make 10 – what, technically, we might call an 'addend', for example 6 + $\square$ = 10. The extension from 6 + 4 = 10, to 60 + 40 = 100 and to 400 + 600 = 1,000 then becomes straightforward.

Number bonds for 10 and 100 are useful in subtraction, given that this can be done by counting on through tens, hundreds and thousands.

The number bonds for 9 and 11 can be taught as they relate to 10.

Teaching number doubles for digits less than 10 can be a useful strategy for rapid recall in mental arithmetic. When learners can remember doubles, they can easily be moved on to doubles plus or minus one, for example 6 + 5 = (5 + 5) + 1, or 7 + 8 = (8 + 8) – 1.

Grauberg (2002, p. 66) suggests that, where students experience this kind of difficulty, it is important to provide them with:

a working model that can illustrate the underlying structure of the decimal system clearly and memorably. They need a tool at their fingertips, a picture in their minds, ready for use.

One way to do this is to support the student to conceptualise a 'field of 100', consisting of a square with 10 rows of 10 dots marked on it, each row of 10 with a gap in the middle. Students can then see straight away that 10 is made of 5 + 5. After that, by covering one of the dots in one row, it can consist of 9 + 1, and so on. Similarly, numbers can be counted in tens and students can see the relationship between 10, 20, 30 and so on to 100:

> Numbers are thus seen as two-dimensional geometrical shapes, as 'quantity pictures' rather than as points on a number line. (Grauberg, 2002, p. 66)

This arrangement of dots is useful for supporting students' understanding of the position on numbers under 100 within this arrangement of dots.

Using Cuisenaire rods is another way to build up a concept of base 10, using groupings of 1, 5, 10 and 50.

Games can be a good way of engaging children and young people. For example, board games with number tracks, such as snakes and ladders, have been found to be effective for improving number recognition and understanding the relative magnitudes of numbers for young children (Ramani & Siegler, 2008). There are a number of computer-based mathematics games which use images and movement to try to improve numeracy. However, the use of computer games on their own is not generally recommended, but may be helpful in addition to face-to-face teaching.

Mathematical terminology

Many of those who experience difficulties in acquiring, understanding and using number symbols also experience difficulties in the use of mathematical terms. Such terminology may prove difficult for a variety of reasons. First, there is the sheer amount of words, signs and symbols to be learned. Then the way words are used inside and outside the context of mathematics is often ambiguous. In addition, there are so many mathematical terms that are synonymous.

Synonyms

In the area of mathematics, there are many synonyms: different words meaning the same thing. Weavers (2003, p. 35) notes how the most basic arithmetical computations can be signalled with a range of terms. For example, some alternative terms for

- 'add' are '+', 'sum of', 'plus', 'and', 'altogether', 'addition', 'more than';
- 'subtract' are 'take away', 'minus', 'difference between', 'less', 'smaller than';
- 'multiply' are '×' (often confused with '+'), 'times', 'product of', 'lots of';
- 'divide' are '÷', 'share', 'how many in', 'how much each';
- 'equals' are '=', 'becomes', 'is the same as', 'makes'.

An important question for teachers would be how to teach learners the meaning of these synonyms. The number of new terms needs to be restricted to a very few that the student can remember the next day and the next week and practised very regularly.

Homonyms

Homonyms are words that are spelt the same and sound the same, but have different meanings. Sometimes the same word in mathematics can require a different calculation. For example, 'What is 10 more than 40?' means something different from 'How many more than 10 is 40?'. It will require careful explanation, perhaps assisted by concrete materials, to explain the different calculations required here, especially to a learner who experiences difficulties in mathematics.

Some words have different meanings in mathematics from other contexts: 'volume' can refer to quantity or sound; the 'face' can refer to a clock 'face', the 'face' of a three-dimensional object or a person's 'face'. Learners may need their own memory cues, perhaps devised by themselves, to remember what each of these means.

Relational signs: Adding, subtracting, balancing

Primary schools in particular have a lot of equipment that can be used to play games in adding, subtracting and balancing. Without an understanding of what adding and subtracting mean in action, there seems little point in trying to encourage the use of the symbol '+' or '−'. The equals sign, '=', is often interpreted to children as 'makes', but, mathematically, as we are all aware, 'makes' does not mean what a child would understand from his/her use of materials in play contexts.

A major question is how to move from the action to competent use of the abstract symbols. One way to do this might be to put in an additional step by encouraging children to devise their own symbols for the actions first. Once they are confident in using their own personally-devised abstract symbols, these can gradually be substituted with the conventional symbols – one at a time, if necessary.

Multiplication

Numbers of educators have stressed how important it is that learners should understand the meaning of operations in the area of mathematics. The concept of multiplication can be problematic for some learners if they do not see it as repeated addition of the same numbers, as Chinn (2012) points out. Three pairs of socks in the market costing £4 each can be understood as £4 + £4 + £4, so 3 lots of £4, or 3 × £4.

Times table facts should be learned, if at all possible, not for its own sake but to reduce what we might call 'cognitive load'. This concept is related to 'working memory', the part of our mind that processes what we are currently doing and that can only deal with a limited amount of information at any one time. Having times tables at automatic level means that we have more opportunity to think about aspects of a problem other than the mechanical calculation. Chanting tables in rhythm is one way in which tables are commonly taught. However, for some learners the string of numbers may be too long to hold in memory. One way to help overcome this that the current author has found very successful is to teach students in short sequences that overlap, for example 1×2 to 5×2, then 5×2 to 9×2, then 9×2 to 12×2. One sequence should be practised until the student is very confident with it. For example:

$1 \times 2 = 2; 2 \times 2 = 4; 3 \times 2 = 6; 4 \times 2 = 8; 5 \times 2 = 10.$

When the learner is entirely confident, the next overlapping sequence will be:

$5 \times 2 = 10$; $6 \times 2 = 12$; $7 \times 2 = 14$; $8 \times 2 = 16$; $9 \times 2 = 18$

The final sequence will be:

$9 \times 2 = 18$; $10 \times 2 = 20$; $11 \times 2 = 22$; $12 \times 2 = 24$

Depending on the learners, sequences can be shortened, but should always overlap. The rationale behind this is that when the learner recites the whole table, the overlaps will lead him/her into the next sequence.

Another way to reduce cognitive load is to show learners how to draw their own table squares and use these as a visual means of supporting themselves to multiply. They should be reminded to leave the top left-hand square blank. Number facts for the 0 times, 1 times, 5 times and 10 times can be filled in first because they are the easiest; 2 times can follow next. **Students might need to be reminded that 0 × any number is 0.** See Table 11.1.

Table 11.1 Example of table square to be completed by learners

	0	1	2	3	4	5	6	7	8	9	10	11	12
0	0	0	0	0	0	0	0	0	0	0	0	0	0
1	0	1	2	3	4	5	6	7	8	9	10	11	12
2	0	2	4	6	8	10	12	14	16	18	20	22	24
3	0												
4	0												
5	0	5	10	15	20	25	30	35	40	45	50	55	60
6	0												
7	0												
8	0												
9	0												
10	0	10	20	30	40	50	60	70	80	90	100	110	120
11	0												
12	0												

Weavers (2003), among others, also suggests that children should use 'table squares' for multiplication of two numbers up to 10 because they display obvious patterns of numbers which learners might find memorable.

Problem-solving for teachers and learners

As we noted in a previous chapter, addressing the difficulties in learning experienced by learners at a level in the education system may be seen as a question of problem-solving, where the teacher makes a deliberate effort to get to know the learner, thinks about the difficulties s/he experiences, reflects on the demands of the particular area and then matches the learner's strengths and areas of difficulty against the demands of the curriculum area.

Learners may have spent a long time on repetition and drill with the result that s/he has little understanding of mathematical concepts or the conventions used in mathematical problem-solving. Mathematical word problems are complex because students need to understand the context in which the problem is set, the logic of the word problem, and also the mathematical procedures that are required to reach a solution.

A useful starting point is to ensure that pupils understand the problem in the first place. It might be helpful to encourage them to talk to each other about what they think it means – to inter-think (Littleton & Mercer, 2013) – partly to check understanding of the logic of the problem and partly also to ensure that they have read the text properly. Alternatively, or in addition, learners might close their eyes and visualise the problem. Then they might either use concrete objects such as counters or blocks, or draw a picture, to represent the problem before attempting to work out the solution.

Web activity WA11.1
Preparing for the lesson

On the website we have uploaded a suggested framework for thinking about how to prepare for mathematics lessons for mixed-attainment classes. You should access this now.

Multi-sensory teaching by using all the senses simultaneously wherever possible, will, again, help many students, for example talking students through processes while they are carrying them out, repeating the sequences they should follow aloud and encouraging them to do this also can be very helpful.

LEARNING POINT
CONSIDERING WAYS TO APPROACH
PROBLEM-SOLVING

Read the list below. How useful might this be as a protocol for teaching learners how to approach problem-solving in mathematics?

- Consider carefully what the learner has already learned before teaching new skills or concepts.
- Problems may need to be read very slowly with an emphasis on each individual word so that the learner has an opportunity to think about what the problem means before s/he tries to work it out.
- Teach students to think aloud, and/or discuss with peers the steps involved in solving problems.
- Encourage the learners to draw charts or sketches to solve problems.

- Use graph paper to help line up numbers.
- Use authentic examples that connect mathematics to real life.
- Use concrete objects such as coins, blocks and puzzles to teach new concepts or approaches to problem-solving.
- Check frequently to make sure the learner understands the work.
- Encourage learners to use flowcharts to organise information or help break down mathematics problems into steps. For example, model for learners how to solve problems in logical steps:
  o Draw a series of vertical boxes.
  o Write the problem in the top one.
  o Think about the steps needed to complete the problem.
  o Put only one step in each box in a logical order.
  o Complete the problem, step by step.
  o Write the solution in the bottom box.

Understanding 'place value'

An understanding of place value in mathematics is important at any stage in the education system beyond the earliest stages, not simply in the mathematics classroom but across other curriculum areas. If we take one example from the secondary curriculum, in geography lessons learners may be expected to cope with the concept of population density expressed in thousands per square mile. If these learners do not understand place value, they cannot be expected to understand population density of, for example, heavily populated conurbations. It would be hardly surprising in this situation if learners found concepts such as this so frustratingly complex and difficult that their behaviour became disruptive.

Taking a multi-sensory approach and using concrete equipment, such as base ten blocks, Dienes materials – unit cubes, 'longs' of 10 cm cubes, and 'flats' of 100 cm cubes – or similar materials for much longer than the teacher might have anticipated, is one way to address lack of understanding of place value, providing that this can be done without embarrassing the learners.

The use of zero as a place holder in a multi-digit line can be difficult to comprehend – without understanding the whole concept of place value.

LEARNING POINT
CONSIDERING DIFFICULTIES IN THE USE OF ZERO

Read the text below and note down:

- how the difficulty experienced by the learner might be explained;
- how you would address the learner's difficulties if you were the teacher.

(Continued)

A 14-year-old learner in a bottom mathematics set in a secondary school asked his teacher: 'How can 44 times nought possibly equal nought? How can 44 times anything equal nothing when you've started with 44 and made it bigger by multiplying?' (adapted from Wearmouth, 2009, p. 138).

The teacher realised that the young man did not really understand the concept of multiplication and realised she would have to do something about this.

As a short-term measure she took a handful of nothing and put it down on the desk 44 times to illustrate that there are occasions when multiplying does not necessarily result in making a number 'bigger'.

What would you have done?

Negative numbers

Counting backwards and understanding and dealing with the concept of negative numbers can be quite challenging for some learners (Chinn, 2012).

Web activity WA11.2
Negative numbers

On the website you will find suggestions about activities that may support learners who experience difficulties in this area.

Concept of money

Understanding the concept of money, and competence in calculations and problem-solving, is another important area that some learners might find problematic. First, there is the issue of money as a system of tokens, each of which stands for a particular value that can be exchanged for goods, and so on. Second, there is the question of understanding all the difficulties with numbers that might be experienced by the learner.

Diennes equipment or other concrete materials can be used in activities here, as suggested above. Rods and cubes can be made up into bundles representing the value of the money in the decimal system first, and then a gradual transition can be made to toy money and then to the real thing.

Concept of time

Acquiring a concept of time is not the same as learning to tell the time. The concept of time is abstract and complex (Piaget, 1969), with multiple meanings: points in time, duration or frequency of events, or intervals in-between. The reference point for many indicators of time is inconsistent. 'Late' can refer to a point in the morning when someone should have arrived earlier, or simply mean a point at night. The passage of time seems to distort in the mind, depending on the event and the degree of participants' engagement or interest in it.

No concept of time is concrete (Grauberg, 2002). However, these days, visual timetables are often used in schools for use with learners who experience cognitive difficulties (Selikowitz, 2008). Using a timer of some sort, for example a sand timer, to see how much of an activity can be completed before it runs out can help with the sense of time passing in the initial stages. Or learners might be asked to focus on the intervals between regular sounds, tapping or striking a percussion instrument for example, to encourage a sense of the duration of time. Or teachers might encourage children to act out a regular sequence of events in their own lives, represent them as a series of pictures on cards (Bruner's iconic mode), and ask the learners to arrange the cards in the correct sequence. A digital clock or watch is simpler than a traditional clock face to tell the time. However, the numbers on a digital timepiece simply change and do not offer a sense of the passage of time in the same way that the hands of the traditional clock do as they move round in the twelve-hour cycle.

Dyscalculia: Specific numeracy difficulties

Up to around 60% of individuals who identify as dyslexic experience difficulty in understanding and acquiring mathematical concepts and learning computational skills despite ability in other areas (Joffe, 1983; Henderson, 1998; Miles & Miles, 2004). The term 'dyscalculia' is often used to describe such a difficulty.

Web activity WA11.3
Activities addressing difficulties in information-processing

Many of the difficulties experienced by dyslexic students in information processing also affect their progress in mathematics learning, for example:

- left–right orientation difficulties;
- sequencing problems;
- poor spatial awareness;
- slow speed in information processing.

We have uploaded suggestions for activities that address these areas on the website. You might choose to access these now.

Support from parents and families

The available evidence suggests that parental/family support is an important factor in helping children with dyscalculia to improve numeracy (Peninsula Cerebra Research Unit, 2018). Parents and families can also play a role by helping a child to create a positive self-image as a successful mathematics learner, and to help reduce anxiety around maths. Activities involving the provision of home–school mathematics boxes with games and/or other mathematics materials has become increasingly popular. A number of published materials, for example Numicon (see below), might be used in a home–school initiative. In other schools, it may be that the teacher has to create them him/herself.

LEARNING POINT
AN EXAMPLE OF A MULTI-SENSORY PROGRAMME, 'NUMICON'

Numicon (Oxford University Press) is a commercially-produced multi-sensory programme that is designed to teach children number using structured visual representations to make the number system both visual and tactile. Its aim is to make the stable order of the number system clear to children. The materials include coloured plastic shapes, coloured pegs and baseboards, which fit together, and allow children to explore the relationships between numbers. The shapes represent numbers 1–10, with each shape being 'one' bigger than the previous number.

You will find an article by Nye, Buckley and Bird (2005) outlining the rationale underpinning Numicon and evaluating its effectiveness at: https://assets.cdn.down-syndrome.org/pubs/a/updates-352.pdf (accessed 20.06. 2020). You should access this now, and reflect on potential usefulness of the programme to you in your context.

In some schools, parents and families may be accustomed to coming into the school to discuss with teachers what they can do to help their offspring, while others will not. Achieving a positive working relationship with families often requires a great deal of sensitivity on the part of schools, especially if parents or carers are not confident in mathematics learning themselves. It is really important that families are thoroughly familiar and confident with the materials and how to use them before working with them at home with their children, and also that they have access to the school to talk through any issues that may arise.

Web activity WA11.4
Considering home–school numeracy partnerships

On the website we have uploaded an activity related to home–school partnerships to support learners' mathematics acquisition. You should access this now.

Conclusion

There is evidence to suggest the importance of building a child's confidence with mathematics. Research suggests that high teacher expectations are helpful in improving a child's mathematical ability. One way of doing this is to focus on developing strengths while offering positive encouragement and support for addressing weaknesses.

Teachers who are effective in supporting the mathematical learning of those students who experience difficulties show an interest in what students have to say, listen to their ideas, avoid sarcasm and do not allow students to put each other down. These teachers make an effort to make mathematics problems interesting and give the impression that they value all students' contributions (Stipek et al., 1998). In this way they create an environment where students are prepared to take risks because they know that it is safe to do so.

Multi-sensory methods of teaching can be helpful for improving aspects of mathematics.

After reading this chapter, what do you consider the most important things that teachers of mathematics should know and be able to do to encourage the mathematical learning of young people who experience difficulties in mathematics acquisition?

In Chapter 11 we move on to issues of adaptation of teaching, or what we might call differentiation, in classrooms to ensure that all children are included.

Further reading

Theory and practice

Bird, R. (2021) *The Dyscalculia Toolkit: Supporting Learning Difficulties in Maths*. London: Sage.

Chinn, S. (ed.) (2017) *Routledge International Handbook of Dyscalculia and Mathematical Learning Difficulties*. London: Routledge.

Chinn, S. (2018) *Maths Learning Difficulties, Dyslexia and Dyscalculia* (2nd edn). London: Jessica Kingsley.

Chinn, S., Goddard, F., & Henning, L. (2017) *Numicon Big Ideas*. Oxford: Numicon/Oxford University Press.

Dennis, M. S., Sharp, E., Chovanes, J., Thomas, A., Burns, R. M., Custer, B., & Park, J. (2016) A meta-analysis of empirical research on teaching students with mathematics learning difficulties. *Learning Disabilities*, 31(3), 156–168.

Doabler, C. T., & Fien, H. (2013) Explicit mathematics instruction: What teachers can do for teaching students with mathematics difficulties. *Intervention in School and Clinic*, 48(5), 276–285.

Gersten, R., Jordan, N. C., & Flojo, J. R. (2005) Early identification and interventions for students with mathematics difficulties. *Journal of Learning Disabilities*, 38(4), 293–304.

Useful websites

Association of Teachers of Mathematics: www.atm.org.uk/

Maths on Toast: www.mathsontoast.org.uk/

National Centre for Excellence in the Teaching of Mathematics: www.ncetm.org.uk/

National Numeracy: www.nationalnumeracy.org.uk/

Touch, Type, Read and Spell (n/d) Students struggling with math: www.readandspell.com/struggling-with-math#:~:-text=Many%20kids%20have%20trouble%20with,it%20more%20difficult%20than%20others.&text=There%20are%20a%20number%20of,apply%20and%20perform%20mathematical%20operations.

12

INCLUSIVE PRACTICES IN SCHOOLS AND CLASSROOMS

Major questions addressed in this chapter are:

- What can an inclusive classroom look like that makes effective curriculum access for all its learners?
- Are there any principles that could guide decisions about inclusive classroom practice and pedagogy?
- Is teaching that encourages progress in learning and behaviour for young people with special educational or additional learning or support needs necessarily qualitatively different from that of all other learners? If so, in what way(s)?

Key terms

Inclusive teaching environments, differentiation, curriculum adaptation, teacher support teams, 'Lesson Study', restorative practice

Introduction

In a previous chapter, we noted how legislation across the UK requires settings, schools and colleges to include all young people with special and/or additional learning or support needs. In general terms, we might all agree, as Wearmouth (2016, 2017) comments, that effective whole-setting/school/college inclusive provision means high aspirations for the achievement of all. Indeed, in England, the 2014 Children and Families Act mandates that provision should enable all learners with special education needs to achieve the 'best possible' – not simply 'satisfactory' – outcomes. In England also, the National Curriculum Inclusion Statement reaffirms that teachers should plan to set 'suitable challenges' with 'high expectations for every pupil' (§4.1), including those 'who have low levels of prior attainment or come from disadvantaged backgrounds'. This means using appropriate assessment to respond to pupils' needs and overcome potential barriers to learning. 'Potential areas of difficulty should be identified and addressed at the outset of work' (§4.4). Achieving this requires evaluation of the effectiveness of provision at all levels in enhancing opportunities and progress, leadership teams who aim to improve general provision to meet a wider range of needs, and teachers who evaluate achievement and well-being regularly, and make changes in provision where required as a result of this.

The focus of the current chapter is on the kind of learning environments, and the kind of pedagogies, that can be responsive to the learning and positive behaviour of all young people. This will include discussion of the role of what constitutes the most expensive resource in most settings, schools and colleges for learners who experience difficulties: teaching/learning support assistants.

Inclusive learning environments

As we have commented in previous chapters, it is probably at classroom level that the most important interactions between teachers and learners take place (Department of Education and Science, 1989). The current marketisation of education, fuelled by league tables in some areas of the UK, and competition and accountability for resources, can potentially make the creation of inclusive climates in schools and classrooms problematic – but nevertheless still possible – with a really determined whole-school and whole-staff effort.

Web activity WA12.1
Considering important features of inclusion in educational institutions

On the website we have uploaded perceptions of important features of 'inclusion' in educational institutions, together with a reflective activity. You might choose to access this material at this point.

Inclusive teaching approaches

Drawing on the work of Wells (1999), Swanwick (2019, p. 83) argues that the construction of knowledge is 'a social activity on many levels'. Language is 'the most powerful cultural tool in the human repertoire for making sense and sharing experience'. Humans learn through action that, importantly, is mediated by language as the most 'ubiquitous, flexible and creative of all the meaning-making tools available' (Mercer & Littleton, 2007, p. 2). Swanwick goes on to discuss the so-called 'dialogic theory of learning', based on putting into classroom practice the work of Vygotsky (1978), in particular the concept of the zone of proximal development. Classroom teaching based on this theory of learning focuses on ways in which teachers and learners share activities for the purpose of co-constructing knowledge. In 'dialogical meaning-making' the learner is seen to play an active role in constructing personal understanding through the process of dialogic interchange (Bakhtin, 1981, 1984). Implications of this approach can be seen reflected in Lyle's (2008, p. 230) comments that dialogic teaching '[...] explores learner's thought processes [...] treats students' contributions', including answers to teachers' questions, as an 'ongoing cognitive quest [...] [*that*] nurtures student's engagement, confidence [...] responsibility'. Along similar lines, Alexander's (2006) list of essential features of effective dialogic teaching include:

- teachers and students addressing learning tasks together, listening to each other and considering alternative viewpoints;
- students articulating ideas without fear of embarrassment about being wrong, and giving each other mutual support;
- teachers and students building on their own and others' ideas and linking them into coherent lines of thinking;
- teachers, as the more-knowledgeable others, planning dialogic teaching with particular goals in view.

From this perspective, all learners are active, all think about their learning, and have views and feelings about it. Vygotsky (1978, p. 57) proposed two planes where the learning process happens:

- the interpersonal, 'between the people' plane, and
- the intrapersonal, within the individual plane, where s/he thinks about new concepts, knowledge and skills, and appropriates them to him/herself.

The process through which an individual 'takes up and makes use of" (Newman, Griffin & Cole, 1989, p. 15) literacy, language and other tools available in society is called 'appropriation' (Leont'ev, 1981; Wertsch, 1991). Outward 'interpsychological' relations become the inner, 'intrapsychological' functions and, through this process of appropriation, the learner develops ways of thinking that are the norm in specific practices such as that associated with literacy. Hence the very well-known quote:

> Each function in the child's cultural development appears twice: first on the social level, and later on the individual level; first between people (interpsychological), and then inside the child (intrapsychological). (Vygotsky, 1978, p. 57)

Cognitive development, that is the progressive building of learning skills required for learning, such as attention, memory, thinking, problem-solving and language, depends on the presence of mediators during interactions between the individual and the environment. In schools, teachers-as-mediators can prompt, guide, reward, punish, model, and so on, the use of abstract cultural tools, as, for example, language and literacy.

The view that the learning process can be conceptualised on two planes, inter- and intrapsychological, implies that everything in the learning environment matters, especially the actions of the teacher. Learners need 'dialogic space' to enable scaffolding and learning on the intrapersonal plane (Wearmouth, 2017), that is, metaphorical 'space' where discussion can take place between learners and the more informed other(s), and between learners and peers through 'inter-thinking' (Littleton & Mercer, 2013). They also need time for personal reflection on the intrapersonal plane for appropriation of skills and knowledge (such as aspects of literacy and numeracy) that they have begun to acquire intermentally (in discussion with more-informed others) (Newman et al., 1989). There should also be respectful relationships among and between learners and adults to encourage feelings of safety in talking about their work (Wearmouth et al., 2011).

Compatible with this view of learning is the view of Riddick et al. (2002) in relation to 'dyslexia-friendly teachers'. Available support and organisation for teaching dyslexic children varies across settings and schools. However, within their own context all teachers can endeavour to create a dyslexia-friendly classroom by doing the following (Riddick et al., 2002, p. 22):

- create a positive image of dyslexia;
- make it OK for children to be dyslexic;
- teach in a multi-sensory manner;
- put a child in a set or group matched to their intellectual rather than literacy ability;
- believe the child can succeed and have high expectations;
- mark written work for content and not presentation (or mark them separately);
- give constructive advice on written presentation (not 'be less messy' or 'you must be more careful', etc.);
- be familiar with the child's individualised educational programme (IEP) (if a secondary school, have an organised system for reminding self which children in a class/set have IEPs);
- consult the child about their targets and how they would like any classroom-based support to be delivered;
- enable access to and output from the curriculum (prepared notes, workbooks, videos, information and communication technology (ICT), etc.);
- through teaching approach and organisation, reduce chances for visible public indicators of the child's difficulties (i.e. do not say 'Hands up who has finished');
- never ask a dyslexic child to read out loud without ascertaining in private if they are happy to do so;
- identify and appreciate the child's strengths or particular interests/expertise;
- ensure the child receives more positive than negative feedback and that they receive at least as much attention and positive feedback as other children in the class (e.g. is their work displayed as often as other children's work?).

Use of checklists to evaluate inclusive classroom practice

Checklists, against which inclusive practice in classrooms can be evaluated, can be very useful.

Web activity WA12.2
Learning from colleagues in a safe environment

On the website we have uploaded a template for auditing classroom organisation and behaviour. You might choose to access this now.

Curriculum adaptation and differentiation

As we have discussed before, all learners are entitled to fair access to the curriculum in a setting, school or college. In some special contexts, every learner may have his/her own curriculum that is differentiated to address individual needs and designed to encourage and monitor progress. It is really important to have high expectations of all learners in classrooms, irrespective of age, stage or identified need. In England, for example, the National Curriculum inclusion statement (Department for Education, 2014c) requires that:

> 4.1 Teachers should set high expectations for every pupil. [...] They have an even greater obligation to plan lessons for pupils who have low levels of prior attainment or come from disadvantaged backgrounds. Teachers should use appropriate assessment to set targets which are deliberately ambitious.

Teachers and classroom assistants need to be aware of which learners have individual plans and be conversant with their content so that they can take adequate account of learners' needs. However, rather than assuming that something different has to be organised for every individual, a more pragmatic process would be to focus first on strategies that ensure the inclusivity of the approach to teaching and learning, for example by increasing the range of teaching approaches, what in England is called 'Quality First Teaching'. This means adjusting learning objectives to suit individual learners' needs, and teaching that employs, for example, open and closed tasks, short and long tasks, visual, auditory or kinaesthetic activities. It also means acknowledging that the learning environment itself can support, or create barriers to, learning. Where learners experience auditory difficulties, attention must be paid to the acoustic environment, as discussed in Chapter 8, for example. Rooms with high benches and stools, or with little room between tables and chairs, may be very difficult for learners with physical impairments.

Disability legislation requires 'reasonable adjustments' where needed to enable fair access to learning and teaching programmes. Some young people who experience difficulties in learning can work on the same learning objectives as others in the class, as long as the teacher plans appropriate access strategies, for example, alternatives to written recording, and/or provision of appropriate resources of various kinds. For instance, if a barrier to a mathematics lesson on problem-solving is a dyslexic one, learners who lack competence and confidence in number facts may need the use of a calculator. However, learners who experience fine motor co-ordination difficulties, and cannot draw shapes and graphs accurately, may benefit from the use of a computer with appropriate software to draw shapes and graphs. Those with difficulty in understanding and using abstract symbols may benefit from the use of concrete materials of some kind, as discussed in previous chapters. In the chapters above, we have discussed other techniques for responding to the individual needs of young people according to their strengths, interests and the difficulties they experience, for example mind-mapping, returning to previous conceptual learning, multi-sensory approaches, reduction in speed of teaching and moving from one topic to the next, enabling additional time to absorb concepts and answer questions, use of visual and tactile supports for learning, and scribing by a classroom assistant or other helper.

Teachers themselves might be encouraged to try out ideas and assess results to extend their own experience and understanding. Strategies resulting in improved learning and/or behaviour can then be interpreted not as failures but as experiments leading towards solutions.

Tracking back

In mainstream classrooms, planning to meet the identified learning needs of individuals should take place within the planning process for the whole-class or whole-subject curriculum. For some learners, 'tracking back' is an effective method of deciding on appropriate learning objectives. The starting point for this is the relevant age-related objective for the whole class. Once this is decided, the teacher can track back through the learning programme for the particular subject to find a related objective for learners who experience difficulties that will challenge but at the same time be realistic. If tracking back takes place during the planning for a half-termly series of activities, the teacher can plan activities that are shared between learners. Maintaining the age-appropriate context of the learning objectives is really important to ensure access to a broad curriculum.

LEARNING POINT
DEVELOPING A DIFFERENTIATED APPROACH IN THE CLASSROOM

The Middletown Centre for Autism (2022) has provided a very useful step-by-step example of an approach to differentiating the curriculum in the classroom for autistic learners. This is available at https://best-practice. middletownautism.com/approaches-of-intervention/differentiating-the-curriculum/ (accessed 01.04.2022). We would like you to access this material now. As you do so, please note down the principles and techniques that you consider might apply to approaches for adapting or differentiating curricula as enacted in the classroom for learners who experience other kinds of difficulties in learning.

How closely might you follow this particular example in your own context?

What other approaches to classroom adaptation would you have to make to enable fair curriculum access for learners you know who experience difficulties in learning and/or sensory impairments?

Peer support for teachers

The link between the quality of teaching and student behaviour was also clearly acknowledged in a report on behaviour in schools, the Steer Report (Department for Education and Skills, 2005) 'Section 2: Principles and practice: What works in schools', which identified practical examples of ways to promote good behaviour and that can be adopted by all schools. The report notes the importance of consistently applied policy and practice, and an understanding that good behaviour will not necessarily just happen. It needs to be taught by staff who model what they want through their own behaviour and who have access to training and support in behaviour and classroom management. The Elton Report (Department of Education and Science, 1989) recommends the introduction of peer support groups to develop the trust and confidence needed for mutual observation and consultancy. Two examples of initiatives that incorporated peer support among teachers are Teachers Support Teams and Lesson Study.

Teachers Support Teams

Provision of support for classroom teachers through Teachers Support Teams (TSTs) (Creese, Norwich & Daniels, 2013) was an initiative set up at the Institute of Education in the 1990s. It was designed to address the issue in some schools of classroom teachers lacking confidence in their ability to provide appropriately differentiated programmes of study for their learners and feeling stressed or disaffected as a result. Class teachers were enabled to request support and advice from a team of peers on how to provide effectively and appropriately for young people with SEN(D) in mainstream classrooms. Effectively, a TST was a school-based group 'for teachers to exchange ideas, air feelings and work on problem-solving issues relating to teachers' work in the classroom' (Creese et al., 2013, p. 6). It provided a forum for teachers to 'share knowledge and skills, and to express and receive collegial and emotional support' as well as 'to learn specific methods and have access to different teaching approaches [...] and [...] an opportunity to air frustrations around disheartening behavioural issues' (p. 6). The TST in a school usually comprised the SENCo, a senior teacher and another class teacher. The referring teacher collaborated with the team to understand the problem and, together, work out an 'appropriate form of intervention related to learning and behaviour difficulties' (p. 5). The system 'involved 'a sharing of expertise between colleagues rather than some teachers acting as experts to others' (p. 5). Meetings lasted between 30 and 45 minutes, usually during lunchtime or after school. Most of the referrals were about behaviour problems, although many were about learning difficulties. The support included providing emotional encouragement, specific approaches to managing behaviour, teaching strategies and consulting others.

Referring teachers reported that experience with TSTs led to increased confidence and some improved behaviour and learning, while TST members themselves believed that they had gained much from the TST experience.

Lesson Study

Lesson Study is a professional development programme that involves teachers working in small groups to plan lessons that address a shared learning goal for pupils. They then deliver these lessons while their peers observe, and refine the lesson plans based on feedback and review. The focus of peer observations is on the learning of particular pupils rather than the teacher.

Murphy et al. (2017) describe how this programme was implemented in a project running between 2013 and 2015 in 181 schools in England. The implementation of the Lesson Study cycle in schools started with an initial group meeting where the three teachers planned the order in which they were observed and which lessons the other teachers in the team observed. The first teacher then taught three 'research lessons' observed by the other two teachers, who focused on pupil learning, rather than the teacher. After each of these lessons, there was a follow-up discussion that reviewed the class and joint planning for the next session in terms of content structure and delivery. In the planning, two 'case pupils' were selected that were typical of a group of pupils in the class so that the impact of the lessons on pupils with identified barriers to learning could be monitored. There was also input from the case pupil directly in the form of teacher–pupil interviews. Teachers were expected to keep records of the training sessions and were also expected to write up pupil case studies after each round of Lesson Study. This process was repeated after each of the research lessons. Over the course of the academic year, there were three cycles of Lesson Study with each teacher taking the turn of being observed.

Use of support staff in classrooms

Most schools employ teaching/classroom assistants (TAs), learning support assistants (LSAs) and other support staff – 'paraprofessionals' – in classrooms, and roles vary. Ideally, partnerships should be positive and be built on a common understanding of how to address the difficulties in learning that some learners might face, but such relationships are not created automatically. They often develop out of accommodations made by all parties as they negotiate their ways of working.

In the past 25 years there has been a large investment in increasing levels of support staff. Between 1997 and 2003 there was a 99% increase in TAs in English schools but, for a long time, limited research evidence about their impact and effectiveness. The evidence that existed was mostly based on teachers' reports. Findings from a study in England that evaluated the effectiveness of TAs in schools, the Deployment and Impact of Support Staff (DISS) project (Blatchford et al., 2004), indicated that there was a positive impact on teachers' workloads, levels of stress and job satisfaction. Most of TAs' time, but comparatively little teachers' time, was spent working with small groups or with individuals, usually those with SEN or who were lower attaining. TAs often led interventions out of the main classroom. They tended to be focused on finishing a set task, rather than on open questioning and discussion, and encouraging independent learning. Teachers, on the other hand, tended to extend learning through specific feedback and more detailed explanations of new concepts. Thus, learners became dependent on support from the TAs rather than autonomous. Most importantly, in general, learners who received the greatest support from TAs made less progress than peers who had less TA support. This remained the case even when there had been consideration of factors such as SEN, English as an additional language, free school meals and prior attainment (Webster, Russell & Blatchford, 2016).

One conclusion of the project was that the lack of impact on learners' achievement related to the way decisions were 'made about how TAs are used, albeit with the best of intentions, by schools and teachers' (Webster et al., 2016, p. 2). Some of the recommendations from this report relate to deployment, practice and the preparedness of support staff:

- deployment relates to the extent to which school-level vision for the use of TAs informs the way in which TAs are deployed in classrooms;
- practice relates to the kind of interactions TAs have with learners;
- preparedness relates to TAs' training for their roles, preparation to equip teachers with the necessary skills to manage support staff and time for joint planning, feedback and consideration of how to deploy TAs effectively.

In further studies, the recommendations from DISS were put into effect. The evaluations showed that the trials conducted by each school improved how senior management and teachers in schools thought about the deployment of TAs. Deployment, preparedness and practice all improved with the focus on these areas.

Making classrooms inclusive

Differentiation and adaptation of lesson activities, tasks and resources needs to take account of the full range of learning needs among children in the classroom and any requirements on individual learning plans. This includes current reading and numeracy levels, consideration of possible visual and auditory difficulties, interest level of the poems and mathematical tasks that are used, consideration of student grouping in the classroom, prior experiences of students, and the potential range of applications of ICT that might support learning, and so on. Resources include the human as well as the material. In classrooms where there are teaching assistants, discussion and preparation with those assistants and any other adults prior to the sequence of lessons is vital.

Inclusive programmes

In previous chapters we have discussed approaches to maintaining order in schools that are based on behaviourist understandings of learning and behaviour. In many countries, restorative justice is becoming increasingly common as an alternative means of preventing, managing and controlling behaviour. Restorative justice is concerned to move away from a retributive justice approach and the primacy of assigning blame and punishment to an alternative means of preventing, managing and controlling behaviour by finding a mutually agreeable way forward by negotiation.

Over the years, within special education practice in many countries, there has been a variety of provision for students whose behaviour is seen as 'difficult', 'disturbed' or 'disruptive'. Interventions have been retributive, punitive and harsh, rehabilitative or therapeutic. In countries, such as those in the UK, that have adopted a principle of universal education for all their young people, the national policy contexts have had to reconcile principles of individuality, distinctiveness and diversity with principles of inclusion and equal opportunities. There are occasions in schools when the rights of individual students may conflict with the rights and entitlements of the majority. This issue may be particularly stark where individual behaviour is seen to have an adverse effect on others. This issue of disciplinary exclusion, for example, raises an important issue of whose rights should be paramount: the individual's right to education or a student community's right to schooling in contexts that are safe and affirming, without disruption by the challenging behaviour of individuals. The real dilemma for schools is how to act in a situation that is beset by often irreconcilable tensions.

The main focus in a restorative justice approach is on 'putting things right' between all those involved rather than punishing. The process of restorative justice has been introduced into a number of schools, in New Zealand and in the UK for example, where it can be seen as embodying a set of important skills required by mediators and facilitators but underpinned by a third view as an ethos or philosophy:

> that encompasses the values of respect, openness, empowerment, inclusion, tolerance, integrity and congruence [...] and a philosophy which gives central importance to building, maintaining and, when necessary, repairing relationships and community. (Hopkins, 2004, p. 20)

Below we outline the way in which restorative practices were implemented by the Scottish Government.

Restorative practices in Scotland

In 2004, The Scottish Executive established a 30-month pilot project in restorative practices in three local authorities. An evaluation of the implementation over the first two years indicates that restorative practice 'can offer a powerful and effective approach to promoting harmonious relationships in school and to the successful resolution of conflict and harm'.

The research indicated that the atmosphere in most of the schools became calmer and learners became more positive about their school experience. They thought staff were fair and listened to 'both sides of the story'. Indeed, 'a small number of schools had raised attainment and in several there was a decrease in exclusions, in-school discipline referrals and out of school referrals' (Scottish Executive, 2004, www.webarchive.org.uk/wayback/archive/20170701074158/ http://www.gov.scot/Publications/2007/08/23161140/2, accessed 30.10.2021).

Schools experienced some challenges in implementing restorative practice instead of the more conventional punitive approaches. In primary and special schools, for example, these included recruiting staff open to the approach, convincing some parents of its value and communicating with all the stakeholders when a restorative solution was reached to ensure that it was understood and 'owned' by everyone.

In secondary schools, challenges included the need to revise disciplinary procedures to facilitate restorative approaches, key staff remaining committed to a restorative approach if change was slow, and provision of structured opportunities for trained staff to develop confidence to train others.

In both primary and secondary sectors, key features predisposing to successful implementation included:

> readiness for change, and also balance of clarity and flexibility about identification of aims [...] good quality training and leadership [...] where schools saw a need for change and were already committed to improving school ethos by creating and sustaining positive relationships throughout the school community. [...] A crucial part of readiness was

[...] a sense of agency among those involved; they had the capacity to make them better. (McCluskey et al., 2008 p. 412)

Overall, when introduced in schools with at least some receptive staff and when the initiative was supported by enthusiasm, leadership and staff development, there was a positive impact on relationships in school. This was evidenced through a reduction in playground incidents, discipline referrals, exclusion and use of external behaviour support.

Web activity WA12.3
Cultural underpinnings of restorative practices

On the website we have uploaded an example of restorative practice in New Zealand. You might choose to access this now.

Restorative circles

A circle is an example of restorative practice that is used in some educational institutions to develop relationships and build community or to respond to wrongdoing, conflicts and problems. Circles give people an opportunity to speak and listen to one another safely in an atmosphere of respect and equality. 'Circle time' (Mosley, 1998) and morning meetings (Charney, 1992) have been widely used in primary schools for many years, and more recently in secondary schools and higher education (Mirsky, 2007, 2011; Wachtel & Wachtel, 2012).

Circles may use a sequential format where one person speaks at a time. The chance to speak moves in one direction around the circle. Each person must wait till his/her turn. No one is allowed to interrupt. Alternatively, a talking piece – a small object, for example a conch shell as in *Lord of the Flies* (Golding, 1954) – is passed from person to person to facilitate this process. Only the person who is holding the talking piece may speak (Costello, Wachtel & Wachtel, 2010). Both the circle and the talking piece have roots in ancient and indigenous practices (Mirsky, 2004a, 2004b).

The sequential circle encourages participants to talk less and listen more. Typically, it is organised around topics raised by the circle facilitator. The format maximises the opportunity for the voices of those who are usually inhibited by more assertive people to speak without interruption. Individuals who want to respond to something that has been said must be patient and wait until it is their turn to speak (Costello et al., 2010).

Conclusion

In the various countries of the UK, legislation functions to strengthen and extend the legal requirement to ensure the availability and effectiveness of high-quality provision for special and/or additional learning and support needs and disabilities. All teachers in settings, schools and colleges, newly qualified and experienced, are expected to provide effective learning opportunities for all their pupils, including those who have special and/or additional learning and support needs and disabilities. Making appropriate provision for all young people in settings, schools and colleges is challenging, but not insurmountable.

As you reflect on the content of this chapter, what do you consider to be the hallmarks of an inclusive school, classroom and teacher?

In Chapter 13 we turn to issues of professional relationships between schools/colleges, and families, and between schools/colleges and outside agencies.

Further reading

Inclusive classrooms

Allen, M. (2021) *Leading Inclusion in a Secondary School: No Pupil Left Behind*. London: David Fulton.

Briggs, S. (2016) *Meeting Special Educational Needs in Primary Classrooms: Inclusion and How to Do It* (2nd edn). London: David Fulton.

Canavan, G. (2016) *Supporting Pupils on the Autism Spectrum in Primary Schools*. London: Routledge.

Crossley, N., & Hewitt, D. (2021) *Inclusion: A Principled Guide for School Leaders*. London: Routledge.

Reid, G. (2006) *Dyslexia and Inclusion: Classroom Approaches for Assessment, Teaching and Learning* (2nd edn). London: Routledge.

Teacher collaboration

Creese, A., Daniels, H., & Norwich, B. (1997) *Teacher Support Teams in Primary and Secondary Schools*. London: David Fulton.

Dudley, P. (ed.) (2015) *Lesson Study: Professional Learning for Our Time*. London: Routledge.

Norwich, B., & Jones, J. (eds) (2014) *Lesson Study: Making a Difference to Teaching Pupils with Learning Difficulties*. London: Bloomsbury.

Restorative practice in schools

Bradford, N., & LeSal, D. (2021) *A Real-world Guide to Restorative Justice in Schools: Practical Philosophy, Useful Tools, and True Stories*. London: Jessica Kingsley.

Hansberry, B. (2016) *A Practical Introduction to Restorative Practice in Schools: Theory, Skills and Guidance*. London: Jessica Kingsley.

13

WORKING IN PARTNERSHIP WITH FAMILIES AND OUTSIDE AGENCIES

Major questions addressed in this chapter are:

- What rights do families across the UK have in relation to decision-making over their children's education?
- What kind of partnership work between settings, schools, colleges and families is effective in meeting the needs of children and young people in education?
- What is the range of people with whom teachers might expect to work in support of children who experience some sort of difficulty? What is their likely role?
- Are there any principles for effective collaborative working of which we should be aware?

Key terms

Home–school partnerships, parental rights, multi-agency collaboration, child protection

Introduction

The chapter begins by outlining statutory rights and potential roles of parents and families in the education system, and goes on to reflect on practitioners' views of essential features of setting/school/college partnerships with learners' homes. It continues with discussion of professional relationships and partnership work between schools/colleges, parents and families, and between schools/colleges and outside agencies. It considers the role of specialist external agencies in supporting the provision for SEND in schools and colleges: when and how to seek advice. In doing so, it acknowledges challenges in relation to partnership work – with examples of what can happen in practice, effective and ineffective.

Parental and families' rights

In a number of different countries across the world parents and carers are formally acknowledged as, potentially, an important source of additional support in addressing difficulties in learning and/or behaviour experienced by their children. The right of parents and/or carers to be consulted at every stage of decision-making about their children is enshrined in law across the UK, as we discussed in Chapter 4. In Wales, for example, the new 2018 Act requires that the views, wishes and feelings of children, their parents and young people are considered at all stages of the Individual Development Plan (IDP) process. In a similar vein, the SEND supplement (Department of Education Northern Ireland (DENI), 2005, §1.15) reads:

> Schools should welcome and encourage parents to participate throughout their child's career in the school and [...] schools must tell parents when special educational provision is being made for a child because the child is considered by the school as having SEN.

There is statutory provision for families who are dissatisfied with the way in which their children's needs have been addressed across the UK also. In Scotland, for example, the Education (Additional Support for Learning) (Scotland) Act 2004 sets out rights for parents and families, establishes mechanisms for resolving differences for families and authorities through mediation and dispute resolution, and has established the Additional Support Needs Tribunals (Scotland). The legislation was amended by the Education (Additional Support for Learning) (Scotland) Act 2009. The amendments related, among other issues, to the provision of a new national advocacy service for parents and young people.

Legal entitlement is not always reflected in reality. In 2009, when the Lamb Enquiry into special educational needs and parental confidence in the system was published, families were entitled to be involved with decision-making in relation to assessment and provision for their children. However, Lamb concluded that:

> Failure to comply with statutory obligations speaks of an underlying culture where parents and carers of children with SEN can too readily be seen as the problem and as a result parents lose confidence in schools and professionals. [...] As the system stands it often creates 'warrior parents' at odds with the school and feeling they have to fight for what should be their children's by right; conflict in place of trust. (Lamb, 2009, 1.1)

Lamb (2009, 1.4) recommended a new framework in England for the provision of SEN and disability information that 'puts the relationship between parent and school back at the heart of the process' and 'trades adherence to a "laundry list" of rules for clear principles to guide that relationship'. These recommendations are clearly reflected in the terms of the Children and Families Act 2014 in England.

As we noted in Chapter 9, a number of guides for parents and carers have been issued to support families to understand their entitlements in the most recent legislation, for example *The Parents' Guide to Additional Support for Learning* (Enquire, 2014), which is funded by the Scottish government, and the *Special Educational Needs and Disability (SEND) – A Guide for Parents and Carers* (Department for Education, 2014d) published in England. Parents' and families' rights are made very clear in these *Guides*. For example, the *Guide* in England (DfE, 2014d, p. 11) sets out the basic principles that parents and families:

> [...] should have a real say in decisions that affect their children, should have access to impartial information, advice and support and know how to challenge decisions they disagree with.

Regular assessments of the progress of all learners and gathering of information should include discussion early on with both student and parents so that all can be clear about the pupil's areas of strength and difficulty, any concerns the parent(s) might have, the outcomes agreed for the child and the next steps. Parents and families are advised in the *Guide* (pp. 8–9):

> If you think your child has SEN, you should talk to your child's early education setting, school, college or other provider. They will discuss any concerns you have, tell you what they think and explain to you what will happen next.

Parental/family engagement with settings, schools and colleges

While law is specific in setting out families' and learners' entitlements, in practice it is still not always easy to access appropriate provision. The Parliamentary Select Committee's report on special educational provision in England in October 2019 was scathing in its criticism on what was commonly on offer:

> Parents and carers have to wade through a treacle of bureaucracy, full of conflict, missed appointments and despair. We want to see a neutral role introduced, the purpose of which would be to arrange meetings, co-ordinate paperwork and be a source of impartial advice to parents. We believe that this would help reduce conflict in the system and remove much of the responsibility that seems to fall on parents' shoulders. (Great Britain, Parliament, House of Commons, 2019, p. 3)

Family support outside the setting, school or college

Settings, schools and colleges have a lot of power to affect the well-being of learners and their families and carers through the expectations that they have of the home context. If we take the example of effective provision for young people with hearing impairments, the National Deaf Children's Society (NDCS) is very clear about the need to take close account of the family circumstances:

> The 'best' communication approach for any child and family is the one which works for them, both fitting in with the family's culture and values and, most importantly, allowing the child to develop good self-esteem, a positive self-image, successful relationships [...] in all aspects of her [*sic*] life. (NDCS, 2010b, p. 50)

Where a child uses British Sign Language (BSL), it is useful if the rest of the family, classmates and teachers learn to sign also.

Learners may well benefit very effectively from support for them at home with programmes organised or suggested by the setting, school or college. There are a number of literacy programmes or techniques currently in common use in home–school partnerships in different countries which are designed to enable parents and carers to support the literacy development of students who experience difficulties. If families and schools are to work together to support the learning of students who experience difficulties in literacy development, it is crucial that educators have a clear view of how to establish home–school links in ways which take account of:

- the ability of families from a diversity of social and cultural backgrounds to support children's literacy acquisition;
- the home–school power relationships that are implied by different partnership models.

The surmise that the homes of poor working-class and ethnic minority-culture families are less good environments for children to acquire literacy than those of culturally-dominant, middle-class families was common until recent years. In the 1970s and 1980s, the results of a number of studies suggested that achievement on standardised tests of reading related strongly to social class. For example, tests of reading attainment were carried out on 7-year-old children born in one week in 1958 as part of the National Child Development Study (Davie, Butler & Goldstein, 1972). Of these children, 30% showed relatively poor achievement. This correlated highly with a number of home factors, including social class. However, the assumption of a clear reciprocal relationship between low levels of parental literacy and poor literacy development of their children is not fully supported by research. For example, Hewison and Tizard's (1980) study of the reading attainment of 7-year-old working-class children in Dagenham, Essex, showed that half the parents of working-class children who were competent readers regularly heard them read, although none of the parents had been encouraged by the school to do so. Subsequently, a number of research studies were set up to investigate the hypothesis that parental support at home for school-related literacy had a significant effect on the improvement of children's reading.

Case study: Evidence of the effectiveness of family support for children's reading

In the Haringey Project (Hewison & Tizard, 1980), at a time when poor reading achievement seems automatically to have been associated with membership of the lower classes, every child in two top infant classes chosen at random from two multiracial inner-city schools in London was heard reading from books sent home by the class teachers for two years. A highly significant improvement among pupils who were heard reading at home in comparison with other pupils was indicated in the results. There was no comparable improvement among those pupils who received extra tuition in school. Since that time numbers of home–school literacy projects have also demonstrated the potential effectiveness of family support for children's literacy learning.

We have included some of the programmes that lend themselves to home use in Chapter 10.

As with difficulties in literacy acquisition, it may very well be worth considering how to form working partnerships with parents and families to support young people to overcome barriers to their mathematics learning, for example by using home–school mathematics boxes with games and/or other mathematics materials. Some schools will already have very good, effective partnerships with families who may be accustomed to coming into the school to discuss with teachers what they can do to help their offspring, while others will not. Whatever the case, it is really important that families are thoroughly familiar and confident with the materials and how to use them before working with them at home with their children, and also that they have access to the school to talk through any issues that may arise.

LEARNING POINT
FEATURES OF EFFECTIVE PARTNERSHIPS WITH PARENTS AND FAMILIES

A group of special educational needs co-ordinators working in educational institutions across the age range who were studying on a professional development course in the East Midlands of England recently made the following comments about what they felt are essential features of effective partnerships with parents and families.

Schools getting to know families really well, understand their backgrounds and engage positively with parents/guardians to ensure they are actively involved with all decision making/communication, so they are confident that they:

- know they are listened to by the school;
- can support their children and feel a part of the community;
- understand their responsibility and that of the school.

To what extent, from your experience, would you agree with them?

Is there anything you would add to this list?

Work with external agencies

For teachers, parents and families, knowing when and how to interact with the range of professionals, inside and outside the setting, school or college, who may become involved with their children can be complex and, at times, time-consuming, but is nevertheless very important for welfare and progression. There are two particular areas in schools where work with other professionals is important: child protection and support for learning and behaviour.

Child protection

Over time, since the 1980s, various governments in the UK have viewed multi-agency collaborative working practices as paramount for the safety of children, and recommendations have been made about professional development in joint working practices for professionals working in health, social services, education, and others (Dunhill, 2009). Despite this, reports from many child protection reviews within the UK over the past 20 years (Reder & Duncan, 2003; Brandon et al., 2009; Laming, 2009; Rochdale Borough Safeguarding Children Board, 2012) have concluded that a lack of communication and collaboration between agencies has contributed to the death or abuse of a child.

In terms of child welfare, there is a long history of problems in inter-agency work in, for example, exchanging information or disputes over responsibility for offering particular services. Victoria Climbié was a child known to be at risk by both education and social services. Her tragic death at the hands of a family member is illustrative of systems failure and re-emphasised the need for closer co-operation between agencies. The government published a formal response to the report investigating her death, and a Green Paper, *Every Child Matters* (HM Treasury, 2003), was followed by the Children Act 2004. The 'Every Child Matters' agenda (Department for Education and Skills, 2004) sought to resolve the difficulties by unifying children's services, and all local education authorities and other services were combined to form local authorities (LAs).

In 2009, however, significant problems in the 'day-to-day reality of working across organisational boundaries and cultures, sharing information to protect children' were identified in the Laming Report (Laming, 2009, para 1.6). Laming noted that training issues remained (para 1.5) and that 'Staff across frontline services [...] need to be able to notice signs of distress in children of all ages, but particularly amongst very young children who are not able to voice concerns and for whom bedwetting, head-banging and other signs may well be a cry for help' (para 3.1). Children's safety and well-being is dependent on this.

Each profession is different in terms of its values (i.e. what is considered most important), vocabulary, criteria for understanding risk, knowledge and expertise, recording and sharing of information within legal or institutional frameworks, length of training, prestige or status, expertise as a practitioner and the aspects of life experience that inform practice.

The issue of professional identity is of crucial importance in considering how to establish effective collaboration among the various agencies. Working together may lead to greater understanding of the roles of other professions (Whiting, Scammell & Bifulco, 2008). However, it may also often result in a sense of threat to the individual's sense of his/her own professional identity with a consequent decrease in collaboration within the multi-agency team (Hudson, 2002). Particularly in teams with no clearly defined responsibilities, communication may be at a surface level, but with underlying tensions resulting in avoidant behaviours and little action by the group (Stuart, 2012).

Web activity WA13.1
Auditing essential factors in multi-agency partnerships

In a systematic literature review (Atkinson, Jones & Lamont, 2007), a number of factors were identified as essential to effective multi-agency practice. We have uploaded a summary of this list on the website, and an activity related to this. You might like to have a look at this material now.

Support for learning and behaviour

It is highly likely that a student and his/her family will be involved with other agencies in addition to the school if s/he experiences more complex and severe difficulties (as well as some medical conditions associated with learning problems), especially if these have been identified before school age. All young people are different. Without the involvement of others, it may not be possible for families or schools either to sort out the complex interaction of factors which result in difficulty in learning, or know how they might begin to address this.

Table 13.1 outlines some of the different individuals that practitioners and families might expect to work with and gives an indication of their job role.

Table 13.1 Examples of professional roles in supporting children and young people in settings, schools and colleges

Title	Job role
I. Education	
SEN, additional needs or support needs advisory teacher	The advisory teacher, or Lead Professional or co-ordinator in Scotland, may support the links between the settings, parents, schools, social care and health services by developing and disseminating good practice, supporting the development and delivery of training both for individual institutions and on a wider basis and developing links with existing networks to support children making transitions across phases. They may work with advice and support services, to promote effective work with families of learners with needs of various kinds.
Educational psychologist	Educational psychologists (EPs) have knowledge and understanding of children's development, learning and behaviour. They provide support through the assessment of an individual learner's learning and/or behavioural needs and may advise on appropriate learning resources and plans to meet needs in settings, schools and colleges.
Teacher for the hearing impaired (HI)/teacher for the visually impaired (VI)	The teacher for sensory-impaired learners assesses, advises practitioners in settings, schools and colleges, and often teaches deaf and/or blind children and young people in the place of learning. S/he works closely with health and social care and other agencies (where appropriate) following diagnosis and may collaborate with voluntary agencies, for example the National Deaf Children's Society, the Royal National Institute for Blind People. S/he also works with hospitals to ensure children and young people with sensory impairments receive the most appropriate assessment.

(Continued)

Table 13.1   (Continued)

Title	Job role
Learning support assistants/teaching assistants	A learning support assistant (LSA) or teaching assistant (TA) works in the classroom under the direction of a qualified teacher to support individual learners or small groups. The class teacher should always maintain responsibility for the progress of all his/her learners in the classroom
Portage and early support	Portage is a home-based education service for families with a child or children from birth to 5 years with complex additional needs. Portage works closely with a wide number of other professionals from social care, health and the voluntary sector. Portage will offer advice and support to the pre-school setting where the child is attending and may support the child through the transition process into pre-school or school when the time comes.
2. Health	
Paediatrician	A paediatrician is a specialist doctor who looks after babies and children. S/he is often involved, particularly early on, when there are concerns that a child may have an impairment or disability. A paediatrician can make referrals as needed for further medical investigations and diagnosis, for example to other paediatric specialists, therapists, psychologists and specialist nursing services.
Speech and language therapists (SLTs)	Speech and language therapists (SLTs) assess speech, language and communication problems to help children better to communicate. They operate in homes, Early Years settings and schools, providing specialist assessments, support and advice to parents/carers and teachers.
Physiotherapists	Children's physiotherapists are health care professionals who provide specialist assessment and intervention to children and young people who have a range of physical and movement difficulties which limit their mobility, function and/or independence. They may work in a range of locations: clinics, school and pre-school settings, homes, and respite or voluntary care settings.
Occupational therapists (OTs)	Occupational therapists are health professionals who may work with a variety of children with educational needs, disability and complex health difficulties, and work in the setting that is most appropriate for the child, young person or their family/carers.
3. Social care	
Social worker	Social workers tend to specialise in either adult or children's services. Among possible roles are: • ensuring that schools have a contact for seeking social work advice on children who may have needs in education; • co-ordinating social services advice for any statutory assessments, transition reviews and annual reviews, as appropriate; • ensuring social services provision is made for any children with needs, where appropriate.

Across the UK, statutory assessment of children and young people's special educational needs and disabilities and/or additional support needs requires effective inter-agency collaboration in order to ensure that they are supported with the special/additional provision that they need in order to engage with the school or college curriculum and make good progress. In Scotland, the *Supporting Children's Learning Code of Practice: Revised* (Scottish Government, 2017, §11) notes that 'The Act[1] promotes integrated working across agencies, in assessment, intervention, planning, provision and review'. In Scotland, also, the individual plan that results from statutory assessment is termed 'a co-ordinated support plan':

> a number of children and young people have additional support needs arising from complex or multiple factors which require a high degree of co-ordination of support from education authorities and other agencies in order that their needs can be met. This support is co-ordinated through the provision of a co-ordinated support plan under the Act. (Scottish Government, 2017, p. 74, §1)

To achieve the level of effective inter-agency collaboration that is required, the Code in Scotland (p. 30, §8) reads:

> Education authorities need to play their part in ensuring that there is effective communication, collaboration and integrated assessment, planning, action and review when other agencies are involved.

In England, the new Education, Health and Care Plans, introduced by the Children and Families Act, 2014, by definition also require a similar degree of collaboration, albeit that previous attempts at this have often been problematic. The 2015 *Code of Practice*, for example, reads:

> 1.22 If children and young people with SEN or disabilities are to achieve their ambitions and the best possible educational and other outcomes, including getting a job and living as independently as possible, local education, health and social care services should work together to ensure they get the right support.

> 1.23 When carrying out their statutory duties under the Children and Families Act 2014, local authorities **must** do so with a view to making sure that services work together where this promotes children and young people's wellbeing or improves the quality of special educational provision (Section 25 of the Children and Families Act 2014). Local authorities **must** work with one another to assess local needs. Local authorities and health bodies **must** have arrangements in place to plan and commission education, health and social care services jointly for children and young people with SEN or disabilities.

The *Code* in England (Department for Education/Department of Health (DfE/DoH), 2015) offers statutory advice about joint commissioning arrangements between education, health and social care:

> 3.9 Joint commissioning arrangements **must** cover the services for 0–25 year old children and young people with SEN or disabilities, both with and without EHC plans. Services will include specialist support and therapies, such as clinical treatments and delivery of

---

[1]This is the Education (Additional Support for Learning) (Scotland) Act 2004.

medications, speech and language therapy, assistive technology, personal care (or access to it), Child and Adolescent Mental Health Services (CAMHS) support, occupational therapy, habilitation training, physiotherapy, a range of nursing support, specialist equipment, wheelchairs and continence supplies and also emergency provision. [...]

3.10 Local authorities, NHS England and their partner CCGs **must** make arrangements for agreeing the education, health and social care provision reasonably required by local children and young people with SEN or disabilities. In doing so they should take into account provision being commissioned by other agencies, such as schools, further education colleges and other education settings. Partners should commission provision for children and young people who need to access services swiftly [...].

When EHC Plans were piloted (DfE, 2014b, p. 14), a number of 'Key challenges and enabling factors' were identified in relation to multi-agency working. Some were seen as 'fundamental to the new process' (p. 14). The first challenge was 'ensuring sufficiency and consistency of multi-agency working'. Another was the 'sharing of information between agencies and with families' (p. 15).

It seems that the much-hoped-for collaboration is often not happening, as the 2019 report of the Parliamentary Select Committee notes:

[...] many of the eagerly anticipated initiatives are not living up to their ambition and name. The role of health providers is pivotal, but unsurprisingly, the meshing of two systems has not worked. Unless health and social care are 'at the table', we are no further on, and the Education, Health and Care Plan is no more than a Statement by another name. In a similar vein, we want to see greater joint working between the health and education sectors, beginning firmly with the development of a joint outcomes framework to measure how the health aspects of support for children and young people with SEND are being delivered locally. But ultimate responsibility for this monitoring should sit with government, not an inspectorate.

We are seeing serious gaps in therapy provision. We need to see professionals trained and supported so that they are able to support all pupils; these huge gaps in therapy provision across the country are letting down all pupils, but particularly those on SEN Support. (Great Britain, Parliament, House of Commons, 2019, pp. 3–4)

In Wales, the most recent legislation, the Additional Learning Needs (ALN) Act shows a deliberate intention to ensure that external services do actually collaborate effectively. This Act places a duty on all local health boards to designate an officer to have responsibility for co-ordinating the health board's functions in relation to children and young people with ALN. That person is known as the Designated Education Clinical Lead Officer (DECLO). The DECLO must either be a registered medical practitioner or a registered nurse or another health professional. The Local Health Board must only designate an officer as a DECLO it considers to be suitably qualified and experienced in the provision of health care for children and young people with ALN. Further, the Education Tribunal for Wales ('the Tribunal') will have the power to make legally-binding decisions on local authorities and further education institutions (FEIs). In doing so, it will be able to require an NHS body to provide evidence regarding health-related aspects of an appeal and can make recommendations to an NHS body about the exercise of its functions under the Act.

Effective collaborative working practices

For teachers, parents and families, knowing when and how to interact with the range of professionals, inside and outside the school, who may become involved with a particular child is very important to the student's welfare and progress.

Web activity WA13.2
Consideration of the inclusiveness of meetings

On the website we have uploaded suggestions about effective practices in formal meetings between external agencies, staff and families, together with an activity. You might choose to access this material now.

Conclusion

Across the UK, families have statutory rights to be involved in their children's education and any discussion about special educational, or additional learning or support provision. Entitlement is not the same as reality, however, and there is evidence in some parts of the UK that 'the distance between young people's lived experience, their families' struggles and Ministers' desks is just too far' (Great Britain, Parliament, Select Committee on Education, 2019, p. 3).

Families can do a lot to support their children at home. Settings, schools and colleges have a lot of power to affect the lives of learners and their families and carers through the kind of consultation arrangements, assessment and provision that they make and the expectations that they have of the home context. To carry out their responsibilities effectively and include young people who experience difficulties, there is a level above which good will is not enough, and they themselves need additional resourcing.

Crucial to the success of implementing the terms of legislation relating to special educational, additional learning, or support needs in settings, schools and colleges across the UK is the effectiveness of multi-agency working across children's services, health and education. Assessment of children and young people's special educational needs and disabilities and/or additional support needs, whether statutory or not, may require effective inter-agency collaboration in order to ensure that they are supported with the special/additional provision that they need to engage with the school or college curriculum and make good progress.

From your own experience what would you say are the main issues that settings, schools and colleges should take into account when setting up, or reviewing, partnerships with parents and families so that everyone feels respected and their views are taken into account properly?

Further reading

Guides for families

Department for Education (DfE) (2014) *Special Educational Needs and Disability (SEND): A Guide for Parents and Carers.* London: DfE.

Education Authority Northern Ireland (2020) *Special Educational Needs (SEN).* Available at: www.eani.org.uk/parents/special-educational-needs-sen

Enquire (2017) *The Parents' Guide to Additional Support for Learning.* Edinburgh: Enquire.

Welsh Government (2018) *Additional Learning Needs and Education Tribunal (Wales) Act Fact Sheet 5.* Cardiff: Welsh Fovernment. Available at: https://gov.wales/sites/default/files/publications/2018-06/aln-factsheet-how-will-the-act-affect-children-young-people-and-parents-carers.pdf

Partnership with parents and families

Axford, N., Berry, V., Lloyd, J., Moore, D., Rogers, M., Hurst, A., Blockley, K., Durkin, H., & Minton, J. (2019) *How Can Schools Support Parents' Engagement in their Children's Learning? Evidence from Research and Practice.* London: Education Endowment Foundation.

Education Support Partnership (n/d) *How Schools and Families Can Work Better Together.* Available at: www.education-support.org.uk/sites/default/files/resources/how_schools_and_families_can_work_better_together_0.pdf

Useful websites

American Federation of Teachers (n/d) *Building Parent–Teacher Relationships:* www.readingrockets.org/article/building-parent-teacher-relationships

Independent Parental Special Educational Advice:

www.ipsea.org.uk

School–Home Support: www.schoolhomesupport.org.uk/

POSTSCRIPT

Provision for special and/or additional learning and support needs and disabilities in Early Years settings, schools and colleges continues to be high priority for teachers and other educators, governors, parents and politicians. Since 2000, several pieces of legislation relating to disability equality have been passed across the UK.[1] Most recently, the Equality Act 2010 stresses planned approaches to eliminating discrimination and improving access and is nationwide (including private education), imposing duties on schools and local authorities. This means that organisations such as settings, schools and colleges are expected to be proactive in anticipating and responding to the needs of disabled students. Revised legislation related to provision for special and/or additional learning and support needs and disabilities for young people was introduced in England, from birth to 25 years, in Part 3 of the Children and Families Act 2014; in Wales by the Additional Learning Needs and Education Tribunal (Wales) Act 2018; in Scotland by the Education (Additional Support for Learning) (Scotland) Act 2009; and in Northern Ireland by a Special Educational Needs and Disability Act (Northern Ireland) 2016. In each nation, up-to-date Codes of Practice have been, or will be, devised to explain the duties of settings, schools and colleges under the relevant law.

In this book we have taken the view that, as Bruner (1996) noted over 20 years ago, what we experience in education is fundamental to the formation of 'Self'. By this we mean what we think about ourselves and our potential for learning and achieving, what we believe others think of us, and so on. Settings, schools and colleges judge learners, and learners respond by judging themselves in the way they have been judged. Children and young people identified as needing special or additional learning, support or provision in educational institutions are human beings with the same degree of humanity, individuality and entitlement to respect, dignity, excitement and engagement in learning as their peers. What happens in educational institutions therefore plays a critical part in shaping students' ability, responsibility and skill in initiating and completing actions, that is, their 'self-efficacy'. In this way, it contributes to the construction of feelings, positive or negative, about being able to cope with the world of education and, in turn, the global community.

---

[1]This does not apply in Northern Ireland, where policy related to disability is devolved to the Northern Ireland Assembly.

GLOSSARY

Additional learning needs (ALN)   In Wales, this term has a legal definition and refers to learning, physical or sensory needs experienced by some children and young people that make it harder to learn than most others of the same age.

Additional support needs   In Scotland, this term has a legal definition and refers to the support needed by some children and young people that is additional to, or different from, that received by children or young people of the same age to ensure they can access, and benefit from, education. These needs may be long or short term.

Alternative and Augmentative Communication (AAC)   Any method of communicating that is an alternative to, or supplements, regular methods of communicating, for example speech, where there is some kind of difficulty that makes this problematic.

Attachment theory   This concerns relationships between human beings. The most important tenet is that primary caregivers who are available and responsive to an infant's needs allow the child to develop a sense of security.

Attention deficit/hyperactivity disorder (AD/HD)   A 'condition' marked by behaviour such as inattentiveness, hyperactivity and impulsiveness. Formal identification is through assessment by qualified professionals.

Autistic spectrum disorder (ASD)   A developmental condition that involves persistent difficulties in social interaction, speech and non-verbal communication, and restricted/repetitive behaviours.

Behaviourism   A theory that assumes that all behaviour is learnt through interaction with the environment. A stimulus from the environment can cause a reflex action; events occurring simultaneously with the stimulus may elicit the same response (classical conditioning). Or individuals can learn from the consequences of an action through reinforcement of it (operant conditioning).

Bloom's Hierarchy (Taxonomy)   A framework used to define and classify different levels of human thinking, learning and understanding.

Bullying in educational establishments   The actions of perpetrators who have greater physical or social power than their victim(s) and behave aggressively towards him/her through verbal or physical means.

Child protection   The safeguarding of young people from violence, exploitation, abuse and/or neglect.

Code of Practice Sets out professional behaviour and conduct expected of professionals, including mandatory requirements such as those laid down through legislation in the areas of special educational, additional learning or support needs.

Cognitive difficulties Difficulties with the mental processes involved in acquiring knowledge, manipulating of information and reasoning. This includes perception, memory, learning, attention, decision making and language acquisition.

Comprehension Ability to understand something.

Constructivist learning theories Theories in education that recognise how learners construct new understandings and knowledge, and integrate these with pre-existing knowledge.

Counselling Provision of a safe space to talk to a trained professional about issues and concerns, and explore thoughts, feelings and behaviour. There are different types of counselling therapies, depending on the needs of the individual.

Criterion-referencing Use of tests and assessments that are designed to measure student performance against a fixed set of predetermined criteria or learning standards.

Culture Social behaviour and norms found in human societies, together with the knowledge, beliefs, arts, laws, customs and habits of the individuals in these societies.

Decoding The use of letter–sound relationships to pronounce written words.

Differentiation Tailoring teaching approaches and curriculum to meet individual learning needs, for example adapting content, process, anticipated outcomes or the learning environment.

Disability Legally defined in the UK Equality Act (2010) as a physical or mental impairment that has a 'substantial' and 'long-term' negative effect on an individual's ability to carry out normal daily activities.

Dyscalculia A specific, persistent and unexpected difficulty in understanding numbers and acquiring number-ness which can lead to a range of barriers to progressing in mathematics learning and achievement.

Dyslexia A specific difficulty in learning, primarily affecting accurate and fluent word reading and spelling, most often involving problems in phonological awareness, verbal memory and the speed of verbal processing.

Dyspraxia A difficulty that affects movement and co-ordination.

Equality of opportunity A state of fairness in which all individuals are treated in the same way with access to the same resources.

Equity in education A state where all learners receive the resources they need as individuals to be successful in education, beginning with the acknowledgement that some learners require more than others to access the curriculum.

Eugenics   A set of beliefs and practices that aimed to improve the genetic composition of the human race historically by selective breeding to achieve these goals, excluding people and groups judged to be inferior, or promoting those judged to be superior.

Formative assessment in education   A method of assessing learners and providing feedback on current progress and structured feedforward for next steps during the learning process rather than at the end of a topic. It can be carried out through, for example, targeted questioning or peer- and self-assessment that promotes reflection by both learner and teacher.

Frame of reference   A set of assumptions and attitudes that filter perceptions that individuals use to construct meaning. This can include, for example, beliefs, preferences, values and culture that influence human understanding and judgement.

Human Rights legislation   Laws that protect rights that are inherent to all human beings, regardless of gender, nationality, place of residency, sex, ethnicity, religion, colour and other categorisation. The Human Rights Act (1998) sets out the fundamental rights and freedoms that everyone in the UK is entitled to. It incorporates the rights set out in the European Convention on Human Rights (ECHR) into domestic British law.

Inclusive education   Recognition of all learners' entitlements to an education that respects diversity, enables participation, removes barriers, and anticipates and responds to a variety of individual learning needs and preferences.

Labelling theory   The belief that individuals' identity and behaviour may be influenced by the labels used to describe them. It is associated with the concept of stereotyping.

Lesson Study   A Japanese model of teacher-led research in which a triad of teachers target an identified area for development for their learners, and collaboratively research, plan, teach and observe a series of lessons, using ongoing discussion, reflection and expert input to monitor and improve their pedagogy.

Motivation   An important driving factor influencing actions, willingness to carry out activities and personal goals.

Multi-agency collaboration   Co-operation between several organisations to provide services to meet individuals' identified needs.

Multi-sensory impairment   Impairment in both sight and hearing.

Norm-referenced (standardised) testing   The process of evaluating the learning of individuals by ranking them against the performance of their peers. Norm-referenced scores are usually reported as a percentage or a percentile ranking.

Phonics   A technique for teaching reading by identifying symbols with sounds in an alphabetic writing system.

Picture Exchange Communication System (PECS)   A kind of Augmentative and Alternative Communication that uses visual symbols to teach the learner to communicate with others.

Pragmatic language impairment (PLI)   Difficulty in using language appropriately in social situations.

Profound and multiple learning difficulty (PMLD)   A severe learning disability and other difficulties that may include seeing, hearing, speaking and moving, and that significantly affect the ability to communicate and be independent.

Reading age   The term often used for an individual's reading level when compared against the expectations for an individual of the same age.

Reasonable adjustments   A term used to refer to the legal duty to take positive steps to ensure that disabled learners can fully participate in the education provided by an educational institution so that they can enjoy the facilities and services that are provided for other learners.

Restorative practice   A strategy that seeks to repair relationships that have been damaged through anti-social behaviour, for example bullying, rather than to punish. It sets out to do this by encouraging a sense of remorse and agreement about restorative action on the part of the offender, and forgiveness by the victim.

Social constructivism   A social learning theory that posits that learning takes place primarily in social and cultural settings and that individuals are active participants in the creation of their own knowledge. All knowledge develops as a result of social interaction and language use, and is a shared, rather than an individual, experience.

Special educational needs (SEN)   A legal term used in England and Northern Ireland that refers to individuals from 0 to 25 years old with learning problems or disabilities that make it harder for them to learn than most peers of the same age, and that require special provision so that these learners can access the curriculum on offer.

Specific learning difficulty   A difficulty with some specific aspect of learning.

Standard deviation   A statistic that measures the spread of scores in a set of data relative to the mean score.

Treatment and Education of Autistic and related Communication Handicapped Children programme (TEACCH)   A structured teaching approach designed for individuals with autism and communication disabilities and their families and carers.

REFERENCES

Academies Commission (2013) *Unleashing Greatness: Getting the Best from an Academised System*. London: Academies Commission.

Adams, C., & Lloyd, J. (2007) The effects of speech and language therapy intervention on children with pragmatic language impairments in mainstream school. *British Journal of Special Education*, 34(4), 226–233.

Adams, M. J. (1994) *Beginning to Read: Thinking and Learning about Print*. Cambridge, MA: MIT Press.

Aitken, S. (2000) Understanding deafblindness. In S. Aitken, M. Buultjens, C. Clark, J. T. Eyre & L. Pease (eds), *Teaching Children who are Deafblind*. London: David Fulton.

Aitken, S., & Millar, S. (2002) *Listening to Children with Communication Support Needs*. Glasgow: Sense Scotland.

Alexander, R. (2006). *Towards dialogic teaching* (3rd edn). New York: Dialogos.

American Psychiatric Association (APA) (2013) *Diagnostic and Statistical Manual of Mental Disorders (5th edn)* (DSM-5). Arlington, VA: APA.

Anderson, L. W., Krathwohl, D. R., Airasian, P. W., Cruikshank, K. A., Mayer, R. E., Pintrich, P. R., Raths, J., & Wittrock, M. C. (eds) (2001) *A Taxonomy for Learning, Teaching, and Assessing: A Revision of Bloom's Taxonomy of Educational Objectives*. Boston, MA: Allyn & Bacon.

Anthony, G., & Walshaw, M. (2007) *Effective Pedagogy in Mathematics/Pàngarau: Best Evidence Synthesis Iteration*. Wellington: Ministry of Education.

Apel, K., & Masterton, J. (1998) Assessment and treatment of narrative skills: What's the story? In *RTN Learning Book*. Rockville, MD: American Speech-Language-Hearing Association.

Applebee, A. N. (1993) *Literature in the Secondary School: Studies of Curriculum and Instruction in the United States* (NCTE Research Report No. 250). Urbana, IL: National Council of Teachers of English.

Askew, M., Brown, M., Rhodes, V., Johnson, D., & Wiliam, D. (1997) *Effective Teachers of Numeracy*. London: Kings College.

Asok, A., Bernard, K., Roth, T. L., Rosen, J. B., & Dozier, M. (2013) Parental responsiveness moderates the association between early-life stress and reduced telomere length. *Development Psychopathology*, 25(3), 577–585.

Asperger, H. (1944) Die 'Autistischen Psychopathen' im Kindesalter. *Arch Psychiatr Nervenkr*, 117, 76–136.

Asperger, H. (1944/1991) Autistic psychopathy in childhood. In U. Frith (ed.), *Autism and Asperger Syndrome* (pp. 37–92). Cambridge: Cambridge University Press.

Assessment Reform Group (1999) *Assessment for Learning: Beyond the Black Box*. Cambridge: University of Cambridge School of Education.

Atkinson, M., Jones, M., & Lamont, E. (2007) *Multi-Agency Working and its Implications for Practice: A Review of the Literature*. Slough: Centre for British Teachers (CfBT) Education Trust.

Audit Commission and Her Majesty's Inspectorate (1992) *Getting in on the Act Provision for Pupils with Special Educational Needs*. London: HMSO.

Autism Education Trust/Centre for Research in Autistic Education (CRAE) (2011) *What is Good Practice in Autism Education?* London: Autism Education Trust/CRAE.

Baer, D. M., Wolf, M. M., & Risley, T. R. (1968) Some current dimensions of applied behavior analysis. *Journal of Applied Behavior Analysis*, 1, 91–97.

Bakhtin, M. M. (1981) *The Dialogic Imagination: Four Essays by M. M. Bakhtin* (Ed. M. Holquist, Trans. C. Emerson & M. Holquist). Austin, TX: University of Texas Press.

Bakhtin, M. M. (1984) *Problems of Dostoevsky's Poetics* (Ed. & Trans. C. Emerson). Minneapolis, MN: University of Minnesota Press.

Bandura, A. (1982) Self-efficacy mechanism in human agency. *American Psychologist*, 37(2), 122–147.

Bandura, A., & Schunk, D. H. (1981) Cultivating competence, self-efficacy, and intrinsic interest through proximal self-motivation. *Journal of Personality and Social Psychology*, 41(3), 586–598.

Barclay, L., Herlich, S. A., & Sacks, S. Z. (2010) Effective teaching strategies: Case studies from the alphabetic braille and contracted braille study. *Journal of Visual Impairment & Blindness*, 104, 753–764.

Bargiela, S., Steward, R., & Mandy, W. (2016) The experiences of late-diagnosed women with autism spectrum conditions: An investigation of the female autism phenotype. *Journal of Autism and Developmental Disorders*, 46(1), 3281–3294.

Barkley, R. A. (2015) *Attention-Deficit Hyperactivity Disorder: A Handbook for Diagnosis and Treatment* (4th edn). New York: Guilford Press.

Barron, S. (1992) *There's a Boy in Here: Emerging from the Bonds of Autism*. London: Simon & Schuster.

Bartholomew, H. (2003) Ability grouping and the construction of different types of learner in mathematics classrooms. In L. Bragg, C. Campbell, G. Herbert & J. Mousley (eds), *Mathematics Education Research: Innovation, Networking, Opportunity* (Proceedings of the 26th Annual Conference of the Mathematics Education Research Group of Australasia (MERGA), Vol. 1, pp. 128–135). Sydney: MERGA.

Barton, D. (1995) *Literacy: An Introduction to the Ecology of Written Language*. Oxford: Blackwell.

Beattie, R. (2006) The oral methods and spoken language acquisition. In P. Spencer & M. Marshark (eds), *Advances in the Spoken Language Development of Deaf and Hard-of-Hearing Children*. New York: Oxford University Press.

Bell, J. (2010) *Doing Your Research Project: A Guide for First-time Researchers in Education, Health and Social Science* (5th edn). Maidenhead: Open University Press.

Benn, C., & Chitty, C. (1996) *Thirty Years On: Is Comprehensive Education Alive and Well or Struggling to Survive?* London: David Fulton.

Bennathan, M. (2000) 'Children at risk of failure in primary schools', in M. Bennathan & M. Boxall, *Effective Intervention in Primary Schools: Nurture Groups* (2nd edn). London: Routledge

Bennathan, M., & Boxall, M. (2012) *Effective Intervention in Primary Schools: Nurture Groups* (2nd edn). London: Routledge.

Bereiter, C., & Scardamalia, M. (1986) Educational relevance of the study of expertise. *Interchange*, 17(2), 10–19.

Best, E. (2020) *Audiobooks and Literacy*. London: National Literacy Trust.

Bishop, D. V. M., & Adams, C. (1992) Comprehension problems in children with specific language impairment: Literal and inferential meaning. *Journal of Speech and Hearing Research*, 35(1), 119–129.

Bishop, D. V. M., & Norbury, C. F. (2002) Exploring the borderlands of autistic disorder and specific language impairment: A study using standardised diagnostic instruments. *Journal of Child Psychology and Psychiatry*, 43(7), 917–929.

Bishop, R., Berryman, M., & Wearmouth, J. (2014) *Te Kotahitanga: Towards Effective Education Reform for Indigenous and Other Minoritised Students*. Wellington: New Zealand Council for Educational Research (NZCER).

Black, A., Bessudnov, A., Liu, Y., & Norwich, B. (2019) Academisation of schools in England and placements of pupils with special educational needs: An analysis of trends, 2011–2017, *Frontiers in Education*, 4(3). Available at: https://www.frontiersin.org/articles/10.3389/feduc.2019.00003/full (accessed 05.07.2022).

Black, P., & Wiliam, D. (1998) Assessment and classroom learning. *Assessment in Education*, 5(1), 7–74.

Blairmires, G., Coupland, C., Galbraith, T., Parker, J., Parr, A., Simpson, F., & Thornton, P. (2016) *Supporting Children with Sensory Impairment*. London: David Fulton.

Blatchford, P., Bassett, P., Brown, P., Martin, C., Russell, A., Russell, A., & Webster, R. (2004) *Deployment and Impact of Support Staff Project*. London: Institute of Education.

Bliss, J., Askew, M., & Macrae, S. (1996) Effective teaching and learning: Scaffolding revisited. *Oxford Review of Education*, 22(1), 37–61.

Bloom, B. S., & Krathwohl, D. R. (1956) *Taxonomy of Educational Objectives: The Classification of Educational Goals*. Compiled by a committee of college and university examiners. Handbook I: Cognitive Domain. New York: Longmans, Green.

Boaler, J., Wiliam, D., & Brown, M. (2000) Students' experiences of ability grouping: Disaffection, polarisation and the construction of failure? *British Educational Research Journal*, 26(5), 631–648.

Board of Education (1926) *Report of the Consultative Committee on the Education of the Adolescent* ('The Hadow Report'). London: HMSO.

Board of Education (1938) *Report of the Consultative Committee on Secondary Education with Special Reference to Grammar Schools and Technical High Schools* ('The Spens Report'). London: HMSO.

Bombèr, L. M. (2007) *Inside I'm Hurting: Practical Strategies for Supporting Children with Attachment Difficulties in Schools*. Duffield: Worth Publishing.

Bond, G. L., & Dykstra, R. (1967) The co-operative research program in first-grade reading instruction. *Reading Research Quarterly*, 2, 5–142.

Bondy, A., & Frost, L. (1994) The picture exchange communication system. *Focus on Autistic Behavior*, 9, 1–19.

Bowlby, J. (1944) Forty-four juvenile thieves: Their characters and home-life. *International Journal of Psychoanalysis*, 25, 19–52.

Bowlby, J. (1952) A two-year-old goes to hospital. *Proceedings of the Royal Society of Medicine*, 46, 425–427.

Boxall, M. (2002) *Nurture Groups in School: Principles and Practice*. London: Paul Chapman.

Brandon, M., Bailey, S., Belderson, P., Gardner, R., Sidebotham, P., Dodsworth, J., Warren, C., & Black, J. (2009) *Understanding Serious Case Reviews and Their Impact: A Biennial Analysis of Serious Case Reviews 2005–07*. London: Department for Children, Schools and Families.

British Psychological Society (BPS) (1996) *Attention Deficit Hyperactivity Disorder (ADHD): A Psychological Response to an Evolving Concept*. Leicester: BPS.

Broadfoot, P. (2011) *Assessment, Schools and Society*. London: Routledge.

Brown, D., & Thomson, C. (2000) *Cooperative Learning in New Zealand Schools*. Wellington: Dunmore Press.

Bruner, J. (1966) *Toward a Theory of Instruction*. Cambridge, MA: Harvard University Press.

Bruner, J. (1996) *The Culture of Education*. Cambridge, MA: Harvard University Press.

Burman, D., Nunes, T., & Evans, D. (2006) Writing profiles of deaf children taught through British Sign Language. *Deafness and Education International*, 9, 2–23.

Burns, M. K., VanDerHeyden, A. M., & Boice, C. H. (2008) Best practices in delivering intensive academic interventions. In A. Thomas & J. Grimes (eds), *Best Practices in School Psychology* (5th edn). Bethesda, MD: National Association of School Psychologists.

Buzan, T. (2000) *The Mind Map Book*. London: Penguin.

Cameron, L., & Murphy, J. (2002) Enabling young people with a learning disability to make choices at a time of transition. *British Journal of Learning Disabilities*, 30, 105–112.

Carroll, J. M., & Snowling, M. J. (2004) Language and phonological skills in children at high risk of reading difficulties. *Journal of Child Psychology and Psychiatry and Allied Disciplines*, 45(3), 631–640.

Cejas, I., & Quittner, A. L. (2019) Effects of family variables on spoken language in children with cochlear implants. In H. Knoors & M. Marschark (eds), *Evidence-based Practices in Deaf Education* (pp. 111–128). Oxford: Oxford University Press.

Central Advisory Council for Education (1963) *Half Our Future* ('The Newsom Report'). London: HMSO.

Central Advisory Council for Education (1967) *Children and their Primary Schools* ('The Plowden Report'). London: HMSO.

Charney, R. (1992) *Teaching Children to Care: Management in the Responsive Classroom*. Greenfield, MA: Northeast Foundation for Children.

Childnet International and the Department for Children, Schools and Families (DCSF) (2007/2008) *Let's Fight It Together: What We Can All Do to Prevent Cyberbullying*. London: Childnet International and the DCSF.

Chinn, S. (2012) *The Trouble with Maths: A Practical Guide to Helping Learners with Numeracy Difficulties* (2nd edn). London: Routledge.

Chitty, C., & Dunford, J. E. (1999) *State Schools: New Labour and the Conservative Legacy*. London: Woburn Press.

Clark, C., Dyson, A., Millward, A., & Skidmore, D. (1997) *New Directions in Special Needs*. London: Cassell.

Clark, C., & Picton, I. (2019) *Children Young People and Digital Reading*. London: National Literacy Trust.

Clark, C., & Teravainen, A. (2017) *Celebrating Reading for Enjoyment: Findings from Our Annual Literacy Survey 2016*. London: National Literacy Trust.

Clay, M. (1979) *Reading: The Patterning of Complex Behaviour*. Auckland: Heinemann.

Clay, M. (1991) *Becoming Literate: The Construction of Inner Control*. Auckland: Heinemann.

Cole, T. (1989) *Apart or a Part? Integration and the Growth of British Special Education*. Milton Keynes: Open University Press.

Cole, T. (1990) The history of special education: Social control of humanitarian progress? *British Journal of Special Education*, 17(3), 101–107.

Cooper, P., & Barbara, B. (2011) *From Inclusion to Engagement: Helping Students Engage with Schooling through Policy and Practice*. Chichester: Wiley-Blackwell.

Costello, B., Wachtel, J., & Wachtel, T. (2010) *Restorative Circles in Schools: Building Community and Enhancing Learning*. Bethlehem, PA: International Institute for Restorative Practices.

Coulter, S., Kynman, L., Morling, E., Grayson, R., & Wing, J. (2015) *Supporting Children with Dyspraxia and Motor Co-ordination Difficulties*. London: David Fulton.

Council of Europe (CoE) (1952) *Protocol 1 to the European Convention for the Protection of Human Rights and Fundamental Freedoms*. Strasbourg: CoE.

Cowling, K., & Cowling, H. (1993) *Toe by Toe*. Basildon, UK: Toe by Toe.

Cragg, L., & Gilmore, C. (2014) Skills underlying mathematics: The role of executive function in the development of mathematics proficiency. *Trends in Neuroscience and Education*, 3(2), 63–68.

Creese, A., Norwich, B., & Daniels, H. (2013) *Teacher Support Teams in Primary and Secondary Schools*. London: David Fulton.

Cross, M. (2004) *Children with Emotional and Behavioural Difficulties and Problems: There is Always a Reason*. London: Jessica Kingsley.

Cumberland, P., Pathai, S., & Rahi, J (2010) Prevalence of eye disease in early childhood and associated factors: Findings from the Millennium Cohort Study. *Ophthalmology*, 117(11), 2184–2190.

Dammeyer, J. (2019) Mental health and psychosocial well-being. In H. Knoors & M. Marschark (eds), *Evidence-based Practices in Deaf Education* (pp. 477–493). Oxford: Oxford University Press.

Davey, R., & Parkhill, F. (2012) Raising adolescent reading achievement: The use of sub-titled popular movies and high interest literacy activities. *English in Aotearoa*, 78(October), 61–71.

Davie, R., Butler, N. R., & Goldstein, H. (1972) *From Birth to Seven: The Second Report of the National Child Development Study* (1958 Cohort). London: Longman in association with the National Children's Bureau.

Davis, P. (2003) *Including Children with a Visual Impairment in Mainstream Schools: A Practical Guide*. London: David Fulton.

de Shazer, S. (1985) *Keys to Solution in Brief Therapy*. New York: W. W. Norton.

de Shazer, S. (1988) *Investigating Solutions in Brief Therapy*. New York: W. W. Norton.

de Shazer, S., Dolan, Y., Korman, H., McCollum, E., Trepper, T., & Berg, I. K. (2007) *More than Miracles: The State of the Art of Solutions-focused Brief Therapy*. New York: Haworth.

Demetriou, C. (2011) The attribution theory of learning and advising students on academic probation. *NACADA Journal*, 31(2), 16–21.

Department for Children, Schools and Families (DCSF) (2005) *Primary National Strategy (PNS): Speaking Listening Learning: Working with Children Who Have Special Educational needs* (Ref. 1235/2005). London: Qualifications and Curriculum Authority.

Department for Education (DfE) (1994) *The Code of Practice for the Identification and Assessment of Special Educational Needs.* London: DfE.

Department for Education (DfE) (2013a) *The National Curriculum in England Key Stages 1 and 2 Framework Document.* London: DfE.

Department for Education (DfE) (2013b) *Use of Reasonable Force: Advice for Headteachers, Staff and Governing Bodies.* London: DfE.

Department for Education (DfE) (2014a) *Supporting Pupils at School with Medical Conditions: Statutory Guidance for Governing Bodies of Maintained Schools and Proprietors of Academies in England.* London: DfE.

Department for Education (DfE) (2014b) *Special Educational Needs and Disability Pathfinder.* London: DfE.

Department for Education (DfE) (2014c) *National Curriculum for England Inclusion Statement.* London: DfE.

Department for Education (DfE) (2014d) *Special Educational Needs and Disability (SEND) – A Guide for Parents and Carers.* London: DfE.

Department for Education (DfE) (2018) *Bullying in England, April 2013 to March 2018.* London: DfE. Available at: https://assets.publishing.service.gov.uk/government/uploads/system/uploads/attachment_data/file/754959/Bullying_in_England_2013-2018.pdf (accessed 24.02.2020).

Department for Education (DfE) (2019) *Statistical First Release (SFR): Special Educational Needs in England.* London: DfE.

Department for Education and Skills (DfES) (2004) *Every Child Matters: Change for Children.* London: DfES.

Department for Education and Skills (DfES) (2005) *Learning Behaviour: The Report of The Practitioners' Group on School Behaviour and Discipline* ('The Steer Report'). Nottingham: DfES.

Department for Education/Department of Health (DfE/DoH) (2015) *Special Educational Needs and Disability Code of Practice: 0 to 25 Years.* London: DfE/DoH.

Department of Education and Science (DES) (1968) *Psychologists in the Education Services: Report of the Working Party* ('The Summerfield Report'). London: HMSO.

Department of Education and Science (DES) (1978) *Special Educational Needs, Report of the Committee of Enquiry into the Education of Handicapped Children and Young People* (Cmnd. 7212) ('The Warnock Report'). London, DES.

Department of Education and Science (DES) (1989) *Discipline in Schools: Report of the Committee of Enquiry Chaired by Lord Elton* ('The Elton Report'). London: DES.

Department of Education, Northern Ireland (DENI) (1998) *Code of Practice on the Identification and Assessment of Special Educational Needs.* Bangor: DENI.

Department of Education, Northern Ireland (DENI) (2005) *Supplement to the Code of Practice on the Identification and Assessment of Special Educational Needs.* Bangor: DENI

Department of Health (DoH) (2011) *No Health without Mental Health: A Cross-government Mental Health Outcomes Strategy for People of All Ages.* London: DoH.

Dirks, E. (2019) The caregiving environment. In H. Knoors & M. Marschark (eds), *Evidence-based Practices in Deaf Education* (pp. 417–436). Oxford: Oxford University Press.

Dixit, R. (2006) *Child Development: Birth to Adolescence.* Bhopal: Indra.

Donaldson M. (1984) *Children's Minds.* London: Fontana.

Douglas, J. W. B. (1964) *The Home and the School.* St Albans: Panther.

Down, J. L. H. (1866) Observations on an ethnic classification of idiots. *Clinical Lecture Reports, London Hospital 3*, pp. 259–262. www.neonatology.org/classics/down.html (accessed 21.05.2015).

Duke, N. K., & Pearson, P. D. (2002) Effective practices for developing reading comprehension. In A. E. Farstrup & S. J. Samuels (eds), *What Research Has to Say about Reading*. Newark, NJ: International Reading Association.

Dumortier, D. (2004) *From Another Planet: Autism from Within*. London: Paul Chapman.

Dunckley, I. (1999) *Managing Extreme Behaviour in Schools*. Wellington: Specialist Education Services.

Dunhill, A. (2009) *What is Communication? The Process of Transferring Information*. Exeter: Learning Matters.

Dunn, L., Parry, S., & Morgan, C. (2002) *Seeking quality in criterion referenced assessment*. Paper presented at the Learning Communities and Assessment Cultures Conference, University of Northumbria, 28–30 August.

DuPaul, G. J., & Stoner, G. (2014) *ADHD in the Schools: Assessment and Intervention Strategies* (3rd edn). New York: Guilford Press.

Dwivedi, K., & Gupta, A. (2000) 'Keeping cool': Anger management through group work. *Support for Learning*, 15(2), 76–81.

Dyson, A. H. (1997) *Writing Superheroes: Contemporary Childhood, Popular Culture, and Classroom Literacy*. New York: Teachers College Press.

Dyson, A. H. (2003) 'Welcome to the Jam': Popular culture, school literacy, and the making of childhoods. *Harvard Educational Review*, 73(3), 328–361.

Dyspraxia Foundation (2020) *What is Dyspraxia?* Hitchin: Dyspraxia Foundation. Available at: https://dyspraxiafoundation.org.uk/about-dyspraxia (accessed 03.04.2020).

Education Department (1898) *Report of the Departmental Committee on Defective and Epileptic Children* ('The Sharpe Report'). London: HMSO.

Education Department of Western Australia (1997) *First Steps: Reading Development Continuum*. Perth: Rigby Heinemann.

Ehri, L. C. (2002) Reading processes, acquisition and instructional implications. In G. Reid & J. Wearmouth (eds), *Dyslexia and Literacy: Research and Practice*. Chichester: Wiley.

Eldridge Jr, R. G. (1995) The possibility of knowledge and reality without science. In B. Hayes & K. Camperell (eds), *Linking Literacy: The Past, Present and Future*. Logan, UT: American Reading Forum.

Englert, C., & Raphael, T. (1988) Constructing well-formed prose: Process, structure and metacognition in the instruction of expository writing. *Exceptional Children*, 54, 513–520.

Enquire (2014) *The Parents' Guide to Additional Support for Learning*. Edinburgh: Enquire.

Exner, C. E. (2005) Development of hand skills. In J. Case-Smith (ed.), *Occupational Therapy for Children* (5th edn) (pp. 304–355). St Louis, MO: Mosby.

Fani, T., & Ghaemi, F. (2011) Implications of Vygotsky's Zone of Proximal Development (ZPD) in teacher education: ZPTD and self-scaffolding. *Procedia – Social and Behavioral Sciences*, 29, 1549–1554.

Felitti, V. J., Anda, R. F., Nordenberg, D., Williamson, D. F., Spitz, A. M., Edwards, V., Koss, M. P., & Marks, J. S.. (1998) Relationship of childhood abuse and household dysfunction to many of the leading causes of death in adults: The Adverse Childhood Experiences (ACE) Study. *American Journal of Preventive Medicine*, 14(4), 245–258.

Fellinger, J., Holzinger, D., Sattel, H., Laucht, M., & Goldberg, D. (2009) Correlates of mental health disorders among children with hearing impairments. *Developmental Medicine & Child Neurology*, 51(8), 635–641.

Fletcher-Campbell, F. (2005) Moderate learning difficulties. In A. Lewis & B. Norwich (eds), *Special Teaching for Special Children* (pp. 180–191). Maidenhead: Open University Press.

Foucault, M. (1980) Power/knowledge. In C. Gordon (ed.), *Power/Knowledge: Selected Interviews and Other Writings 1972–1977* (pp. 109–133). New York: Pantheon.

Fraivillig, J., Murphy, L., & Fuson, K. (1999) Advancing children's mathematical thinking in everyday mathematics classrooms. *Journal for Research in Mathematics Education*, 30(2), 148–170.

Frederickson, N., & Cline, T. (2015) *Special Educational Needs, Inclusion and Diversity* (3rd edn). Maidenhead: Open University Press/McGraw-Hill.

Frederickson, N., Warren, L., & Turner, J. (2005) 'Circle of Friends': An exploration of impact over time. *Educational Psychology in Practice*, 21(3), 197–217.

Froebel, F. (1826/2005) *The Education of Man* (Trans. W. N. Hailmann). Mineola, NY: Dover.

Fulcher, G. (1989) *Disabling Policies: A Comparative Approach to Educational Policy and Disabilities*. London: Falmer Press.

Furlong, V. J. (1985) *The Deviant Pupil: Sociological Perspectives*. Milton Keynes: Open University Press.

Gaastra, G. F., Groen, Y., Tucha, L., & Tucha, O. (2017) The effects of classroom interventions on off-task and disruptive classroom behavior in children with symptoms of attention-deficit/hyperactivity disorder: A meta-analytic review. *PLoS One*, 11(2). Available at: www.ncbi.nlm.nih.gov/pmc/articles/PMC4757442/ (accessed 05.07.2022).

Galloway, D. M., & Goodwin, C. (1987) *The Education of Disturbing Children: Pupils with Learning and Adjustment Difficulties*. London: Longman.

Galton, M., & MacBeath, J. (2015) *Inclusion: Statements of intent,* A report to the National Union of Teachers on the current state of special educational needs and disability provision. Cambridge: NUT/Cambridge University.

Gay, G. (2010) *Culturally Responsive Teaching: Theory, Research and Practice*. New York: Teachers' College Press.

Gerhardt, S. (2004) *Why Love Matters* (2nd edn). London: Routledge.

Gersch, I. (1995) Involving the child. In *Schools' Special Educational Needs Policies Pack*. London: National Children's Bureau.

Gifford, S., & Rockliffe, F. (2012) Mathematics difficulties: Does one approach fit all? *Research in Mathematics Education*, 14(1), 1–15.

Gillard, D. (2021) *Education in England: A Brief History*. Available at: www.educationengland.org.uk/history/chapter08.html (accessed 26.10.2021).

Glick, H., & Sharma, A. (2017) Cross-modal plasticity in developmental and age-related hearing loss: Clinical implications. *Hearing Research*, 343, 191–201.

Glynn, T., & Bishop, R. (1995) Cultural issues in educational research: A New Zealand perspective. *He Pūkengo Kōrero*, 1(1), 37–43.

Glynn, T., Wearmouth, J., & Berryman, M. (2006) *Supporting Students with Literacy Difficulties: A Responsive Approach*. Maidenhead: Open University Press.

Goldberg, L. R., & Richberg, C. M. (2004) Minimal hearing impairment: Major myths with more than minimal implications. *Communication Disorders Quarterly*, 24, 152–160.

Golding, W. (1954) *Lord of the Flies*. London: Faber and Faber.

Goodman, K. S. (1996) *On Reading*. Portsmouth, NJ: Heinemann.

Gordon, A. (1961) Mongolism (correspondence). *The Lancet*, 1(7180), 775.

Goswami, U., & Bryant, P. (2007) *Children's Cognitive Development and Learning* (Primary Review Research Survey 2/1a). Cambridge: University of Cambridge Faculty of Education.

Gotink, R. A., Meijboom, R., Vernooij, M. W., Smits, M., & Hunink, M. G. (2016) 8-week mindfulness-based stress reduction induces brain changes similar to traditional long-term meditation practice – a systematic review. *Brain and Cognition*, 108(October), 32–41.

Grandin, T. (1996) *Emergence: Labelled Autistic*. New York: Warner Books.

Grandin, T., & Panek, R. (2013) *The Autistic Brain: Thinking across the Spectrum*. Boston, MA: Houghton Mifflin Harcourt.

Grauberg, E. (2002) *Elementary Mathematics and Language Difficulties*. London: Whurr.

Graves, A., Montague, M., & Wong, Y. (1990) *The effects of procedural facilitation on story composition of learning-disabled students*. Paper presented at the Annual Meeting of the American Educational Research Association, San Francisco.

Graves, D. (1983) *Writing: Teachers and Children at Work*. Exeter, NH: Heinemann.

Great Britain, Parliament, House of Commons (1807) *Hansard* (Vol. 9). London: Parliament.

Great Britain, Parliament, House of Commons (2019) *Report from the Select Committee on Education Special Educational Needs and Disabilities Inquiry.* London: Parliament.

Great Britain, Parliament, Select Committee on Education (1838) *Report from the Select Committee on Education of the Poorer Classes.* Shannon: Irish University Press.

Green, H., McGinnity, A., Meltzer, H., Ford, T., & Goodman, R. (2005) *Mental Health of Children and Young People in Great Britain, 2004.* Basingstoke: Palgrave Macmillan.

Greenhalgh, P. (1994) *Emotional Growth and Learning.* London: Routledge.

Greeno, J. G. (1998) The situativity of knowing, learning, and research. *American Psychologist,* 53(1), 5–26.

Gregory, E. (1996) *Making Sense of a New World.* London: Paul Chapman.

Gutman, L., & Vorhaus, J. (2012) *The Impact of Pupil Behaviour and Wellbeing on Educational Outcomes.* London: Department for Education.

Haberstroh, S., & Schulte-Körne, G. (2019) The diagnosis and treatment of dyscalculia. *Deutsches Ärzteblatt International,* 116(7), 107–114.

Hage, C., & Leybaert, J. (2006) The effect of cued speech on the development of spoken language. In P. Spencer & M. Marshark (eds), *Advances in the Spoken Language Development of Deaf and Hard-of-Hearing Children.* New York: Oxford University Press.

Hall, J. (2008) Mental deficiency – changing the outlook. *The Psychologist,* 21(11), 1006–1007.

Hanko, G. (1994) Discouraged children: When praise does not help. *British Journal of Special Education,* 21(4), 166–168.

Hargreaves, D. H. (1967) *Social Relations in a Secondary School.* London: Routledge.

Haring, N. G., Lovitt, T. C., Eaton, M. D., & Hansen, C. L. (1978) *The Fourth R: Research in the Classroom.* Columbus, OH: Charles E. Merrill.

Harlow, H. F. (1962) Development of affectional patterns in infant monkeys. In B. M. Foss (ed.), *The Determinants of Infant Behavior* (Vol. II, pp. 75–88). New York: Wiley.

Harris, M., & Moreno, C. (2006) Speech reading and learning to read: A comparison of 8-year-old profoundly deaf children with good and poor reading ability. *Journal of Deaf Studies and Deaf Education,* 11, 189–201.

Hattie, J. (2002) What are the attributes of excellent teachers? In B. Webber (ed.), *Teachers Make a Difference: What is the Research Evidence?* Proceedings of the New Zealand Association of Research in Education Conference (NZARE) (pp. 3–26). Wellington: NZARE.

Hawton, K., Rodham, K., Evans, E., & Weatherall, R. (2002) Deliberate self-harm in adolescents: Self-report survey in schools in England. *British Medical Journal,* 325, 1207–1211.

Hayden, S., & Jordan, E. (2015) *Language for Learning in the Primary School.* London: David Fulton.

Hayes, J. R., & Flower, L. S. (1986) Writing research and the writer. *American Psychologist,* 41(10), 1106–1113.

Hayes, R., & Whittaker, P. (2016) *Understanding and Supporting Pupils with Moderate Learning Difficulties in the Secondary School.* London: David Fulton.

Heath, S. B. (1983) *Ways with Words: Language Life, and Work in Communities and Classrooms.* New York: Cambridge University Press.

Heilbronn, R. (2016) Freedoms and perils: Academy schools in England. *Journal of Philosophy of Education,* 50(3), 306–318.

Heimler, H., Pavani, F., & Amedi, A. (2019) Implications of cross-modal and intramodal plasticity for the education and rehabilitation of deaf children and adults. In H. Knoors & M. Marschark (eds), *Evidence-based Practices in Deaf Education* (pp. 323–363). Oxford: Oxford University Press.

Helme, S., & Clarke, D. (2001) Identifying cognitive engagement in the mathematics classroom. *Mathematics Education Research Journal,* 13(2), 133–153.

Henderson, A. (1998) *Maths for the Dyslexic: A Practical Guide.* London: David Fulton.

Hewison, J., & Tizard, J. (1980) Parental involvement and reading attainment. *British Journal of Educational Psychology,* 50(3), 209–215.

Hiebert, J., Carpenter, T., Fennema, E., Fuson, K. C., Wearne, D., Murray, H., Olivier, A., & Human, P. (1997) *Making Sense: Teaching and Learning Mathematics with Understanding*. Portsmouth, NH: Heinemann.

Higashida, N. (2013) *The Reason I Jump*. London: Hodder and Stoughton.

Hill, H., Rowan, B., & Ball, D. (2005) Effects of teachers' mathematical knowledge for teaching on student achievement. *American Educational Research Journal*, 42(2), 371–406.

Hintermair, M. (2006) Parental resources, parental stress, and socioemotional development of deaf and hard of hearing children. *Journal of Deaf Studies and Deaf Education*, 11(4), 493–513.

HM Treasury (2003) *Every Child Matters*. London: HM Treasury.

Holmes, J. (1993) *John Bowlby and Attachment Theory*. London: Routledge.

Hopkins, B. (2004) *Just Schools: A Whole School Approach to Restorative Justice*. London: Jessica Kingsley.

Howard-Jones, N. (1979) 'On the diagnostic term "Down's disease"', *Medical History*, 23(1), 102–4.

Hudson, B. (2002) Interprofessionality in health and social care: The Achilles' heel of partnership? *Journal of Interprofessional Care*, 16(1), 7–11.

Hughes, A. M. (2015) *Developing Play for the Under 3s: The Treasure Basket and Heuristic Play*. London: Routledge.

Institute for Public Policy Research (IPPR) (2014) *Whole System Reform: England's Schools and the Middle Tier*. London: IPPR.

Joffe, L. S. (1983) School mathematics and dyslexia: A matter of verbal labelling, generalisation, horses and carts. *Cambridge Journal of Education*, 13, 22–27.

Johnson, M. (2002) 'Multisensory teaching of reading in mainstream settings', in J. Wearmouth, J. Soler & G. Reid (eds), *Addressing Difficulties in Literacy Development* (pp. 269–81). London: RoutledgeFalmer.

Joint Council for Qualifications (JCQ) (2021) *Adjustments for Candidates with Disabilities and Learning Difficulties*. London: JCQ.

Jordan, R. (1999) *Autistic Spectrum Disorders: An Introductory Handbook for Practitioners*. London: David Fulton.

Jordan, R., & Powell, S. (1995) *Teaching and Understanding Children with Autism*. Chichester: Wiley.

Kanner, L. (1943) Autistic disturbances of affective contact. *Nervous Child*, 2, 217–250.

Kilpatrick, J., Swafford, J., & Findell, B. (eds) (2001) *Adding It Up: Helping Children Learn Mathematics*. Washington, DC: National Academy Press.

Kirby, A. H. P. (1914) *Legislation for the Feeble-minded*. London: John Bale, Sons & Danielsson.

Klin, A., Sparrow, S., Marans, W. D., Carter, A., & Volkmar, F. R. (2000) Assessment issues in children and adolescents with Asperger syndrome. In A. Klin, F. R. Volkmar & S. Sparrow (eds), *Asperger Syndrome*. New York: Guilford Press.

Koenig, A. J., & Holbrook, M. C. (2000) Ensuring high-quality instruction for students in braille literacy programs. *Journal of Visual Impairment & Blindness*, 94, 677–694.

Kofler, M. J., Rapport, M. D., & Alderson, R. M. (2008) Quantifying ADHD classroom inattentiveness, its moderators, and variability: A meta-analytic review. *Journal of Child Psychology and Psychiatry*, 49, 59–69.

Kozulin, A. (2003) Psychological tools and mediated learning. In A. Kozulin, B. Gindis, V. S. Ageyev & S. M. Miller (eds), *Vygotsky's Educational Theory in Cultural Context* (pp. 15–38). Cambridge: Cambridge University Press.

Krutetskii, V. A. (1976) *The Psychology of Mathematical Abilities in School Children* (Trans. J. Kilpatric & I. Wirszup). Chicago, IL: University of Chicago Press.

Lamb, B. (2009) *Report to the Secretary of State on the Lamb Inquiry Review of SEN and Disability Information*. London: Department for Children, Schools and Families.

Laming, Lord (2009) *The Protection of Children in England: A Progress Report*. London: HMSO.

Lampert, M. (1990) When the problem is not the question and the solution is not the answer: Mathematical knowing and teaching. *American Educational Research Journal*, 27(1), 29–63.

Lantolf, J. P., & Aljaafreh, A. (1996) Second language learning in the zone of proximal development: A revolutionary experience. *International Journal of Educational Research*, 23, 619–632.

Lave, J., & Wenger, E. (1998) *Communities of Practice: Learning, Meaning, and Identity*. Cambridge: Cambridge University Press.

Lawson, J., & Silver, H. (1973) *A Social History of Education in England*. London: Routledge.

Lee, W. (2008) *Speech, Language and Communication Needs and Primary School-aged Children*. I CAN Talk Series, Issue 6. London: I CAN.

LeFevre, D., Moore, D., & Wilkinson, I. (2003) Tape-assisted reciprocal teaching: Cognitive bootstrapping for poor decoders. *British Journal of Educational Psychology*, 73(1), 37–58.

Leinonen, E., Letts, C., & Smith, R. (2000) *Children's Pragmatic Communication Difficulties*. London: Whurr.

Leont'ev, A. N. (1981) *Problems of the Development of Mind*. Moscow: Progress Publishers.

Lewis, A. (2002) Accessing through research interviews the views of children with difficulties in learning. *Support for Learning*, 17(3), 110–116.

Lifton, R. J. (2000) *The Nazi Doctors: Medical Killing and the Psychology of Genocide*. New York: Basic Books.

Lindsay, G., Dockrell, J., & Strand, S. (2008) Longitudinal patterns of behaviour problems in children with specific speech and language difficulties: Child and contextual factors. *The British Journal of Educational Psychology*, 77(4), 811–828.

Littleton, K., & Mercer, N. (2013) *Interthinking: Putting Talk to Work*. London: Routledge.

Loomes, R., Hull, L., & Mandy, W. P. L. (2017) What is the male-to-female ratio in autism spectrum disorder? A systematic review and meta-analysis. *Journal of the American Academy of Child and Adolescent Psychiatry*, 56(6), 466–474.

Lorenz, L. (1952) *King Solomon's Ring*. London: Methuen.

Lovaas O. I. (1987) Behavioral treatment and normal educational and intellectual functioning in young autistic children. *Journal of Consulting and Clinical Psychology*, 55, 3–9.

Lowe, R. (1867) *Primary and Classical Education*. Edinburgh: Edmonston and Douglas.

Loxley, A., & Thomas, G. (2007) *Deconstructing Special Education and Constructing Inclusion*. Maidenhead: Open University Press.

Lunzer, E. A., & Gardner, W. K. (1979) *The Effective Use of Reading*. London: Heinemann Educational.

Lyle, S. (2008). Dialogic teaching: Discussing theoretical contexts and reviewing evidence from classroom practice. *Language and Education*, 22(3), 222–40.

Lyons, K. E., & DeLange, J. (2016) Mindfulness matters in the classroom: The effects of mindfulness training on brain development and behavior in children and adolescents. In K. Schonert-Reichl & R. Roeser (eds), *Handbook of Mindfulness in Education: Mindfulness in Behavioral Health*. New York: Springer.

Macintyre, C. (2014) *Identifying Additional Learning Needs in the Early Years* (2nd edn). London: Routledge.

Mason, H. (1997) Assessment of vision. In H. Mason, S. McCall, C. Arter, M. McLinden & J. Stone (eds), *Visual Impairment: Access to Education for Children and Young People* (chapter 6). London: David Fulton.

Mason, H. (2001) *Visual Impairment*. Tamworth: National Association of Special Educational Needs (NASEN).

McCluskey, G., Lloyd, G., Kane, J., Riddell, S., Stead, J., & Weedon, E. (2008) Can restorative practices in schools make a difference? *Educational Review*, 60(4), 405–417.

McLaughlin, C., Holliday, C., Clarke, B., & Ilie, S. (2013) *Research on Counselling and Psychotherapy with Children and Young People: A Systematic Scoping Review of the Evidence for its Effectiveness from 2003–2011*. Lutterworth: British Association for Counselling & Psychotherapy (BACP).

McLeod, J. (1998) *An Introduction to Counselling* (2nd edn). Buckingham: Open University Press.

McNaughton, S., Glynn, T., & Robinson, V. (1987) *Pause, Prompt and Praise: Effective Tutoring of Remedial Reading*. Birmingham: Positive Products.

Meichenbaum, D., & Turk, D. (1976) The cognitive-behavioural management of anxiety, anger and pain. In P. O. Davidson (ed.), *The Behavioural Management of Anxiety, Anger and Pain*. New York: Brunner/Mazel.

Mencap (undated) *About Profound and Multiple Learning Disabilities*. London: Mencap.

Mercer, N., & Littleton, K. (2007) *Dialogue and the Development of Children's Thinking: A Sociocultural Approach*. London: Routledge.

Mesibov, G. (2015) *What is TEACCH?* Available at: www.autismuk.com/training/what-is-teech/ (accessed 05.07.2022).

Mesibov, G. B., Shea, V., & Schopler, E. (2004) *The TEACCH Approach to Autism Spectrum Disorders*. London: Springer.

Middletown Centre for Autism (2022) Differentiating the curriculum. Available at: https://best-practice.middletownautism.com/approaches-of-intervention/differentiating-the-curriculum/ (accessed 05.07.2022).

Miles, T. R., & Miles, E. (2004) *Dyslexia and Mathematics* (2nd edn). London: Routledge.

Milgram, S. (1963) Behavioural study of obedience. *Journal of Abnormal and Social Psychology*, 67, 371–378.

Milgram, S. (1974) *Obedience to Authority: An Experimental View*. New York: Harper & Row.

Miller, O., & Ockleford, A. (2005) *Visual Needs*. London: Continuum.

Ministry of Education (MoE) (1945) *The Nation's Schools*. London: MoE.

Ministry of Education (MoE) (1946) *Special Educational Treatment*, Ministry of Education Pamphlet No. 5. London: HMSO.

Ministry of Education (MoE) New Zealand (2005) *Effective Literacy Practice*. Wellington: Learning Media.

Mirsky, L. (2004a) *Restorative Justice Practices of Native American, First Nation and Other Indigenous People of North America: Part One*. Retrieved from www.iirp.edu/pdf/natjust1.pdf

Mirsky, L. (2004b) *Restorative Justice Practices of Native American, First Nation and Other Indigenous People of North America: Part Two*. Retrieved from www.iirp.edu/pdf/natjust2.pdf

Mirsky, L. (2007) SaferSanerSchools: Transforming school culture with restorative practices. *Reclaiming Children and Youth*, 16(2), 5–12.

Mirsky, L. (2011, May 26) *Restorative Practices: Whole-school Change to Build Safer, Saner School Communities*. Retrieved from: www.iirp.edu/news/1891-restorative-practices-whole-school-change-to-build-safer-saner-school-communities

Moeller, M. P., Tomblin, J. B., Yoshinaga-Itano, C., Connor, C., & Jerger, S. (2007) Current state of knowledge: Language and literacy of children with hearing impairment. *Ear and Hearing*, 28, 740–753.

Moll, L. C., & Greenberg, J. B. (1990) Creating zones of possibilities: Combining social contexts for instruction. In L. C. Moll (ed.), *Vygotsky and Education: Instructional Implications and Applications of Sociohistorical Psychology* (pp. 319–348). New York: Cambridge University Press.

Montgomery, J. K., & Kahn, N. L. (2003) You are going to be an author: Adolescent narratives as intervention. *Communication Disorders Quarterly*, 24(3), 143–52.

Moores, D. (2001) *Educating the Deaf*. Boston, MA: Houghton Mifflin.

Moores, D. (2008) Research in Bi-Bi instruction. *American Annals of the Deaf*, 153, 3–4.

Morris, M., & Smith, P. (2008) *Educational Provision for Blind and Partially Sighted Children and Young People in Britain: 2007*. London: Royal National Institute for Blind People.

Mosley, J. (1996) *Quality Circle Time in the Primary Classroom: Your Essential Guide to Enhancing Self-esteem, Self-discipline and Positive Relationships*. Cambridge: Learn, Develop, Achieve (LDA).

Mosley, J. (1998) *Turn your School Round: Circle-Time Approach to the Development of Self-esteem and Positive Behaviour in the Primary Staffroom, Classroom and Playground*. Wisbech: Learn, Develop, Achieve (LDA).

Mountain, V. (2016) Play therapy – respecting the spirit of the child. *International Journal of Children's Spirituality*, 21(3/4), 191–200.

Muir, R., & Clifton, J. (2014) *Whole System Reform: England's Schools and the Middle Tier*. London: IPPR.

Murphy, R., Weinhardt, F., Wyness, G., & Rolfe, H. (2017) *Lesson Study Evaluation Report and Executive Summary*. London: Education Endowment Foundation.

Myhill, D., & Warren, P. (2005) Scaffolds or straitjackets? Critical moments in classroom discourse. *Educational Review*, 57(1), 55–69.

National Assembly for Wales (NAW) (2014) *White Paper: Legislative Proposals for Additional Learning Needs*. Cardiff: NAW.

National Assembly for Wales (NAW) (2018) *Implementing the Additional Learning Needs and Education Tribunal (Wales) Act 2018*. Cardiff: NAW.

National Assembly for Wales (NAW) (2019) *Support for Children and Young People with Multi-sensory Impairment in Educational Settings*. Cardiff: NAW.

National Association of Head Teachers (NAHT) (2003) *Policy Paper on Special Schools*. London: NAHT.

National Autistic Society (NAS) (2019) *Asperger syndrome and other terms*. London: NAS. Available at: www.autism.org.uk/advice-and-guidance/what-is-autism/asperger-syndrome (accessed 05.07.2022).

National Autistic Society (NAS) (2021) *Advice and guidance*. Available at: www.autism.org.uk/advice-and-guidance (accessed 05.07.2022).

National Deaf Children's Society (NDCS) (2008) *Acoustics Toolkit*. London: NDCS.

National Deaf Children's Society (NDCS) (2010a) *How Do Hearing Aids Work?* Available at: www.ndcs.org.uk/information-and-support/childhood-deafness/hearing-aids/how-do-hearing-aids-work/ (accessed 28.03.2020).

National Deaf Children's Society (NDCS) (2010b) *Communicating with Your Deaf Child*. London: NDCS.

National Deaf Children's Society (NDCS) (2015a) *Communicating with Your Deaf Child*. London: NDCS.

National Deaf Children's Society (NDCS) (2015b) *Supporting the Achievement of Hearing-impaired Children in Early Years Settings*. London: NDCS.

National Deaf Children's Society (NDCS) (2020) 'Levels of deafness'. Available online at: www.ndcs.org.uk/information-and-support/childhood-deafness/what-is-deafness/levels-of-deafness/

National Institute for Health and Care Excellence (NICE) (2011) *Autism: Recognition Referral and Diagnosis of Children and Young People on the Autism Spectrum*. Clinical Case Scenarios for Professionals Working with Children and Young People. London: NICE.

National Institute for Health and Care Excellence (NICE) (2017) *Autism in Under 19s: Recognition, Referral and Diagnosis*. London: NICE.

National Research Council (US) Division of Behavioral and Social Sciences and Education (2001) *Early Childhood Development and Learning: New Knowledge for Policy*. Washington, DC: National Academies Press.

Nawotka, E. (2019) Bologna 2019: Audiobook Sales Show Global Growth. *Publishers Weekly*, 11 April. Available at: www.publishersweekly.com/pw/by-topic/childrens/childrens-industry-news/article/79769-bologna2019-audiobook-sales-show-global-growth.html

Newman, D., Griffin, P., & Cole, M. (1989) *The Construction Zone: Working for Cognitive Change in School*. New York: Cambridge University Press.

Newton, C. & Wilson, D. (1999) *Circle of Friends*. Dunstable: Folens Publishers Ltd.

Newton, C., Taylor, G., & Wilson, D. (1996) Circles of friends. *Educational Psychology in Practice*, 11(4), 41–48.

Nind, M. (1999) Intensive interaction: A useful approach? *British Journal of Special Education*, 26(2), 96–102.

Noddings, N. (1995) *Philosophy of Education*. Oxford, and Boulder, CO: Westview Press.

Norbury, C. F. & Bishop, D. V. M. (2003) Narrative skills in children with communication impairments. *International Journal of Language and Communication Impairments*, (38), 287–313.

Nye, J., Buckley, S., & Bird, G. (2005) Evaluating the Numicon system as a tool for teaching number skills to children with Down syndrome. *Down Syndrome News and Update*, 5(1), 2–13.

O'Connor, M. C. (1998) Language socialisation in the mathematics classroom: Discourse practices and mathematical thinking. In M. Lampert & M. Blunk (eds), *Talking Mathematics in School: Studies of Teaching and Learning* (pp. 17–55). Cambridge: Cambridge University Press.

Oliphant, J. (2006) Empowerment and debilitation in the educational experience of the blind in nineteenth-century England and Scotland. *History of Education*, 35(1), 47–68.

Organisation for Economic Co-operation and Development (OECD) (2016) PISA 2018 draft analytical frameworks Retrieved from www.oecd.org/pisa/data/PISA-2018-draft-frameworks.pdf (accessed 15.04.2020).

Organisation for Economic Co-operation and Development (OECD) (2018) *Equity in Education: Breaking Down Barriers to Social Mobility.* Retrieved from www.oecd.org/pisa/Equity-in-Education-country-note-UK.pdf

Owen, R. (1824) *Outline of the System of Education at New Lanark.* Glasgow: University Press.

Owen, R. (1841) *Address on Opening the Institution for the Formation of Character at New Lanark, delivered on 1st January, 1816, being the First Announcement of the Discovery of the Infant School System.* London: Home Colonization Society.

Owen, R. (1857) *The Life of Robert Owen Written by Himself* (Vol. 1, Part 1). London: Effingham Wilson.

Padden, C., & Gunsals, D. (2003) How the alphabet came to be used in a sign language. *Sign Language Studies,* 4, 1–13.

Palincsar, A. S. (1998) Social constructivist perspectives on teaching and learning. *Annual Review of Psychology,* 49, 345–375.

Palincsar, A. S., & Brown, A. L. (1984) Reciprocal teaching of comprehension-fostering and comprehension-monitoring activities. *Cognition and Instruction,* 1(2), 117–175.

Park, K. (1997) How do objects become objects of reference? *British Journal of Special Education,* 24(3), 108–114.

Pavey, B. (2016) *Dyslexia and Early Childhood.* London: David Fulton.

Pavlov, I. P. (1928) *Lectures on Conditioned Reflexes: Twenty-five Years of Objective Study of the Higher Nervous Activity (Behaviour) of Animals* (Trans. W. H. Gantt). New York: Liveright Publishing Corporation.

Peeters, T., & Gilberg, C. (1999) The autistic spectrum: From theory to practice. In N. Brace & H. Westcott (eds), *Applying Psychology* (pp. 243–315). Milton Keynes: Open University Press.

Peninsula Cerebra Research Unit (PenCru) (2018) *What's the Evidence? Tools and Strategies to Support Children and Young People with Dyscalculia.* Exeter: University of Exeter Medical School. Available at: www.pencru.org/media/universityofexeter/medicalschool/subsites/pencru/pdfs/Dyscalculia_Whats_The_Evidence_for_publication.pdf (accessed 04.05.2020).

Pestalozzi, J. H. (1801/1894) *How Gertrude Teaches her Children* (Ed. with an introduction by Ebenezer Cooke, Trans. Lucy, E. Holland & Frances C. Turner). London: Swan Sonnenschein.

Piaget, J. (1954) *Construction of Reality in the Child.* New York: Basic Books.

Piaget, J. (1964) Cognitive development in children. *Journal of Research in Science Teaching,* 2(3), 176–186.

Piaget, J. (1969) *The Child's Conception of Time.* London: Routledge Kegan Paul.

Picton, I., & Clark, C. (2015) *The Impact of eBooks on the Reading Motivation and Reading Skills of Children and Young People: A Study of Schools using RM Books.* London: National Literacy Trust.

Pidgeon, K., Parson, J., Mora, L., Anderson, J., Stagnitti, K., & Mountain, V. (2015) Play therapy. In C. Noble & E. Day (eds), *Psychotherapy and Counselling: Reflections on Practice* (pp. 155–172). Oxford: Oxford University Press.

Pohlschmidt, M., & Meadowcroft, R. (2010) *Muscle Disease: The Impact, Incidence and Prevalence of Neuromuscular Conditions in the UK.* London: Muscular Dystrophy Campaign

Polanczyk, G., de Lima, M. S., Horta, B. L., Biederman, J., & Rohde, L. A. (2007) The worldwide prevalence of ADHD: A systematic review and metaregression analysis. *American Journal of Psychiatry,* 164, 942–948.

Pollard, A. (2002) *Reflective Teaching: Effective and Evidence-informed Professional Practice.* London: Continuum.

Porter, J. Ouvry, C., Morgan, M., & Downs, C. (2001) Interpreting the communication of people with profound and multiple learning difficulties. *British Journal of Learning Disabilities,* 29(1), 12–16.

Prasad, V., Brogan, E., Mulvaney, C., Grainge, M., Stanton, W., & Sayal, K. (2013) How effective are drug treatments for children with ADHD at improving on-task behaviour and academic achievement in the school classroom? A systematic review and meta-analysis. *European Child & Adolescent Psychiatry,* 22, 203–216.

Preece, D. (2002) Consultation with children with autistic spectrum disorders about their experience of short-term residential care. *British Journal of Learning Disabilities*, 30(3), 97–104.

Pring, R., & Walford, G. (1996) Comprehensive schools: The history. *Times Higher Education Supplement*, Available at: www.timeshighereducation.com/news/comprehensive-schools-the-history/92186.article (accessed 05.07.2022).

Ramani, G. B., & Siegler, R. S. (2008) Promoting broad and stable improvements in low-income children's numerical knowledge through playing number board games. *Child Development*, 79(2), 375–394.

Rapin, I., & Allen, D. A. (1998) The semantic-pragmatic deficit disorder: Classification issues. *International Journal of Language & Communication Disorders*, 33(1), 82–87.

Reason, R., & Boote, R. (1994) *Helping Children with Reading and Spelling*. London: Routledge.

Reder, P., & Duncan, S. (2003) Understanding communication in child protection networks. *Child Abuse Review*, 12(2), 82–100.

Reid, B., & Ayris, L. (2011) *We've Got Great Expectations: The Chance of a Lifetime for Children with Autism.* London: National Autistic Society.

Reid, G. (2017) *Dyslexia in the Early Years*. London: Jessica Kingsley.

Restorative Practices Development Team (2003) *Restorative Practices for Schools.* Hamilton: University of Waikato.

Richardson, M., Moore, D. A., Gwernan-Jones, R., Thompson-Coon, J., Ukoumunne, O., Rogers, M., et al. (2015) Non-pharmacological interventions for attention-deficit/hyperactivity disorder (ADHD) delivered in school settings: Systematic reviews of quantitative and qualitative research. *Health Technology Assessment*, 19(45).

Richmond, W. K. (1978) *Education in Britain since 1944*. London: Routledge.

Riddick, B. (1996) *Living with Dyslexia*. London and New York: Routledge.

Riddick, B. (2010) *Living with Dyslexia: The Social and Emotional Consequences of Specific Learning Difficulties/Disabilities* (2nd edn). London: Routledge.

Riddick, B., Wolfe, J., & Lumsdon, D. (2002) *Dyslexia: A Practical Guide for Teachers and Parents*. London: David Fulton.

Roberts, A. (1981) Chronological and alphabetical bibliographies of lunacy. *Hansard* (Parliamentary History, Vol. 17). Available at: http://studymore.org.uk/7.HTM#1886 (accessed 05.07.2022).

Rochdale Borough Safeguarding Children Board (RBSCB) (2012) *Review of Multi-agency Responses to the Sexual Exploitation of Children*. Rochdale: The Rochdale Borough Safeguarding Children Board.

Rogers, B. (2013) Communicating with children in the classroom. In T. Cole, H. Daniels & J. Visser (eds), *The Routledge International Companion to Emotional and Behavioural Difficulties* (pp. 237–245). London: Routledge.

Rogers, J. (2007) Cardinal number and its representation: Skills, concepts and contexts. *Early Childhood Education and Care*, 178(2), 211–225.

Rosenbaum, P., Paneth, N., Leviton, A. et al. (2007) A report: The definition and classification of cerebral palsy April 2006. *Developmental Medicine Child Neurology* (Suppl), 109, 8–14.

Rosenthal, R., & Jacobson, L. (1968a) *Pygmalion in the Classroom*. New York: Holt, Rinehart and Winston.

Rosenthal, R., & Jacobson, L. (1968) Pygmalion in the classroom. *The Urban Review*, 3, 16–20. Available at: https://superchargeyourlife.de/wp-content/uploads/2017/10/Glaubenssaetze_3_Rosenthal_Jacobson.pdf (accessed 01.07.2020).

Royal College of Ophthalmologists (2015) *Snellen and LogMAR Acuity Testing*. London: Royal College of Ophthalmologists.

Royal National Institute for Blind People (RNIB) (2015) *Learning through Play in the Early Years: Effective Practice Guide*. London: RNIB.

Royal National Institute for Blind People (RNIB) (2018) *Eye Health and Sight Loss Stats and Facts*. London: RNIB. Available at: www.rnib.org.uk/sites/default/files/Eye%20health%20and%20sight%20loss%20stats%20and%20facts.pdf (accessed 28.03.2020).

Royal National Institute for Deaf People (RNID) (2004) *Inclusion Strategies*. London: RNID.

Ruthven, K. (2002) Assessment in mathematics education. In L. Haggarty (ed.), *Teaching Mathematics in Secondary Schools* (pp. 176–191). London: RoutlegeFalmer.

Rutter, M., Tizard, J., & Whitmore, K. (1970) *Education, Health and Behaviour*. London: Longman.

Sahlén, B., Hansson, K., Lyberg Åhlander, V., & Brännström, J. (2019) Spoken language and language impairment in deaf and hard-of-hearing children: Fostering classroom environments for mainstreamed children. In H. Knoors & M. Marschark (eds), *Evidence-based Practices in Deaf Education*. Oxford: Oxford University Press.

Salmon, P. (1995) *Psychology in the Classroom*. London: Cassell.

Scholastic Parents Staff (2019) *Why Audiobooks Are Great for Kids*. Online resource. Available at: www.scholastic.com/parents/books-and-reading/reading-resources/developing-reading-skills/whyaudio-books-are-great-kids.html (accessed 14.04.2020).

Schopler, E. (1997) Implementation of TEACCH philosophy. In D. J. Cohen & F. R. Volkmar (eds), *Handbook of Autism and Pervasive Developmental Disorders* (pp. 767–795). New York: Wiley.

Schopler, E., Reichler, R. J., & Lansing, M. D. (1980) *Individualized Assessment and Treatment for Autistic and Developmentally Disabled Children*. Baltimore, MD: University Park Press.

Schunk, D. H. (1989) Self-efficacy and achievement behaviors. *Educational Psychology Review*, 1, 173–208.

Schunk, D. H., & Zimmerman, B. J. (2003) Self-regulation and learning. In W. M. Reynolds & G. E. Miller (eds), *Handbook of Psychology: Educational Psychology* (Vol. 7, pp. 59–78). Hoboken, NJ: John Wiley & Sons.

Schunk, D. H., & Zimmerman, B. J. (2006) Competence and control beliefs: Distinguishing the means and ends. In P. A. Alexamder & P. H. Winnie (eds), *Handbook of Educational Psychology* (2nd edn, pp. 349–368). Mahwah, NJ: Lawrence Erlbaum Associates.

Scottish Executive (2004) *Restorative Practices in three Scottish Councils: Evaluation of pilot projects 2004-2006*. Available at: www.webarchive.org.uk/wayback/archive/20170701074158; www.gov.scot/Publications/2007/08/23161140/2 (accessed 05.07.2022).

Scottish Government (2017) *Supporting Children's Learning Code of Practice: Revised*. Edinburgh: Scottish Government.

Selikowitz, M. (2008) *Down Syndrome*. Oxford: Oxford University Press.

Shapiro, S., & Cole, L. (1994) *Behaviour Change in the Classroom: Self-management Interventions*. New York: Guilford Press.

Sharp, J. (2009) *Success with your Education Research Project*, London: Sage.

Sheehy, K. (2004) Approaches to autism. In J. Wearmouth, R. C. Richmond & T. Glynn (eds), *Addressing Pupils' Behaviour: Responses at District, School and Individual Levels* (pp. 338–356). London: David Fulton.

Shuayb, M., & O'Donnell, S. (2008) *Primary Review Research Survey 1/2 Aims and Values in Primary Education: England and Other Countries*. Cambridge: Cambridge University Primary Review.

Shulman, L. (1987) Knowledge and teaching: Foundations of the new reform. *Harvard Education Review*, 57(1), 1–22.

Shulman, L., & Shulman, J. (2004) How and what teachers learn: A shifting perspective. *Journal of Curriculum Studies*, 36(2), 257–271.

Shyman, E. (2016) The reinforcement of ableism: Normality, the medical model of disability, and humanism in applied behavior analysis and ASD. *Intellectual and Developmental Disabilities*, 54(5), 366–376.

Simon, B. (1974) *The Two Nations and the Educational Structure 1780–1870*. London: Lawrence & Wishart.

Skinner, B. F. (1938) *The Behaviour of Organisms*. New York: Appleton-Century-Crofts.

Skinner, B. F. (1953) *Science and Human Behavior*. New York: Macmillan.

Skinner, B. F. (1957) *Verbal Behavior*. Englewood Cliffs, NJ: Prentice Hall.

Smith, B. H., Waschbusch, D. A., Willoughby, M. T., & Evans, S. (2000) The efficacy, safety and practicality of treatments for adolescents with attention-deficit/hyperactivity disorder (ADHD). *Clinical Child and Family Psychology Review*, 3, 243–267.

Smith, J., & Elley, W. (1997) *How Children Learn to Write*. Auckland: Paul Chapman Educational Publishing.

Smith, M. (2019) A mother's experiences in the special educational needs system. In J. Wearmouth & A. Goodwyn (eds), *Pupil, Teacher and Student Voice in Educational Institutions: Values, Opinions, Beliefs and Perspectives* (pp. 191–206). London: Routledge.

Social Care Institute for Excellence (SCIE) (2017) *Autism: Improving Access to Social Care for Adults*. London: SCIE. Available at: www.scie.org.uk/autism/transition/adult-services (accessed 22.05.2020).

Spencer, P., & Marschark, M. (2010) *Evidence-based Practice in Educating Deaf and Hard-of-Hearing Students*. Oxford: Oxford University Press.

Sproson, B. (2004) Some do and some don't: Teacher effectiveness in managing behaviour. In J. Wearmouth, T. Glynn, R. C. Richmond & M. Berryman (eds), *Inclusion and Behaviour Management in Schools* (chapter 17). London: David Fulton.

Stanovich, K. (2000) *Progress in Understanding Reading: Scientific Foundations and New Frontiers*. New York & London: Guilford Press.

Stipek, D., Salmon, J. M., Givvin, K. B., Kazemi, E., Saxe, G., & MacGyvers, V. L. (1998) The value (and convergence) of practices suggested by motivation research and promoted by mathematics education reformers. *Journal for Research in Mathematics Education*, 29, 465–488.

Strouse Watt, W. (2003) *How Visual Acuity is Measured*. Available at: https://lowvision.preventblindness.org/2003/10/06/how-visual-acuity-is-measured/(accessed 23.03.2020).

Stuart, K. (2012) Leading multi-professional teams in the children's workforce: An action research project. *International Journal of Integrated Care (IJIC)*, 12, 1–12.

Sullivan, P., Mousley, J., & Zevenbergen, R. (2003) The context of mathematics tasks and the context of the classroom: Are we including all students? *Mathematics Education Research Journal*, 15(2), 107–121.

Swanwick, R. (2019) Dialogic teaching and translanguaging in deaf education. In H. Knoors & M. Marschark (eds), *Evidence-based Practices in Deaf Education* (pp. 81–107). Oxford: Oxford University Press.

Taylor, K. (2007) The participation of children with multi-sensory impairment in person-centred planning. *British Journal of Special Education*, 34(4), 204–211.

Tew, M. (1998) Circle time: A much neglected resource in secondary schools. *Pastoral Care*, September, 18–27.

Thomson, M. (1998) *The Problem of Mental Deficiency: Eugenics, Democracy and Social Policy in Britain, c. 1870–1959*. Oxford: Clarendon Press.

Tomlinson, S. (1988) Why Johnny can't read: Critical theory and special education. *European Journal of Special Needs Education*, 3(1), 45–58.

Topping, K. (1995) *Paired Reading, Spelling and Writing: The Handbook for Teachers and Parents*. London: Cassell.

Topping, K. (1996) Tutoring systems for family literacy. In S. Wolfendale & K. Topping (eds), *Family Involvement in Literacy*. London: Cassell.

Topping, K. (2001) *Thinking, Reading, Writing*. London: Continuum.

Topping, K., Duran, D., & van Keer, H. (2015) *Using Peer Tutoring to Improve Reading Skills*. London: Routledge.

Tye-Murray, N. (2003) Conversational fluency of children who use cochlear implants. *Ear and Hearing*, 24(1 Suppl.), 82S–89S.

Underwood, J. E. A. (1955) *Report of the Committee on Maladjusted Children*. London: HMSO.

United Nations (UN) (1989) *Convention on the Rights of the Child*. Geneva: UN.

van Berkel-van Hoof, L. (2019) Influence of signs on spoken word learning. In H. Knoors & M. Marschark (eds), *Evidence-based Practices in Deaf Education* (pp. 149–169). Oxford: Oxford University Press.

Vissers, C. Th. W. M., & Hermans, D. (2019) Social-emotional problems in deaf and hard-of-hearing children from an executive and theory-of-mind perspective. In H. Knoors & M. Marschark (eds), *Evidence-based Practices in Deaf Education* (pp. 455–476). Oxford: Oxford University Press.

Vygotsky, L. S. (1962) *Thought and Language*. Cambridge, MA: MIT Press.

Vygotsky, L. S. (1978) *Mind in Society: The Development of Higher Psychological Processes*. Cambridge, MA: Harvard University Press.

Vygotsky, L. S. (1981) The genesis of higher mental functions. In J. W. Wertsch (ed.), *The Concept of Activity in Soviet Psychology* (pp. 144–188). Armonk, NY: Sharpe.

Wachtel, J., & Wachtel, T. (2012) *Building Campus Community: Restorative Practices in Residential Life*. Bethlehem, PA: International Institute for Restorative Practices.

Walshaw, M. (2004) The pedagogical encounter in postmodern times: Learning from Lacan. In M. Walshaw (ed.), *Mathematics Education within the Postmodern* (pp. 121–140). Greenwich, CT: Information Age.

Waterland, L. (1985) *Read with Me*. Strand: Thimble Press.

Watson, J. B. (1913) Psychology as the behaviorist views it. *Psychological Review*, 20(2), 158–177.

Wearmouth, J. (1986) Self-concept and learning experience of pupils with moderate learning difficulties. Unpublished Master's thesis, Institute of Education, London University.

Wearmouth, J. (1999) Another one flew over: 'Maladjusted' Jack's perception of his label. *British Journal of Special Education*, 26(1), 15–23.

Wearmouth, J. (2004a) Learning from 'James': Lessons about policy and practice for literacy difficulties in schools' special educational provision. *British Journal of Special Education*, 31(2), 60–67.

Wearmouth, J. (2004b) 'Talking Stones': An interview technique for disaffected young people. *Journal of Pastoral Care in Education*, 22(2), 7–13.

Wearmouth, J. (2009) *A Beginning Teacher's Guide to Special Educational Needs*. Buckingham: Open University Press.

Wearmouth, J. (2016) *Effective SENCo: Meeting the Challenge*. Maidenhead: McGraw Hill.

Wearmouth, J. (2017) *Special Educational Needs and Disabilities in Schools: A Critical Introduction*. London: Bloomsbury.

Wearmouth, J., Berryman, M., & Whittle, L. (2011) Shoot for the moon! Students' identities as writers in the context of the classroom. *British Journal of Special Education*, 38(2), 92–99.

Wearmouth, J., & Butler, C. (2020) Special educational needs co-ordinators' perceptions of effective provision for including autistic children in primary and middle schools in England. *Education 3–13*, 48(3), 258–272.

Wearmouth, J., Glynn, T., & Berryman, M. (2005) *Perspectives on Student Behaviour in Schools: Exploring Theory and Developing Practice*. London: Routledge.

Wearmouth, J., Gosling, A., Beams, J., & Davydaitis, S. (2018) *Understanding Special Educational Needs and Disability in the Early Years*. London: Routledge.

Weavers, J. (2003) Dyslexia and mathematics. In M. Thomson (ed.), *Dyslexia Included* (pp. 33–45). London: David Fulton.

Webster, R., Russell, A., & Blatchford, P. (2016) *Maximising the Impact of Teaching Assistants* (2nd edn). London: Routledge.

Weiner, B. (1979) A theory of motivation for some classroom experiences. *Journal of Educational Psychology*, 71(1), 3–25.

Wells, G. (1999) *Dialogic Inquiry: Towards a Sociocultural Practice and Theory of Education*. Cambridge: Cambridge University Press.

Welsh Government (2021) *The Additional Learning Needs Code for Wales 2021*. Cardiff: Welsh Government.

Werling, D. M., & Geschwind, D. H. (2014) Sex differences in autism spectrum disorders. *Current Opinion in Neurology*, 26(2), 146–153.

Wertsch, J. V. (1991) *Voices of the Mind: A Sociocultural Approach to Mediated Action*. Cambridge, MA: Harvard University Press.

Westby, C. E. (1991) Learning to talk, talking to learn: Oral–literate language difference. In C. S. Simon (ed.), *Communication Skills and Classroom Success* (pp. 334–357). San Diego, CA: College Hill.

Westwood, P. (1997) *Commonsense Methods for Children with Special Educational Needs*. London: Routledge.

Whitaker, P., Barratt, P., Joy, H., Potter, M., & Thomas, G. (2003) Children with autism and peer group support: Using 'circles of friends'. *British Journal of Special Education*, 25(2), 60–64.

Whiting, M., Scammell, A., & Bifulco, A. (2008) The health specialist initiative: Professionals' views of a partnership initiative between health and social care for child safeguarding. *Qualitative Social Work: Research and Practice*, 7(1), 99–117.

Wilkins, M., & Ertmer, D. J. (2002) Introducing young children who are deaf or hard of hearing to spoken language. *Language, Speech and Hearing Services in Schools*, 33, 196–204.

Wilkinson, E. (1947) *The New Secondary Education*. London: HMSO.

Willcutt, E. G. (2012) The prevalence of DSM-IV attention-deficit/hyperactivity disorder: A meta-analytic review. *Neurotherapeutics*, 9, 490–499.

Wing, L., & Gould, J. (1979) Severe impairments of social interaction and associated abnormalities in children: Epidemiology and classification. *Journal of Autism and Developmental Disorders*, 9, 11–29.

Wood, D., Bruner, J., & Ross, G. (1976) The role of tutoring in problem solving. *Journal of Child Psychology and Psychiatry*, 17, 89–100.

Wood, K. C., Smith, H., & Grossniklaus, D. (2001) Piaget's stages of cognitive development. In M. Orey (ed.), *Emerging Perspectives on Learning, Teaching, and Technology*. Athens, GA: University of Georgia.

Woodhouse, J. (1982) Eugenics and the feeble-minded: The Parliamentary debates of 1912–14. *History of Education* 11(2), 127–137.

Woodhouse, J., Davies, N., McAvinchey, A., & Ryan, B. (2014) Ocular and visual status among children in special schools in Wales: The burden of unrecognised visual impairment. *Archives of Diseases in Childhood*, 99, 500–504.

World Health Organization (WHO) (2019) *The International Statistical Classification of Diseases, ICD-11*. Geneva: WHO.

World Health Organization (WHO) (2020) *Deafness and Hearing Loss*. Geneva: WHO. Available at: www.who.int/news-room/fact-sheets/detail/deafness-and-hearing-loss (accessed 25.03.2020).

Wragg, E. C., Wragg, C. M., Haynes, G. S., & Chamberlain, R. P. (1998) *Improving Literacy in the Primary School*. London: Routledge.

Wray, D. (2002) Metacognition and literacy. In G. Reid & J. Wearmouth (eds), *Dyslexia and Literacy: Research and Practice*. Chichester: Wiley.

Wright, D., & Digby, A. (1996) *From Idiocy to Mental Deficiency*. London: Routledge.

Yoder, P. J. (1990) The theoretical and empirical basis of early amelioration of developmental disabilities: Implications for future research. *Journal of Early Intervention*, 14, 27–42.

Yoshinaga-Itano, C. (2003) From screening to early identification and intervention: Discovering predictors to successful outcomes for children with significant hearing loss. *Journal of Deaf Studies and Deaf Education*, 8, 11–30.

Zevenbergen, R., Mousley, J., & Sullivan, P. (2004) Making the pedagogic relay inclusive for indigenous Australian students in mathematics classrooms. *International Journal of Inclusive Education*, 8(4), 391–405.

INDEX